ALLERGY COOKING WITH EASE

Nicolette M. Dumke

ALLERGY COOKING WITH EASE

Nicolette M. Dumke

STARBURST PUBLISHERS

P.O. Box 4123, Lancaster, Pennsylvania 17604

To schedule Author appearances write:
Author Appearances, Starburst Promotions, P.O. Box 4123,
Lancaster, PA 17604 or call (717)-293-0939.

Credits:
Cover design by Bill Dussinger

ALLERGY COOKING WITH EASE

First Printing, September 1992
Second Printing, March 1993
Third Printing, May 1994

ISBN: 0-914984-42-X
Library of Congress Catalog Number 91-67061

Printed in the United States of America

Dedication

To my husband,
Mark,
who encourages me;

To my sons,
Joel and John,
whose dietary needs and desires stimulate creativity;

To my mother,
Mary Jiannetti,
who taught me to love cooking;

And to the memory of my father,
Eugene Jiannetti,
who was my best taster.

Table of Contents

Spelt

Special thanks go to Mr. Wilhelm Kosnopfl, president of Purity Foods, the producers of spelt, for his support which helped make this book possible.

Spelt is a highly nutritious, easily digested grain that is revolutionizing the diets of people around the world, and in particular those who are allergic to wheat. Because of its high gluten content, spelt makes yeast breads that are so light and fluffy that you will have a hard time believing that they are wheat-free. Spelt also makes excellent pasta that, unlike most alternative pastas, does not get mushy upon standing in soups or sauces and can be frozen after cooking without any loss of quality. And best of all, spelt has a delicious, nutty flavor and tastes great in all kinds of foods.

Spelt has a long history. It is mentioned in the Old Testament of the Bible (Exodus 9:31 and Ezekiel 4:9). During the twelfth century, Saint Hildegard or Bingen used it to restore severely ill patients to health in Germany. And now, it is improving the diets of food allergy sufferers. It is higher in protein, carbohydrates, Vitamin A, and several B vitamins than wheat and, because it is more soluble in water than wheat, its nutrients may be more easily absorbed by our bodies. The body's cells are then nourished, strengthened, and prepared for their optimum performance.

Spelt is available as whole grain spelt, spelt flour, and Vita-Spelt™ 100% Wheat-free Pasta.

VITA-SPELT®

PURITY FOODS, INC.
2871 West Jolly Road
Okemos, Michigan 48864
(517) 351-9231

For a complete listing of the spelt recipes in this book, see pages 304 to 307.

Foreword

During the past 35 years I've helped thousands of patients with food allergies and other types of food sensitivities. I've accomplished this goal by putting people on one week trial elimination diets. If and when the person's symptoms improved (as they usually did), the eliminated foods were eaten again *one food per day* and reactions are noted.

Using this program, many of my patients found that they were sensitive to milk, wheat, corn, egg, and other of their favorite foods.

So, they would come back to me and say, "What can I eat and how can I prepare foods for my family?" In responding to these questions over the years, I have used and recommended many different recipes and many books. Yet, I'm always keeping my mind and eyes open in my search to help my patients.

Then, in the summer of 1991, I received the manuscript of Nickie Dumke's *Allergy Cooking With Ease*. I reviewed this book and I liked it. Because I don't claim to be a cook, I passed it along to my allergy colleague, Nell Sellers, who has worked with me and prepared recipes for my patients during the past 30 years. Here are Nell's comments:

"*Allergy Cooking With Ease* is a gem of a book. It incorporates all of the key points I've been telling our patients for years! She even includes starting the day at dinner so you'll have food for breakfast and lunch the next day. Her book includes something for everybody. She agrees that the diet has to be livable or people won't follow it for long."

Features of this book include:
   *Maintaining a positive attitude
   *Diversifying and rotating the diet
   *Providing readers with treats using ingredients which are least likely to cause problems.

Other tips in this book include: Stocking up so as to always have permissable foods on hand to lessen the chances of cheating and making big batches of baked foods and storing them in the freezer for later rotation.

A final word. Nickie Dumke's book isn't only a recipe book. It encourages people to enjoy family, friends, work and recreation. She says in effect, "Be good to yourself. Don't worry if you fall off your diet now and then. You can always pick yourself up and go at it again."

If you or members of your family are troubled by food allergies or sensitivity intolerances, you'll value this book as a treasured friend!

William G. Crook, M.D.

About This Cookbook

The purpose of this cookbook is to provide a wide variety of recipes to meet a wide variety of dietary and social needs, and, whenever possible, to save you time in food preparation.

Because of the wide variety of recipes in this book, not all of the recipes will fit your specific dietary needs. There are grain-free recipes for those who are sensitive to all grains, and recipes using a large variety of grains for those who rotate several grains. There are cracker, muffin, and baking-soda-raised bread recipes for those who cannot tolerate yeast, and yeast bread recipes for those who can. There are recipes sweetened with stevia for those who must abstain from all sweeteners, recipes sweetened with fruit and fruit juices for those who can tolerate fruit sweeteners, and some recipes minimally sweetened with sugar for kids, young and old, who can occasionally tolerate some sugar and may feel deprived without it in some social situations. There are main dish recipes made with game for those allergic to ordinary meats, vegetarian recipes, and recipes that can be made with the meats usually found in your grocery store. Rather than concentrating on the recipes that you cannot use (possibly the majority of them), *be positive* and use those that you *can* use. "Avoid chronic negativity at all costs," as Marge Jones said in the September, 1990 "Mastering Food Allergies" newsletter.

Meeting social needs is as important as meeting dietary needs, especially for children. So this book contains a pumpkin pie recipe and a grain-free stuffing recipe for Thanksgiving, cookie press cookie recipes for Christmas, cake recipes for birthdays, and a large variety of cookie recipes for school lunches, because, after all, children with no dessert in their lunches may swap the nutritious foods that you spent much time preparing for something they should not eat.

The amount of time that must be spent cooking for an allergy diet can seem overwhelming, so as many timesaving tricks as possible are used in these recipes. All of the yeast breads are made with quick-rise yeast. Sources of commercial pastas are given as well as recipes for making your own pasta. And the recipes include canned and frozen vegetables and fruits. But when, for example, canned tomato products could cause problems for individuals who are very sensitive to yeast, the more time-consuming recipes using fresh tomatoes are also provided. Use all of the timesaving tricks and devices that you can and think of the time you spend cooking as an investment in good health for yourself and those you love.

1

"How, Then, Can We Live?"

"How can I live this way?" is a question frequently asked by those with recently diagnosed food allergies. It seems as though your doctor has told you to completely eliminate most of the foods you have normally eaten and to eat the few foods that are left only every fourth or fifth day. As you read package labels in the supermarket, you find that almost everything contains corn, and what doesn't contain corn contains wheat or milk. How can we live and cope with food allergies, and in the process achieve good health? Three things are necessary: the right diet, a practical means of implementing the diet and staying on it, and most important of all, the right attitude.

The right diet is one that eliminates all foods that you are allergic to (at least for a time until you may possibly develop some tolerance to them) and spaces the foods you can eat at infrequent enough intervals so that you do not develop sensitivities to them. The diagnosis of food allergies is beyond the scope of this book and is best left to your doctor. If you are allergic to frequently eaten foods or many foods, you will need professional help to track down which foods are the culprits for you. Once you have determined your individual pattern of sensitivities, the allergen avoidance index on page 272 of this book will help you choose recipes that avoid your major allergens.

The right diet will also introduce you to a variety of new foods. We have all eaten a limited number of foods in the past and think that those foods are all that exist. Therefore, when we find we can no longer eat them, we feel that we may starve. But there are many equally delicious foods that we have never tasted. Along with familiar but less commonly used grains, such as barley, oats, rye, and rice, this book contains recipes using quinoa, amaranth, spelt, teff, millet, cassava, tapioca, water chesnut, and chestnut flours. Also, there are recipes made with unusual sources of protein, such as goat jack or cheddar cheese, goat or sheep feta cheese, game meats, duck, rabbit, and goat, and unusual vegetables, such as belgian endive and jicama.

The right diet includes the right pattern of eating the foods that you tolerate. Different doctors vary in the strictness of the rules of rotation that they wish their patients to follow, but generally, each food family is eaten only every fourth or fifth day. All of the foods in each food family may be kept on the same day of rotation, or some may be eaten on Monday and some on Wednesday, for example, with a day off from that food family between. Some doctors request that their patients eat a particular food only once on its day. Others allow each food to be eaten several times. This second pattern is very practical because it cuts down on the amount of cooking that must be done; cooking can be done in large enough batches to be eaten for more than one meal throughout the day. In order to help you set up a rotation diet, this book gives information about food families, so that you can keep all the foods in each family together on the same day (pages 233 to 262.) Also, you will notice that certain families tend to appear together in the patterns that fit the author's family's rotation schedule, such as grape juice as the sweetener in rye recipes, apple juice in spelt and quinoa recipes, etc. If these patterns do not fit your needs, just substitute another fruit juice with each flour. There are several good books available containing more information on rotation diets, such as If This Is Tuesday It Must Be Chicken by Natalie Golos and Frances Golos Golbitz and The Allergy Self-Help Cookbook by Marjorie Hurt Jones. (See "References", page 271.)

Along with the right diet, we need the practical means to implement and stay on the diet. No diet can improve our health if we cannot stay on it. In order to stay on a diet we need variety. Variety is especially important for children. They may be eating the same combination of foods every fourth or fifth day, but they need to be in different enough forms so that they don't get bored. Often, changing a recipe very slightly and calling it by a different name will improve a child's attitude toward certain foods.

We need to plan ahead and have the right foods available before we get hungry. Hunger, combined with the lack of the right foods to satisfy it immediately, causes most of the problems encountered in trying to stay on a rotation diet. Prepare large batches of crackers, breads, and muffins, using the same sweetener and oil with each flour each time, and freeze them, and you will be prepared when that day of rotation comes around again. If your doctor will allow you to eat foods more than once in each rotation day, start your rotation day at dinnertime, prepare a large portion of the main dish, and eat it for breakfast and lunch too.

We also need to be prepared for those special social occasions. I was recently talking to a person with food allergies who was suffering from a reaction caused by Christmas rum balls that she had eaten. I advised her to be prepared the next time with some Christmas treats that would be allowed on her diet, and told her that I had made a batch of tree-shaped amaranth cookie press cookies for the holidays. She replied, "Yes, but those have sugar in them." That was true, but for me, occasionally eating a little sugar is much better than yielding to the temptation to eat rum balls containing not only sugar but also wheat, butter, eggs, corn, and chocolate, as she had. Be prepared for those special occasions with the most satisfying substitute food you can tolerate.

A final factor in implementing the diet is to try to reduce the amount of work done in preparing all of our food from scratch. If we make our diets more work than we have to, we reduce our chances of being able to follow them. Preparing large batches of baked products, with the same flour, oil and sweetener used together each time, and freezing them, as previously mentioned, is a great timesaving technique. Most main dishes also freeze well. Also, try to use ingredients that save time. If your diet will allow it, use canned and frozen fruits, vegetables, and juices. When making yeast breads, use quick-rise yeast.

"How, then, can we live" with our food allergies? The most important factor of all in coping with food allergies is the right attitude. We can continually talk and think about what we cannot eat and cannot do, but this will depress us and everyone around us. Or we can learn to be content with what we can eat and actually begin to enjoy our food. And when we stick to our diets we may even find that we feel well enough and have enough energy to enjoy other things in life more, such as our families, friends, work, and recreation, and the importance of food in our lives will decrease.

All of us fall off of our diets at times. Do not be too hard on yourself when this happens. Just pick yourself up and start over again. And all parents of allergic children have times of frustration when their children will not eat what they have spent much time preparing. This is just a temporary setback. Freeze the unwanted food until your children forget that they were tired of it, and find another recipe to try.

Finally, be adventurous, inventive, and creative in your cooking. Use this book as a starting point and experiment on your own. Learn as much about cooking with new foods as you can. And consider a cooking class or cookbook worthwhile if you get a single new recipe or idea from it.

2

Know Your Ingredients

When you begin cooking for a rotational allergy diet you will encounter foods that you are not very familiar with. This is an introduction to some of the characteristics of those foods.

FLOURS

While they are very delicious and nutritious, alternative flours are different than wheat, so do not expect things made with them to have a taste or texture identical to wheat-containing baked goods. If you are willing to try new things and have a positive attitude, you will enjoy things made from these flours as you enjoy improved health. For the comparative nutritional values of alternative flours, see ch. 14.

AMARANTH FLOUR:

This flour is not related to the true grains. It is in the same botanical order as quinoa, although it is not in the same food family. It is excellent in baked goods. Purchase it at a store that refrigerates its flour and refrigerate or freeze it at home, since it may develop an unpleasantly strong flavor if stored too long at room temperature.

ARROWROOT:

A fine white powder that looks like cornstarch, arrowroot is excellent as a thickener and tends to hold baked goods together and make them less crumbly. It may be derived from plants in several food families, but when it is purchased in a store, it is usually impossible to determine which plant it came from. Therefore, at our house, we rotate it on the same day as bananas, which is the only commonly eaten food in any of the families.

BARLEY FLOUR:

Barley is a very pleasant tasting gluten-containing grain in the same tribe of the grain family as rye, spelt, wheat, and triticale. Baked goods made with barley flour are excellent, and it is especially good in pie crust.

CAROB:

This plant is in the legume family. The flour made from the pods may be used in baking as a substitute for chocolate. Carob flour or powder is naturally sweet, so it does not require as much additional sweetener in recipes as chocolate does. It tends to form hard lumps upon standing, so you may need to press it through a wire mesh strainer with the back of a spoon before using it. Milk-free unsweetened carob chips are available commercially (See "Sources of Special Foods," ch. 16), and are excellent in cookies. There is also a gum derived from the bean of the carob plant that is used in many commercially prepared foods.

CASSAVA MEAL:

Also called mandioca flour, this comes from the same plant as tapioca, but is very coarse. It is not strongly flavored, and makes good crackers that can be broken up and used as croutons in salads. It may be obtained by mail order for a reasonable price (See "Sources of Special Foods," ch. 16), and therefore is a welcome addition to a diet that must eliminate all grains. (See tuber flours, below, for comments about cassava flour.)

CHESTNUT FLOUR:

Naturally sweet and tasty, this is also a good alternative to grains for the totally grain-free diet. Baked goods made with chestnut flour alone are very crumbly, so it is best to use chestnut flour with a binding ingredient such as bananas or arrowroot. It may be obtained by mail order. (See "Sources of Special Foods," ch. 16.)

CORN:

Corn is not used in any of the recipes in this book, but is included in this listing to warn you that along with corn, corn oil, cornstarch, and corn syrup and sweeteners, you should avoid dextrose and grits in any commercially prepared foods.

GARBANZO FLOUR:

This flour is in the legume family. It has a very pleasant, slightly sweet taste, and is high in protein. It makes excellent tacos and tortillas.

GLUTEN FLOUR and GRAHAM FLOUR:

Both are derived from wheat, and are mentioned so that you may avoid them.

MILLET FLOUR:

Millet is a pleasant-tasting grain flour that is in a tribe of its own in the grain family. Baked goods made with millet flour tend to be very crumbly even when binding ingredients are also used, but it still is an excellent flour to use in baking if you do not mind crumbs.

MILO FLOUR:

Milo is a grain that is commonly used to feed cattle, and may be difficult to locate for human consumption. It is in the same tribe of the grain family as the sugar cane plant. It has a pleasant, bland flavor and is excellent when used in baking. (See "Sources of Special Foods,"ch. 16.)

OAT FLOUR:

This is a very pleasant tasting grain flour. It may tend to be heavy in some baked products, but is still delicious if one is not too particular about heaviness. An occasional batch of oat flour may be gummy in baked goods. Oats are in a tribe of their own in the grain family.

QUINOA FLOUR:

Quinoa flour is a very versatile nongrain flour. Quinoa is excellent in baked goods of all kinds. Although not in the same food family, it is in the same botanical order as amaranth. It is in the same food family as beets, spinach, and chard. Quinoa is an excellent source of high-quality protein and calcium.

RICE FLOUR:

A bland, pleasant tasting grain flour, rice flour tends to be too gritty, especially for the children at our house, in baked goods. It is in a tribe of the grain family with wild rice.

RYE FLOUR:

This is a very versatile grain flour. It contains gluten and behaves much like whole wheat flour in baking. It has a slightly stronger flavor than some of the other grains, but is very tasty. Rye is in the same tribe of the grain family as barley, spelt, kamut, wheat, and triticale.

SEMOLINA FLOUR:

Semolina flour is derived from the endosperm of wheat. It is often used in Jerusalem artichoke pasta and is mentioned so that it may be avoided.

SPELT FLOUR:

A very versatile grain flour, spelt makes excellent yeast breads because it is higher in gluten than wheat. Spelt is very closely related to wheat in its biological classification, being Triticum spelta while bread wheat is Triticum aestivum. In spite of the close relationship, spelt is tolerated by many wheat-sensitive individuals. Muffins and cakes made with spelt flour tend to be a little drier than those made with other grains, and so the recipes may contain slightly more oil.

TAPIOCA FLOUR:

This fine white powder is very similar to arrowroot and may be used interchangeably with it in baking. It behaves very slightly differently than arrowroot in thickening, and may be used in different amounts as a thickener in some recipes. Sauces thickened with tapioca tend to be a little more ropy than those thickened with arrowroot. Tapioca comes from the same plant as cassava.

TEFF FLOUR:

Teff flour is a slightly strong tasting grain flour. It tends to be a little gritty, but still makes very nice baked products. It is in a tribe of its own in the grain family.

TRITICALE:

Triticale is a grain that is a cross between wheat and rye, and is usually not well tolerated by wheat-sensitive individuals.

TUBER FLOURS:

For individuals sensitive to all grains, flours made from a variety of unusual tubers can be very helpful, although they are expensive. White sweet potato, cassava, malanga, and yam flours, along with recipes and instructions for their use, may be obtained by mail order. (See "Sources of Special Foods," ch. 16.)

WATER CHESTNUT STARCH:

While this must be obtained by mail order (See "Sources of Special Foods," ch. 16), it is a useful addition to the diets of individuals who must avoid all grains. Water chestnut starch may be used as a thickener and makes excellent wafers. ("Coconut Milk Wafers," page 37)

LEAVENINGS

Leavenings are the ingredients that make baked products rise, and include baking soda, baking powder, and yeast.

BAKING SODA:

Baking soda is a very pure chemical and is usually allowed on every day of the rotation cycle. It must be used in conjunction with an acid ingredient, such as fruit juice, unbuffered Vitamin C crystals, or cream of tartar, to make baked goods rise.

BAKING POWDER:

Baking powder is a combination of acid and basic components that produces gas that makes baked goods rise in baking. Most commercial baking powder contains cornstarch. Potato-starch-containing baking powder is made for those with food allergies, but sensitivity to potatoes is not uncommon, and therefore potatoes and potato-containing baking powder should not be used daily. Most of the recipes in this book contain a built-in baking powder made of baking soda and unbuffered Vitamin C crystals. It is important to use unbuffered Vitamin C crystals so they can add the acid component to the baking powder.

YEAST:

Yeast is what makes commercial bread rise and is a potent allergen for many individuals. However, in The Yeast Connection Cookbook, Dr. William Crook says that approximately 50% of patients with candidiasis were able to tolerate yeast-containing foods in their diets.[1] Therefore, a section of yeast breads is included in this book, along with tips on baking yeast breads (ch. 4).

OILS

For cooking purposes, most vegetable oils behave the same way and may be used interchangeably. For purposes of health, however, oils differ. A detailed discussion of the health advantages and disadvantages of the various oils is beyond the scope of this book. However, canola oil, in the same family as cabbage, is the lowest in saturated fat and the highest in monounsaturated fat of all the oils currently available.

You should rotate oils and use each kind on the same day as other foods in the same food family. Safflower or sunflower oil may be rotated on the same day as lettuce, soybean or peanut oil on the same day as legumes, rice bran oil on the same day as rice, canola oil on the same day as cabbage, grapeseed oil on the same day as grapes, etc. In addition to these oils, there are enough other oils available, such as avocado, sesame, olive, almond, walnut, etc., to fill almost any rotation pattern.

Coconut oil is the one oil that behaves differently in cooking than other oils. It is high in saturated fat and therefore is solid at room temperature. In some recipes, such as cookie press cookies and ice cream cones, it functions better than any other oil. Because it is high in saturated fats it should not be eaten in large quantities, but according to Harvard authority Dr. Vigen K. Babayan, "There's no danger unless you greatly overdo it. Not all saturated fats are alike, and not all are bad." He says that animal fats and coconut oil are quite different, animal fats being made up of long chains of fatty acids, and coconut oil being made up of shorter-chain fatty acids which do not deposit as easily in blood vessels.[2] There are even reports that medium chain triglycerides, such as coconut oil, may supress the synthesis of fat by the body.[3]

SWEETENERS

The dessert recipes in this book are minimally sweetened. As one gets used to eating little or no refined sugar, one's tastes change and minimally sweetened foods seem like a great treat.

CONCENTRATED SWEETENERS:

Concentrated sweeteners such as BEET SUGAR, CANE SUGAR, MOLASSES, HONEY, and MAPLE SYRUP, have the most effect on blood sugar metabolism and may need to be completely avoided by individuals with candidiasis. They are used in some of the recipes in this book, however, in smaller amounts than in most recipes, as a concession to special social situations, especially those involving children. Beet sugar is in the same family as quinoa and spinach, and cane sugar is in the same family as the grains for purposes of rotation.

FRUIT SWEETENERS:

Fruit sweeteners are used in the majority of the dessert recipes in this book. Frozen fruit juice concentrates may be thawed and used as the liquid in a recipe, adding sweetness and acidity to the leavening process at the same time. Fruit purees improve the texture of many baked products, as well as binding the crumbly ones more firmly together. Date sugar is also a fruit sweetener. It is simply dried ground dates, and behaves more like beet and cane sugars in baking than fruit juices do.

STEVIA:

Stevia is a potently sweet herb that is very helpful in the diets of patients with severe candidiasis. It is derived from the plant Stevia rebaudiana, which is in the composite family. It is available in several forms, as a brownish powder, as a brownish liquid, and as a white powder. The white powder is used in this cookbook, as it is the most pure form of the sweetening agents found in the plant. Stevia has a slight licorice-like taste which is most noticeable in bland recipes, and almost undetectable in recipes containing strongly flavored ingredients such as cranberries and carob.

OTHER INGREDIENTS

Many ingredients not usually found in your kitchen may be used in cooking for an allergy rotation diet. To expand your repertoire of vegetables, see the "Vegetables" chapter of The Yeast Connection Cookbook. To learn about unusual fruits, see "Exploring New Ingredients" in The Allergy Self-Help Cookbook. (See "References," page 271.)

UNBUFFERED VITAMIN C CRYSTALS:

These have already been mentioned as a component in the leavening process. They are also useful to add tartness to salads instead of using vinegar or lemon juice. Different brands of Vitamin C differ in how tasty they are in salads. If available in your area, Vital Life brand is very good for salads. Be sure to purchase a brand of Vitamin C crystals that is free of corn. (See Sources of Special Foods, ch. 16.)

AGAR:

Agar is derived from seaweed, and can be used instead of gelatin for individuals allergic to beef or pork. It is available as a powder or as flakes. Generally speaking, it takes less of the powder than of the flakes to produce gelling.

GUAR GUM:

This ingredient adds fiber to foods. It is added to ice cream recipes as an optional ingredient to promote a smooth texture. In yeast bread recipes that are made with low-gluten flours, the guar gum is essential in order to trap the gas made by the yeast so the bread will rise. (See "Sources of Special Foods," ch. 16.)

ABOUT FOOD FAMILIES

It is essential to know about food families so that you can eat foods from the same family on the same day of your rotation diet. The food family tables beginning on page 233 list all commonly eaten foods. Table 1 lists them alphabetically with their location in Tables 2 and 3. Tables 2 and 3 list them according to their classification into families.

Food families are based on the biological classification of plants and animals used for food, which can be a confusing science. It varies from year to year and from scientist to scientist. Some scientists are "lumpers," who put all the species of what another scientist calls a suborder into the same family, and there are "splitters," who will split what another scientist calls one family into several families. The following tables represent a consensus of opinions from several sources. But for purposes of the rotation diet, the final authorities on what foods to group together are your doctor and your body. For instance, an individual with mild allergies may be able to be liberal and eat one food from the fish suborder Pleuronectoidea, which are sometimes classified to-

gether as a single family, on each day of his rotation cycle (day 1
- turbot, day 2 - halibut, day 3 - flounder, day 4 - sole), or a member
of a different tribe of the grain family each day of his cycle (day
1 - barley, day 2 - oats, day 3 - rice, day 4 - millet). An individual
with severe allergies may have to be more conservative and keep
all members of each of the above groups on the same day of his
rotation cycle.

To use the food family tables, look up the food you are
interested in alphabetically in Table 1. Each food is followed by
the page number that describes its location in Table 2 or 3. You
may find the food in Table 2 or 3 and see what the other members
of its family are so that they may be rotated together. The
complete classification of plants and animals used for food is
included in these tables rather than just a list of food families so
that the relatedness of various food families to each other can be
seen and taken into account in setting up a rotation diet.

1. Crook, William G., M.D. The Yeast Connection Cookbook,
   Professional Books, Jackson, Tennessee 38301, 1989, page 24.

2. Babayan, Vigen K., M.D. "The Denver Post," Food Pharmacy
   Column, March 28, 1990.

3. Kaunitz, Hans, M.D. "Medium Chain Triglycerides (MCT)
   In Aging And Arteriosclerosis," Advances in Human Nutrition,
   Volume 3, Chem-Orbital, Park Forest, Illinois 60466, 1986,
   pages 115-121.

3

Muffins, Crackers, Breakfast Foods, and Breads Made Without Yeast

"What can we eat for breakfast?" "What can I take in my lunch?" These seem like difficult questions when wheat and yeast have been ruled out of your diet. This chapter gives some answers to those questions for people who cannot have yeast or wheat, as well as for those who can occasionally tolerate yeast if it is one of the days when yeast is not allowed on your rotation schedule.

Alternative flours do not have to be sifted before measuring them. (Some of them would not go through the sifter completely.) However, it is important to stir them in case they have settled during storage. Simply stir the flour with a large spoon, lightly spoon it into the measuring cup, and level it off with a knife.

When you make baking soda leavened baked goods, be careful not to overmix as you stir the liquid ingredients into the dry ingredients. Have the necessary baking pans prepared ahead of time; oil and flour them with the same oil and flour used in the recipe. Mix the dry ingredients together in a large bowl and the liquid ingredients together in another bowl. Working quickly, stir the liquid ingredients into the dry ingredients until they are just mixed, put the batter into the pans, and pop them into a pre-heated oven.

To test quick breads and muffins for doneness, insert a toothpick into the center of the pan. If it comes out dry, it is time to remove the pan from the oven. Allow breads to cool completely before you slice them for the freezer.

Pineapple Muffins

Delicately flavorful, these muffins are a hit with young and old alike, especially when you make them with milo flour.

> 2 c. milo flour OR 2 c. teff flour OR 2 1/4 c. spelt flour
> 1 tsp. baking soda
> 1/4 tsp. unbuffered Vitamin C crystals
> 1/2 c. pineapple canned in its own juice or fresh pineapple
>   with juice to cover, pureed
> 1/2 c. pineapple juice concentrate, thawed
> 1/3 c. oil

Mix the flour, baking soda, and Vitamin C crystals in a large bowl. Combine the pureed pineapple, pineapple juice concentrate, and oil and stir them into the dry ingredients until they are just mixed in. Put the batter into an oiled and floured muffin tin, filling the cups about 2/3 full. Bake at 400° for 15 to 20 minutes, or until the muffins begin to brown. Makes about 12 muffins.

This recipe is free of wheat, milk, eggs, corn, soy, yeast, and refined sugar. If the teff flour is used, it is free of gluten.

Apple and Spice Muffins

The chunks of apple are like little treasures in these sweet and spicy grain-free muffins.

> 1 3/4 c. quinoa flour
> 1/4 c. tapioca flour
> 2 tsp. baking soda

1/2 tsp. unbuffered Vitamin C crystals
2 tsp. cinnamon
1 1/2 c. peeled and chopped apples
1 c. unsweetened applesauce
1/4 c. apple juice concentrate, thawed
1/4 c. oil

Mix the dry ingredients together and stir the chopped apples into them. Mix together the applesauce, apple juice, and oil, and add them to the dry ingredients, stirring until just mixed. Put the batter into an oiled and floured muffin tin, filling the muffin cups about 3/4 full. Bake at 375° for 20 to 25 minutes. Makes about 16 muffins.

This recipe is free of all grains (including wheat and corn), gluten, milk, eggs, soy, yeast, and refined sugar.

Pear Muffins

This variation on "Apple and Spice Muffins" will add some variety to your diet.

Prepare "Apple and Spice Muffins," above, except omit the applesauce and apple juice concentrate, and instead use 1 1/4 c. pear juice. (If you purchase pears canned in pear juice, this can be the juice drained from the fruit used in this recipe.) Also, substitute 1 1/2 c. fresh peeled and chopped or canned chopped pears for the chopped apples. If canned pears are used, fold them into the batter after it is mixed instead of mixing them with the dry ingredients.

This recipe is free of all grains (including wheat and corn), gluten, milk, eggs, soy, yeast, and refined sugar.

Oat Muffins

These are a good change from oatmeal for breakfast on days when oats are on your rotation schedule.

2 c. oat flour
1/4 tsp. salt (optional)
1 tsp. baking soda
1/4 tsp. unbuffered Vitamin C crystals
1/4 c. oil
1 c. water

Mix the dry ingredients together in a large bowl. Mix together the water and oil, pour them into the dry ingredients, and stir until they are just mixed in. Put the batter into an oiled and floured muffin tin, filling the cups about 2/3 full. Bake at 400° for 30 to 35 minutes, or until the muffins begin to brown and pull away from the side of the pan. Makes about 10 muffins.

This recipe is free of wheat, milk, eggs, corn, soy, yeast, and refined sugar.

Barley Muffins

These go well with any meal of the day.

2 c. barley flour
1/4 tsp. salt (optional)
1 tsp. baking soda
1/4 tsp. unbuffered Vitamin C crystals
1/4 c. oil
1 1/4 c. water

Mix the dry ingredients together in a large bowl. Mix together the water and oil, pour them into the dry ingredients, and stir until they are just mixed in. Put the batter into an oiled and floured muffin tin, filling the cups about 2/3 full. Bake at 400° for 30 to 35 minutes, or until the muffins begin to brown. Makes about 12 muffins.

This recipe is free of wheat, milk, eggs, corn, soy, yeast, and refined sugar.

Millet Surprise Muffins

These muffins are fragile, but the jelly surprise inside them helps to hold them together.

> 1 c. millet flour
> 3/4 c. tapioca flour
> 3/4 tsp. baking soda
> 1/8 tsp. unbuffered Vitamin C crystals
> 1 tsp. cinnamon
> 3/4 c. apple juice concentrate, thawed
> 1/3 c. oil
> 2 to 3 tbsp. unsweetened all-fruit jelly or jam, such as Poirets
>   Pear-Apple Spread (optional)

Mix the flours, baking soda, Vitamin C crystals, and cinnamon in a large bowl. Combine the juice and oil and stir them into the dry ingredients until just mixed in. Fill 12 oiled and floured muffin cups 1/3 full with the batter, add 1/2 tsp. jelly or jam to the center of each muffin cup, and then top the jelly or jam with additional batter to fill the cups about 2/3 full. Or, omit the jelly or jam and fill the muffin cups 2/3 full with the batter. Bake at 400° for 15 to 20 minutes. Makes about 12 muffins.

This recipe is free of wheat, gluten, milk, eggs, corn, soy, yeast, and refined sugar.

Spelt Surprise Muffins

If pear-apple spread is used rather than a grape-based jelly or jam, this recipe contains only three food families. These muffins are also excellent without the jelly surprise.

> 2 1/2 c. spelt flour
> 1 1/2 tsp. baking soda
> 1/4 tsp. unbuffered Vitamin C crystals
> 1/3 c. oil
> 1 c. apple juice concentrate, thawed
> 2 to 3 tbsp. unsweetened all-fruit jelly or jam, such as
>   Poirets Pear-Apple Spread (optional)

Mix together the flour, baking soda, and Vitamin C crystals in a large bowl. Mix the oil and apple juice concentrate and stir them into the dry ingredients until they are just mixed in. Fill each of 12 oiled and floured muffin cups about 1/3 full of the batter, add 1/2 tsp. of jelly or jam to the center of each muffin cup, and top the jelly with additional batter to fill the muffin cups 2/3 full. Or, omit the jelly or jam and fill the muffin cups 2/3 full of batter. Bake at 350° for 15 to 18 minutes. Makes 12 muffins.

This recipe is free of wheat, milk, eggs, corn, soy, yeast, and refined sugar.

Rye Surprise Muffins

This recipe contains only two food families if the muffins are sweetened with grape juice rather than maple syrup, grapeseed oil is used, and all-grape jelly is used in the center of the muffins.

2 c. rye flour
3/4 tsp. baking soda
1/4 tsp. unbuffered Vitamin C crystals if water and maple syrup are used; 1/8 tsp. with grape juice
1/3 c. grapeseed or any other oil
1 c. unsweetened white grape juice OR 1/4 c. maple syrup plus 3/4 c. water
2 to 3 tbsp. unsweetened all-fruit jelly or jam (optional)

Mix the flour, baking soda, and Vitamin C crystals in a large bowl. Mix the juice or maple syrup plus water with the oil, pour them into the dry ingredients, and stir until they are just mixed in. Fill 12 oiled and floured muffin cups 1/3 full of batter, add 1/2 tsp. jelly or jam to the center of each muffin cup, and top the jelly or jam with additional batter to fill the cups about 2/3 full. Or, omit the jelly or jam and just fill each muffin cup 2/3 full of batter. Bake at 400° for 18 to 20 minutes. Makes about 12 muffins.

This recipe is free of wheat, milk, eggs, corn, soy, and yeast. It is also free of refined sugar if grape juice is used as the sweetener rather than maple syrup.

Blueberry Muffins

This traditional treat is just as delicious as ever when made without wheat, milk, eggs, or sugar.

> 1 c. fresh blueberries or unsweetened frozen blueberries, not thawed
> 1 batch of one of the following recipes:
>> Oat Muffins, page 29
>> Barley Muffins, page 30
>> Spelt Surprise Muffins, omitting the jelly or jam, page 31
>> Rye Surprise Muffins, omitting the jelly or jam, page 32
>> Apple and Spice Muffins, omitting the chopped apple, page 28

Mix the muffin batter as directed in the recipe. Quickly fold in the blueberries. Bake as directed in the recipe. Makes 1 or 2 additional muffins above what the recipe would make without the blueberries.

This recipe is free of wheat, milk, eggs, corn, soy, and yeast. It is free of refined sugar if any of the recipes except the "Rye Surprise Muffin" recipe is used; it is free of refined sugar in the "Rye Surprise Muffin" recipe if grape juice is used rather than maple syrup and water. It is free of all grains and gluten if the "Apple and Spice Muffin" recipe is used.

Banana Muffins

The natural sweetness of the chestnut flour and bananas combine to make this an exceptionally tasty grain-free treat. To obtain chestnut flour, see "Sources of Special Foods," ch. 16.

> 2 1/4 c. chestnut flour, sifted if lumpy
> 1 tsp. baking soda
> 1/2 tsp. unbuffered Vitamin C crystals
> 1/4 tsp. ground cloves (optional)

1 3/4 c. pureed ripe bananas (You may substitute pureed
　　　peaches.)
1/4 c. oil

Mix together the chestnut flour, baking soda, Vitamin C crystals, and cloves in a large bowl. Stir the bananas and oil together, add them to the flour mixture, and stir until they are just mixed in. Spoon the batter into oiled and floured muffin cups, filling them a little over 3/4 full. Bake at 375° for 18 to 20 minutes. Makes 12 to 13 muffins.

This recipe is free of all grains (including wheat and corn), gluten, milk, eggs, soy, yeast, and refined sugar.

Stevia-Sweetened Spice Muffins

Here are muffins for the person who must avoid fruit sweeteners as well as refined sugar. They are also grain-free and made with high-protein flours.

1 3/4 c. amaranth flour plus 1/2 c. arrowroot OR 1 1/2 c.
　　　quinoa flour plus 1/2 c. tapioca flour
2 tsp. baking soda
1/2 tsp. unbuffered Vitamin C crystals
2 tsp. cinnamon (optional)
1/4 tsp. ground cloves (optional)
1/4 tsp. white stevia powder
1 c. water
1/4 c. oil

Stir together the amaranth flour and arrowroot OR the quinoa flour and tapioca starch with the baking soda, Vitamin C crystals, cinnamon, cloves, and stevia powder. Combine the water and oil and stir them into the dry ingredients. (The dough will be stiffer than most muffin batter.) Put the dough onto an oiled and floured muffin tin and bake at 375° for 20 to 25 minutes. Makes 10 to 12 muffins.

This recipe is free of all grains (including wheat and corn), gluten, milk, eggs, soy, yeast, and all sugars.

Quinoa Crackers

These make great snacks, as well as being good with a simple soup or salad meal.

3 c. quinoa flour
1 c. tapioca flour
1/4 c. sesame seeds
2 tsp. baking soda
1/2 tsp. unbuffered Vitamin C crystals
1 tsp. salt
1 1/4 c. water
1/2 c. oil

Mix together the quinoa flour, tapioca flour, sesame seeds, baking soda, Vitamin C crystals, and salt in a large bowl. Combine the water and oil and stir them into the dry ingredients until the dough sticks together, adding a few more tablespoons of water if necessary. Divide the dough into thirds. Roll each third to about 1/8" thickness on an ungreased cookie sheet. Cut the dough into 2" squares and bake at 350° for 15 to 25 minutes, or until the crackers are crisp and lightly browned. Makes about 9 dozen crackers.This recipe is free of all grains (including wheat and corn), gluten, milk, eggs, soy, yeast, and refined sugar.

Graham" Crackers

A traditional favorite made grain-free.

Prepare "Quinoa Crackers," above, except omit the sesame seeds and salt, and substitute an equal amount of thawed apple juice concentrate for the water. Lightly oil the cookie sheets before rolling the dough out on them. Bake at 350° for 10 to 15 minutes, watching the crackers carefully to prevent burning. Remove the crackers from the cookie sheet immediately, using a spatula to pry them off if necessary.

This recipe is free of all grains (including wheat and corn), gluten, milk, eggs, soy, yeast, and refined sugar.

Oat Crackers

These delicious crackers are reminiscent of Scottish shortbread.

4 c. quick oats, uncooked
1/2 tsp. salt (optional)
1/3 c. oil
2/3 c. water

Combine the oats and salt. Add the oil and mix it into the dry ingredients thoroughly. Add the water and mix the dough with a spoon and your hands until the dough sticks together. Divide the dough in half and roll each half to about 1/8 inch thickness on an ungreased cookie sheet. Cut the dough into 1 1/2" to 2" squares. Bake at 350° for 20 to 25 minutes. Makes 4 to 5 dozen crackers.

This recipe is free of wheat, milk, eggs, corn, soy, yeast, and refined sugar.

Saltines

The delicious nutty flavor of spelt shines in these crackers.

2 c. spelt flour
1/2 tsp. salt
1/2 tsp. baking soda
1/4 tsp. unbuffered Vitamin C crystals
1/4 c. oil
1/2 c. water

Combine the flour, salt, baking soda, and Vitamin C crystals. Add the oil and stir until it is thoroughly mixed in to form small crumbs. Add the water two tablespoons at a time, mixing well after each addition. Knead the dough on a lightly floured board for one to two minutes. Divide the dough in half and roll each half out on an oiled baking sheet with an oiled rolling pin to about a 10" by 14' rectangle. The dough should be very thin, about 1/16" to 1/8" thick. Cut the dough into 2" squares and prick each square three times with a fork. Sprinkle the tops of the crackers with additional salt if desired. Bake at 350° for 10 to 14 minutes, or until the crackers are golden brown and crisp. Makes 6 to 7 dozen crackers.

This recipe is free of wheat, milk, eggs, corn, soy, yeast, and refined sugar.

Coconut Milk Wafers

These are an unusual treat with an incredible crunch. They are good to have on hand when the urge to snack on chips hits.

> 1 c. tapioca or water chestnut flour
> 1/4 tsp. baking soda
> 1/8 tsp. Vitamin C crystals
> Coconut milk - 7 to 8 Tbsp. with tapioca flour OR 12
>   to 13 Tbsp. with water chestnut flour
> Melted coconut oil, or any other kind of oil

Mix the tapioca or water chestnut flour, baking soda, and Vitamin C crystals. Add the coconut milk one tablespoon at a time to make a very stiff dough. Drop teaspoonfuls of the dough onto an oiled cookie sheet and flatten them to 1/8" or less thickness with your hand. Bake at 350° for 10 to 15 minutes, or until the edges begin to brown. Turn them over and bake 5 minutes more. Makes 2 to 3 dozen wafers.

This recipe is free of all grains (including wheat and corn), gluten, milk, eggs, soy, yeast, and refined sugar. If the coconut oil is used, this recipe contains only two food families.

Milo Crackers

The slightly coarse texture of milo flour adds to the appeal of these tasty crackers.

1 1/4 c. milo flour
3/4 c. arrowroot
1 tsp. baking soda
1/4 tsp. unbuffered Vitamin C crystals
1/4 to 1/2 tsp. salt, to taste (optional)
1/4 c. oil
1/2 c. water

Combine the milo flour, arrowroot, baking soda, Vitamin C crystals, and salt in a large bowl. Mix together the oil and water and add them to the dry ingredients, mixing with your hands to form a stiff dough. Divide the dough in half and roll each part out onto an ungreased cookie sheet with an oiled rolling pin. Cut the dough into 1 1/2" squares and bake at 350° for 20 to 25 minutes. Makes about 4 dozen crackers.

This recipe is free of wheat, milk, eggs, corn, soy, yeast, and refined sugar.

Canola Seed Crackers

The canola seeds add interest and flavor to both the grain and non-grain versions of these crackers.

Amaranth:

3 c. amaranth flour
1 c. arrowroot
1/4 c. canola seeds (optional)
2 tsp. baking soda
1/2 tsp. unbuffered Vitamin C crystals
1 tsp. salt (optional)
3/4 c. water
1/2 c. canola or other oil

Barley:

4 c. barley flour
1/4 c. canola seeds (optional)

2 tsp. baking soda
1/2 tsp. unbuffered Vitamin C crystals
1 tsp. salt (optional)
7/8 c. water (3/4 c. plus 2 tbsp.)
1/2 c. canola or other oil

Choose one set of ingredients above. Combine the flour(s), canola seeds, baking soda, Vitamin C crystals, and salt in a large bowl. Mix together the water and oil and pour them into the flour mixture. Stir until the dough sticks together, adding another few tablespoons of water if necessary to form a stiff but not crumbly dough. Divide the dough into thirds. Roll each third to about 1/8" thickness on an ungreased cookie sheet and cut the dough into 2" squares. Sprinkle the tops of the crackers lightly with additional salt if desired. Bake at 375° for 15 to 20 minutes, or until the crackers are crisp and lightly browned. Makes about 9 dozen crackers.

The barley version of this recipe is free of wheat, milk, eggs, corn, soy, yeast, and refined sugar. The amaranth version is also free of gluten and all grains.

Chestnut Wafers

With the natural sweetness of chestnut flour, these grain-free crackers can be eaten as a cookie.

2 1/2 c. chestnut flour
1 c. arrowroot
1/2 tsp. baking soda
1/4 tsp. unbuffered Vitamin C crystals
1/4 tsp. salt (optional)
3/4 c. water
1/4 c. oil

Mix the chestnut flour, arrowroot, baking soda, Vitamin C crystals, and salt in a large bowl. Stir together the water and oil and mix them into the dry ingredients, kneading with your hands if necessary. Divide the dough in half and roll each half out to between 1/8" and 1/4" thickness on an oiled cookie sheet. Cut the dough into 1 1/2" squares and bake at 375° for 8 to 12 minutes. Makes about 4 dozen crackers.

This recipe is free of all grains (including wheat and corn), gluten, milk, eggs, soy, yeast, and refined sugar.

Cassava Crackers

These crackers are crunchy and crumbly. Save the crumbs to use in place of croutons in salads or as breading for broiled fish. (See "Crispy Broiled Fish," page 87.) To obtain cassava meal by mail order, see "Sources of Special Foods," ch. 16.

  2 c. cassava meal
  1/2 tsp. baking soda
  1/4 tsp. unbuffered Vitamin C crystals
  1/4 tsp. salt
  3/4 c. water
  1/4 c. oil

Mix the cassava meal, baking soda, Vitamin C crystals and salt together in a large bowl. Combine the water and oil and stir them into the dry ingredients. Roll and press the crumbly mixture firmly into a 12" by 15" pan. (The thickness of the dough layer will be between 1/8" and 1/4".) Cut the dough into 1 1/2" squares and bake at 375° for 35 to 40 minutes. Makes about 3 1/2 dozen crackers.

This recipe is free of all grains (including wheat and corn), gluten, milk, eggs, soy, yeast, and refined sugar.

Quinoa Granola

This granola is good for snacks and to take on outings, as well as for breakfast

  1 1/2 c. quinoa flour
  1/2 c. tapioca flour
  1 1/2 c. chopped nuts

1/2 c. sesame seeds
1 1/2 tsp. cinnamon
1/3 c. oil
3/4 c. unsweetened applesauce
1/4 c. apple juice concentrate, thawed
2/3 c. chopped dried pears, chopped dates, raisins,
    or other dried fruit

Combine the flours, nuts, seeds, and cinnamon in a large bowl. Mix the oil, applesauce, and juice and pour them into the dry ingredients. Stir until the dough sticks together, adding a little more apple juice concentrate or water if necessary. Spread the dough in a lightly oiled 15" by 11" pan. Bake at 300° for 1 hour, or until light brown, breaking the dough into chunks and stirring it every 15 minutes. Cool the granola completely and stir in the dried fruit. Makes about 8 servings of cereal.

This recipe is free of all grains (including wheat and corn), gluten, milk, eggs, soy, yeast, and refined sugar.

Rye Pancakes

Try these and the following pancakes with "Mock Maple Syrup," page 220.

2 c. rye flour
1 tsp. baking soda
1/2 tsp. unbuffered Vitamin C crystals
3 tbsp. oil
2 1/4 c. water or unsweetened white grape juice

Mix together the flour, baking soda, and Vitamin C crystals. Combine the oil and water or juice and stir them into the flour mixture with a wire whisk, adding a few tablespoons more water if necessary to make a thin batter. (This batter may thicken as itstands and may require the addition of more water after part of the pancakes have been cooked.) Heat a lightly oiled griddle over medium heat or an electric griddle to 350°. Pour about 1/8 c. batter for each pancake onto the griddle and cook them until they look dry around the edges on the top and are very brown on the bottom. Turn and cook the other side until brown. Makes about 2 to 2 1/2 dozen 3" pancakes.

This recipe is free of wheat, milk, eggs, corn, soy, yeast, and refined sugar.

Barley Pancakes

These are so delicious that you will never miss the wheat, milk, and eggs.

> 2 c. barley flour
> 1 tsp. baking soda
> 1/2 tsp. unbuffered Vitamin C crystals
> 1/2 tsp. salt (optional)
> 1 tbsp. sugar (optional)
> 3 tbsp. oil
> 2 1/2 to 3 c. water

Mix together the flour, baking soda, and Vitamin C crystals. Combine the oil and 2 1/2 c. of water and stir the liquids into the flour mixture with a wire whisk, adding a few tablespoons more water if necessary to make a thin batter. (This batter has a pronounced tendency to thicken as it stands and may require up to 3 c. total amount of water with the additional tablespoons of water added several times as the pancakes are cooking.) Heat a lightly oiled griddle over medium heat or an electric griddle to 350°. Pour about 1/8 c. batter for each pancake onto the griddle and cook them until they look dry around the edges on the top and are light brown on the bottom. Turn and cook the other side until light brown. Makes about 2 to 2 1/2 dozen 3" pancakes.

This recipe is free of wheat, milk, eggs, corn, soy, and yeast. It is also free of refined sugar if the sugar is omitted.

Spelt Pancakes

The gluten in spelt flour helps these pancakes rise to be the lightest and fluffiest you have ever eaten.

1 c. spelt flour
1 1/2 tsp. baking soda
1/2 tsp. unbuffered Vitamin C crystals
1/2 tsp. salt (optional)
1 c. water OR 1 3/4 c. water plus 1/4 c. thawed
apple juice concentrate OR 1 c. water plus 1 c.
apple juice
3 tbsp. oil

Mix together the flour, baking soda, and Vitamin C crystals. Combine the oil with the water or water and juice and stir them into the flour mixture with a wire whisk, adding a few table-spoons more water if necessary to make a thin batter. (This batter may thicken as it stands and may require the addition of more water after part of the pancakes have been cooked.) Heat a lightly oiled griddle over medium heat or an electric griddle to 350°. Pour about 1/8 c. batter for each pancake onto the griddle and cook them until they look dry around the edges on the top and are light brown on the bottom. Turn the pancakes and cook them until the other side is light brown. Makes about 2 1/2 dozen 3" to 4" pancakes.

This recipe is free of wheat, milk, eggs, corn, soy, yeast, and refined sugar.

Quinoa Pancakes

These pancakes are a delight to those who must avoid all grains. Try them with "Strawberry Sauce," page 195, or "Pineapple Sauce," page 196.

1 1/2 c. quinoa flour
1/2 c. tapioca flour
1 tsp. baking soda
1/2 tsp. unbuffered Vitamin C crystals

1 1/2 tsp. cinnamon (optional)
3 tbsp. oil
2 c. water or apple juice

Mix together the flours, baking soda, Vitamin C crystals, and cinnamon. Combine the oil with the water or juice and stir them into the flour mixture with a wire whisk to make a thin batter. Lightly oil a pancake griddle and heat it over medium heat or heat an electric griddle to 350° Pour out 1/8 to 1/4 c. of batter for each pancake. If the first batch of pancakes you cook is too thick, add an extra 2 to 4 tbsp. of water or juice to the batter until it is thin enough. Cook the pancakes until they are dry on the top and light brown on the bottom, then turn and cook them until the second side is light brown. Makes about 2 dozen 3-inch pancakes or 1 1/2 dozen 4-inch pancakes.

This recipe is free of all grains (including wheat and corn), gluten, milk, eggs, soy, yeast, and refined sugar.

Barley Waffles

These are wonderful for breakfast and at other times during the day, in spite of being a little more time-consuming to prepare than other breakfast foods. For more waffle recipes and general information about preparing waffles refer to pages 135 to 141 of The Yeast Connection Cookbook. (See "References," page 271.)

2 c. barley flour
2 tsp. baking soda
3/4 tsp. unbuffered Vitamin C crystals
1/2 tsp. salt (optional)
2 tbsp. oil
2 1/2 c. water

Preheat a lightly oiled waffle iron to medium-high. While the iron is heating, combine the flour, baking soda, Vitamin C crystals, and salt in a large bowl. Mix the oil and water, stir them into the dry ingredients, and allow the batter to stand for about 10 minutes while the iron is heating. Pour enough batter into the iron to almost reach the edges (about 1 cup for a large iron) and bake for 15 minutes. Do not try to open the iron until each waffle should be almost done. Makes 3 to 4 9" square waffles.

This recipe is free of wheat, milk, eggs, corn, soy, yeast, and refined sugar.

Banana Bread

This sweet and moist bread can be made in either a grain or a nongrain version.

> 3 c. spelt flour OR 2 c. amaranth flour plus 1/2 c.
>   arrowroot
> 2 tsp. baking soda
> 1/2 tsp. unbuffered Vitamin C crystals
> 1/2 tsp. ground cloves (optional)
> 1/2 c. chopped nuts (optional)
> 1 3/4 c. mashed ripe bananas
> 1/4 c. oil

Stir together the flour(s), baking soda, Vitamin C crystals, cloves, and nuts in a large bowl. Combine the mashed bananas and oil and stir them into the dry ingredients until they are completely mixed in, but be careful not to overmix. (The batter will be stiff.) Put the batter into an oiled and floured 9" by 5" loaf pan and bake at 350° for 55 to 60 minutes, or until the bread is lightly browned and a toothpick inserted in the center comes out dry. Remove it from the oven and allow it to cool in the pan for 10 minutes. Remove it from the pan to cool completely. Makes one loaf.

This recipe is free of wheat, milk, eggs, corn, soy, yeast, and refined sugar. If it is made with amaranth flour instead of spelt flour it is also free of gluten and all grains.

Applesauce Bread

This grain-free bread is delicious for breakfast or dessert.

2 c. quinoa flour
1/2 c. tapioca flour
2 tsp. baking soda
1/2 tsp. unbuffered Vitamin C crystals
2 tsp. cinnamon
1/4 c. oil
1 c. unsweetened applesauce
3/4 c. apple juice concentrate, thawed

Combine the flours, baking soda, Vitamin C crystals, and cinnamon in a large bowl. Mix together the oil, applesauce, and juice, and stir them into the dry ingredients until they are just mixed in. Pour the batter into an oiled and floured 8" by 4" loaf pan and bake at 350° for 45 to 55 minutes, or until the bread is brown and a toothpick inserted into the center of the loaf comes out dry. Cool the loaf in the pan for about 10 minutes, and then remove it from the pan to finish cooling. Makes one loaf.

This recipe is free of all grains (including wheat and corn), gluten, milk, eggs, soy, yeast, and refined sugar.

No-Yeast Bread

These breads are a very versatile answer to the question of how to make a sandwich for lunch.

Rye:

3 c. rye flour
1 1/2 tsp. baking soda
1/2 tsp. unbuffered Vitamin C crystals
1 tsp salt (optional)
1/3 c. oil
1 1/2 c. water

Spelt:

    3 1/2 c. spelt flour
    2 tsp. baking soda
    1/2 tsp. unbuffered Vitamin C crystals
    1 tsp. salt (optional)
    1/2 c. oil
    1 1/4 c. water

Barley:

    3 c. barley flour
    1 1/2 tsp. baking soda
    1/2 tsp. unbuffered Vitamin C crystals
    1 tsp. salt (optional)
    3/8 c. oil (1/4 c. plus 2 tbsp.)
    2 c. water

Amaranth:

    3 3/8 c. (3 1/4 c. plus 2 tbsp.) amaranth flour
    1 1/8 c. (1 c. plus 2 tbsp.) arrowroot
    3 tsp. baking soda
    3/4 tsp. unbuffered Vitamin C crystals
    1 1/2 tsp. salt (optional)
    3/8 c. (1/4 c. plus 2 tbsp.) oil
    1 1/2 c. water

Quinoa:

    2 1/4 c. quinoa flour
    3/4 c. tapioca flour
    2 tsp. baking soda
    1/2 tsp. unbuffered Vitamin C crystals
    1 tsp. salt (optional)
    1/4 c. oil
    1 1/2 c. water

Choose one set of ingredients, above. Combine the flour(s), baking soda, Vitamin C crystals, and salt in a large bowl. Stir together the oil and water and mix them into the dry ingredients until they are just mixed in. Put the batter into an oiled and floured 8" by 4" loaf pan. Bake at 350° for 35 to 45 minutes, or until the bread is lightly browned and a toothpick inserted in the center of the loaf comes out dry. Gently remove the loaf from the pan immediately and cool it completely on a wire rack before slicing it for the freezer. Makes one loaf.

This recipe is free of wheat, milk, eggs, corn, soy, yeast, and refined sugar. The amaranth and quinoa versions are also free of gluten and all grains.

No-Yeast Sandwich Buns

These are great with turkey burgers or lentil burgers (page 94), fresh sliced vegetables, and the condiments of your choice (pages 220 to 223).

Prepare one batch of any variety of "No-Yeast Bread," above. Put the batter into oiled and floured glass custard cups, filling them 1/2 to 2/3 full. Bake at 350° for 30 to 40 minutes, or until the buns are lightly browned and a toothpick inserted in the center of one comes out dry. Remove them from the cups immediately and allow them to cool completely. Carefully slice them in half horizontally with a serrated knife. Makes 7 to 11 buns.

This recipe is free of wheat, milk, eggs, corn, soy, yeast, and refined sugar. The amaranth and quinoa versions are also free of gluten and all grains.

Barley Sandwich Bread

If you want to pick your barley bread sandwich up rather than possibly eating it with a knife and fork, try this recipe. The addition of guar gum to this bread makes it less fragile than barley "No-Yeast Bread."

    3 c. barley flour, divided
    2 tsp. guar gum
    1 tsp. salt (optional)
    2 c. water
    3/8 c. oil (1/4 c. plus 2 tbsp.)
    1 1/2 tsp. baking soda
    1/2 tsp. unbuffered Vitamin C crystals

Combine 2 1/2 c. of the flour, the guar gum, and the salt in an electric mixer bowl. Add the water and oil and beat the dough for 3 minutes on medium speed. Combine the remaining 1/2 c. flour with the baking soda and Vitamin C crystals, quickly stir them into the dough mixture in the bowl, and beat it on medium speed for 30 seconds. Put the dough into an oiled and floured 8" by 4" loaf pan and bake at 350° for 55 to 65 minutes, or until a toothpick inserted in the center of the loaf comes out dry. Remove from the pan immediately. Makes 1 loaf.

This recipe is free of wheat, milk, eggs, corn, soy, yeast, and refined sugar.

Spelt Sandwich Bread

Beating the batter for this bread develops the gluten in the spelt flour and gives the bread a firmer texture than spelt "No-Yeast Bread."

    3 1/2 c. spelt flour, divided
    1 tsp. salt (optional)
    1 1/4 c. water
    1/2 c. oil
    2 tsp. baking soda
    1/2 tsp. unbuffered Vitamin C crystals

Combine 3 c. of the flour and the salt in an electric mixer bowl. Add the water and beat on medium speed for 3 minutes or until the dough becomes cohesive and climbs up the beaters. Beat in the oil. Mix together the remaining 1/2 c. flour, baking soda, and Vitamin C crystals and stir or, if necessary, briefly knead them into the dough. Then beat the dough on medium speed for 30 seconds. Put the dough into an oiled and floured 8" by 4" loaf pan. Bake at 350° for 50 to 60 minutes, or until it is brown. Remove it from the pan immediately. Makes one loaf.

This recipe is free of wheat, milk, eggs, corn, soy, yeast, and refined sugar.

Oat Biscuits

These are wonderful fresh out of the oven with stew or soup.

> 2 c. oat flour
> 1 tsp. baking soda
> 1/4 tsp. unbuffered Vitamin C crystals
> 1/2 tsp. salt (optional)
> 1/4 c. oil
> 1/2 c. water

Stir together the flour, baking soda, Vitamin C crystals, and salt. Blend in the oil with a pastry cutter until the mixture is crumbly. Stir in the water and pat the dough to about 1/2" thickness on an oat-floured board. Cut the dough into circles and put them on an ungreased baking sheet. Bake at 400° for 20 to 25 minutes. Makes 10 to 12 biscuits.

This recipe is free of wheat, milk, eggs, corn, soy, yeast, and refined sugar.

Barley Biscuits

The flavor of these barley biscuits is especially delicious when they are hot.

> 2 c. barley flour
> 1 tsp. baking soda
> 1/4 tsp. unbuffered Vitamin C crystals
> 1/2 tsp. salt (optional)

3/8 c. oil (1/4 c. plus 2 tbsp.)
1/2 c. water

Stir together the flour, baking soda, Vitamin C crystals, and salt. Blend in the oil with a pastry cutter until the mixture is crumbly. Stir in the water and pat the dough to about 1/2" thickness on a barley-floured board. Cut the dough into circles and put them on an ungreased baking sheet. Bake at 400° for 20 to 25 minutes. Makes 10 to 12 biscuits.

This recipe is free of wheat, milk, eggs, corn, soy, yeast, and refined sugar.

Spelt Biscuits

These biscuits will split into layers that just invite a little all-fruit jam or jelly, if you can tolerate it.

2 c. spelt flour
1 tsp. baking soda
1/4 tsp. unbuffered Vitamin C crystals
1/2 tsp. salt (optional)
1/4 c. oil
1/2 c. water

Stir together the flour, baking soda, Vitamin C crystals, and salt. Blend in the oil with a pastry cutter until the mixture is crumbly. Stir in the water. Knead the dough about 25 times on a spelt-floured board; then pat or roll it to 3/8" thickness. Cut the dough into circles and put them on an ungreased baking sheet. Bake at 400° for 20 to 25 minutes. Makes about 10 2-inch biscuits.

This recipe is free of wheat, milk, eggs, corn, soy, yeast, and refined sugar.

Spelt-Biscuit Sandwich Buns

These sandwich buns will stand up to almost anything without falling apart.

Prepare "Spelt Biscuit" dough, above, knead it, and roll it out to 1/2 inch thickness. Cut it into 3" to 3 1/2" circles using a large coffee mug. Bake as directed above. Makes 4 to 5 buns.

This recipe is free of wheat, milk, eggs, corn, soy, yeast, and refined sugar.

Teething Biscuits

It is never too young to start rotating the foods of children born into a family with allergic tendencies. These are tough and great for gumming, but watch your children at all times when eating these just in case they manage to gum off a piece that they could choke on.

Quinoa:
1c. quinoa flour
1/2 c. tapioca flour
3 tbsp. oil
1/2 c. apple juice concentrate, thawed

Amaranth:

1 c. amaranth flour
1/2 c. arrowroot
3 tbsp oil
3/8 c. pineapple juice concentrate, thawed

Rye:

1 1/2 c. rye flour
3 tbsp. oil
1/4 c. plus 3 tbsp. grape juice concentrate, thawed

Combine the flour(s) in a bowl. Mix the oil and juice together and stir them into the flour. Knead the dough to absorb all the flour and form a very hard dough. Roll the dough out to 3/8" thickness on a floured board and cut it into 1" by 3" bars with a knife. Transfer the bars to a lightly oiled baking sheet. Bake at 300° for 35 to 40 minutes, or until they begin to brown. Turn off the oven and leave them in for 1 more hour. Makes about 1 1/2 dozen teething biscuits.

This recipe is free of wheat, milk, eggs, corn, soy, yeast, and refined sugar. The quinoa and amaranth versions are also free of gluten and all grains.

4

Yeast Raised Breads and Baked Goods

Yeast raised bread has beeen called "the staff of life." This chapter provides recipes for people who can tolerate yeast-containing foods occasionally but cannot eat the wheat-containing baked goods found at their grocery store.

It is not difficult to make yeast bread and, while it requires intermittent attention over a few hours, the actual amount of time you spend working on it is not that great. Success in making yeast bread depends on two factors: taking good care of the yeast so it will produce gas, and trapping the gas in the dough so the dough will rise properly.

The most important factor in taking good care of the yeast is temperature, both of the liquid used to dissolve the yeast, and of the place the dough is set to rise. A yeast thermometer is a very useful tool for determining the temperature of both the dissolving liquid and the rising place.

For quick-rise yeast, used in the recipes in this book, the temperature of the dissolving liquid should be between 115° and 120°. The yeast dissolves best if you sprinkle it over the whole surface of the liquid rather than adding it in one lump. If you have refrigerated other ingredients used in the recipe, such as oil or flour, allow them to warm up to room temperature before you use them.

You should allow the dough to rise in a warm (85° to 90°) place. The inside of the oven is an ideal place because it is draft-free and can be kept warm regardless of the room temperature. In a gas oven, it is said that the pilot light keeps the inside of the oven at just the right temperature for yeast bread dough to rise. You can use an electric oven for a rising place by heating it to 350° for five minutes as you start making the bread, then turning it off and leaving the door open for long enough to allow it to cool to about 90°, and then closing the door.

Another factor in taking good care of yeast is the provision of some food, usually some type of sugar, to support their metabolism. All of the recipes in this book contain either sugar, honey, maple syrup, or some type of fruit sweetener. The recipes containing fruit sweeteners tend to be a little heavier than those using the more refined sugars. "Spelt Yeast Bread" is an exception to this, being very light in spite of using apple juice to feed the yeast.

Along with keeping the yeast happy, you have to trap the gas they make in order to get yeast bread dough to rise properly. Wheat and spelt flour are naturally high in gluten, a protein found in grains. When you beat or knead wheat or spelt dough, the gluten molecules join together to make long strands of gluten, which trap the gas that the yeast produces. Rye flour contains less gluten than wheat and spelt, but still has enough to allow the bread to rise. Adequate beating and/or kneading is vital to developing the gluten in breads made with these flours so that they will rise properly. Other flours, such as barley, oat, and quinoa, do not contain enough gluten to trap the gas from the yeast on their own. However, you can add guar gum (See "Sources of Special Foods," ch. 16) to the dough to trap the gas, although the bread will not be as light as wheat or spelt bread. Do not allow dough that contains guar gum to rise to more than double its original volume during the final rising period, or it may collapse during baking.

Yeast bread is tested for doneness after baking by different criteria than baking-soda-raised breads. When a loaf of yeast bread is done it will be nicely browned and will have pulled away from the sides of the pan slightly. Remove the bread from the pan immediately after removing it from the oven. If you tap the loaf on the bottom and it sounds hollow, this also indicates that it is done.

Oat Yeast Bread

This bread has a homey and hearty flavor.

1 1/2 c. warm (115°) water
1/2 c. date sugar
1 package quick-rise yeast
2 1/4 c. oat flour
2 1/4 tsp. guar gum
1/2 tsp. salt
3 tbsp. oil
Oatmeal

Mix together the warm water, date sugar, and yeast, and let the mixture stand for about 10 minutes or until it is foamy. Stir together the dry ingredients in a large electric mixer bowl. Add the yeast mixture and oil and beat the dough for three minutes at medium speed. Scrape the dough from the beaters and the sides of the bowl into the bottom of the bowl. Oil the top of the dough and the sides of the bowl, and cover the bowl with a towel. Put the bowl in a warm (85° to 90°) place and let the dough rise for 1 to 1 1/2 hours. Beat the dough again for three minutes at medium speed. Oil an 8" by 4" loaf pan and coat the inside of it with oatmeal. Put the dough in the pan and allow it to rise in a warm place for about 20 minutes, or until it barely doubles. Preheat the oven to 350°. Bake the loaf for about 75 minutes, loosely covering it with foil after the first 15 minutes to prevent excessive browning. Makes one loaf.

This recipe is free of wheat, milk, eggs, corn, soy, and refined sugar.

Quinoa Yeast Bread

Spicy and flavorful, this is a great bread for those who can tolerate yeast occasionally but cannot have grains.

1 c. water
1/2 c. apple juice concentrate, thawed
1 package quick-rise yeast
2 c. quinoa flour
2 1/4 tsp. guar gum
1 tsp. cinnamon (optional)
1/4 tsp. salt
3 tbsp. oil
Sesame seeds

Heat the water and apple juice concentrate to about 115°. Stir in the yeast and let the mixture stand for about 10 minutes or until it is foamy. Stir together the dry ingredients in a large electric mixer bowl. Add the yeast mixture and oil and beat the dough for three minutes at medium speed. Scrape the dough from the beaters and the sides of the bowl into the bottom of the bowl. Oil the top of the dough and the sides of the bowl, and cover the bowl with a towel. Put the bowl in a warm (85° to 90°) place and let the dough rise for 1 to 1 1/2 hours. Beat the dough again for three minutes at medium speed. Oil an 8" by 4" loaf pan and coat the inside of it with sesame seeds. Put the dough in the pan and allow it to rise in a warm place for about 20 minutes, or until it barely doubles. Preheat the oven to 375°. Bake the loaf for about 65 minutes, loosely covering it with foil after the first 15 minutes to prevent excessive browning. Makes one loaf.

This recipe is free of all grains (including wheat and corn), gluten, milk, eggs, soy, and refined sugar.

Raisin Bread

This traditional favorite is excellent when made without grains. "It's raisiny," says my son.

Prepare "Quinoa Yeast Bread," above. After the second beating, stir 1/2 c. raisins into the dough. Put the dough into the pan, allow it to rise the final time, and bake it as directed above. Makes one loaf.

This recipe is free of all grains (including wheat and corn), gluten, milk, eggs, soy, and refined sugar.

Rye Yeast Bread

This sturdy bread is excellent for sandwiches of all kinds.

1/3 c. water
1 c. white grape juice
1 package quick-rise yeast
1 tsp. salt
3 tbsp. oil
4 to 4 1/2 c. rye flour

Warm the water and grape juice to about 115° and stir in the yeast. Let the mixture stand for about 10 minutes or until it is foamy. Stir in the salt, oil, and 2 c. of the flour, and beat it with a spoon or mixer until it is smooth. Add enough of the rest of the flour to make a soft dough. Knead the dough on a floured board for 10 minutes. Place the dough in an oiled bowl, turn it over so the top of the ball is also oiled, and cover it with a towel. Let it rise in a warm (85° to 90°) place for about 45 minutes, or until it is doubled in volume. Shape the dough into a loaf, place it in an oiled 8" by 4" loaf pan, and let it rise in a warm place again for about 30 minutes, or until it doubles in volume. Bake at 425° for 10 minutes, then lower the oven temperature to 350° for an additional 35 to 45 minutes of baking. Remove it from the oven when the loaf is brown and has pulled away from the sides of the pan slightly. Makes one loaf.

This recipe is free of wheat, milk, eggs, corn, soy, and refined sugar.

Rye Sandwich Buns

These are excellent with many types of sandwiches in addition to hamburgers.

Prepare "Rye Yeast Bread" dough, above. After the first rising period, divide the dough into nine pieces. Shape the pieces into flattened balls and place them on an oiled baking sheet. Allow them to rise in a warm place for about 30 minutes, or until they have doubled in volume. Bake at 375° for 20 to 25 minutes, or until they are lightly browned. Slice them in half horizontally with a serrated knife before freezing any that will not be used soon.

This recipe is free of wheat, milk, eggs, corn, soy, and refined sugar.

Quick Barley Yeast Bread

Because this bread dough does well with a single rising period, it can be made more quickly than some of the other yeast breads.

> 2 1/2 c. plus 2 tbsp. warm (115°) water plus 3 tbsp.
>   brown or white sugar OR 2 1/2 c. warm (115°)
>   water plus 3 tbsp. honey OR 1 3/4 c. water
>   plus 3/8 c. orange or pineapple juice concentrate,
>   warmed to 115°
> 1 1/2 packages quick-rise yeast
> 1/4 c. oil
> 1 1/2 tsp. salt
> 3 1/4 tsp. guar gum
> 6 c. barley flour

Mix the water with the sugar, honey, or fruit juice concentrate in a large electric mixer bowl. Stir in the yeast and allow the mixture to stand for about 10 minutes or until it is foamy. Add the oil and salt to the yeast mixture. Stir the guar gum into half of the flour and add this mixture to the liquid ingredients in the mixer bowl. Beat at medium speed for three minutes. Mix in the rest of the flour with the mixer and your hands and knead the dough on a floured board for 5 to 10 minutes. Shape the dough into a loaf and press it into an oiled 8" by 4" or 9" by 5" loaf pan. Place the loaf in a warm (85° to 90°) place and allow it to rise for 20 to 30 minutes, or until the dough is just to the top of the pan. Bake at 375° for 65 to 85 minutes, or until it is golden brown. Makes one loaf.

This recipe is free of wheat, milk, eggs, corn, soy. If made with the fruit juice, it is also free of refined sugar.

Barley Sandwich Buns

While these buns are not exactly light, they are still excellent with hamburgers of all kinds.

Prepare "Barley Yeast Bread" dough, above. After kneading, divide the dough into twelve pieces. Shape the pieces into flattened balls and put them on an oiled baking sheet. Let them rise in a warm place until barely double in volume, about 20 minutes, and bake them at 375° for 45 to 50 minutes, or until they are lightly browned. Makes 12 buns.

This recipe is free of wheat, milk, eggs, corn, soy. If made with the fruit juice, it is also free of refined sugar.

Spelt Yeast Bread

This bread is so light that you will not believe that it is made with an alternative flour. My husband prefers the flavor of spelt bread to that of homemade whole wheat bread.

>2 1/2 c. water plus 1/2 c. thawed apple juice concentrate,
>   warmed to 115° OR 1 c. water plus 2 c. apple juice,
>   warmed to 115°
>2 packages quick-rise yeast
>2 tsp. salt
>1/4 c. oil
>8 to 9 c. spelt flour, divided

Combine the water, juice, and yeast in a large electric mixer bowl and let the mixture stand for about 10 minutes or until it is foamy. Add 4 1/2 c. of the spelt flour and beat on medium speed for 5 to 8 minutes. (During this time the gluten in the dough will develop into long strands and the dough should become cohesive and begin to climb up the beaters.) Beat in the oil and salt. Stir in another 1 to 2 cups of spelt flour. Put the dough on a floured board and knead it for 10 minutes, kneading in enough of the remaining flour to make a firm and elastic dough. Put the dough into an oiled bowl and turn it once so that the top of the ball is also oiled. Cover it with a towel and let it rise in a warm (85° to 90°) place until it has doubled in volume, about 45 minutes to 1 hour. Punch down the dough and shape it into two or three loaves. Put each loaf into an oiled 9" by 5" loaf pan if you made two loaves or an oiled 8" by 4" loaf pan if you made three loaves. (This bread is sometimes difficult to remove from the pan after baking, especially if it has been baked for the full baking time. If you prefer your bread quite brown, you may want to line the pans with parchment or waxed paper after oiling them and also oil the paper.) Let the loaves rise until they have doubled again, about 45 minutes. Bake at 375° for 40 to 45 minutes. Immediately run a knife around the edges of the loaves and remove them from the pans. Cool them on a wire rack. Makes 2 or 3 loaves.

This recipe is free of wheat, milk, eggs, corn, soy, and refined sugar.

Spelt Sandwich or Dinner Buns

These buns are as light and tasty as the best from any bakery.

Prepare "Spelt Yeast Bread" dough, page 60. After the first rising period, divide the dough into 20 to 24 balls for sandwich buns or into about 30 balls for dinner buns. Place them on oiled baking sheets and let them rise until doubled in volume, about 20 minutes. Bake at 375° for 20 to 30 minutes, or until they are nicely browned. Immediately remove them from the baking sheets with a metal spatula. Makes 20 to 24 sandwich buns or about 30 dinner buns.

This recipe is free of wheat, milk, eggs, corn, soy, and refined sugar.

Pita (Pocket) Bread

These are great for pocket sandwiches, or cut them in half and use them for pocket tacos.

> 1/3 batch "Spelt Yeast Bread" dough, page 60
> Oil
> Spelt flour

Make the dough for "Spelt Yeast Bread" as directed in the recipe and let it rise in a warm (85° to 90°) place for 30 to 60 minutes. Punch down the dough and knead it for 3 to 5 minutes on a very lightly oiled board. Using a very lightly oiled rolling pin, roll the dough out to about 1/4" thickness. Fold the dough in half and roll it out to 1/4" thickness again. Repeat this process 15 to 20 times. Cut the dough into eight pieces and roll each piece into a 6" to 7" circle, flouring both sides of each piece well while you are rolling it and when it is finished. Place the circles on floured baking sheets. Bake in a pre-heated 475° oven for 5 to 8 minutes, or until they begin to brown. Immediately remove them from the baking sheet and wrap them with a damp dishcloth to keep them soft. Cool them completely before removing them from the dishcloth. To serve, cut them in half with a saw-toothed bread knife, also using the knife to open any places where the top and bottom did not separate. Makes 8 pitas.

This recipe is free of wheat, milk, eggs, corn, soy, and refined sugar.

Pretzels

These are delicious and nutritious snacks for those who do not need to avoid salt.

> 1/3 batch "Spelt Yeast Bread" dough, page 60
> Salt, coarse if desired

Prepare the "Spelt Yeast Bread" dough and allow it to rise the first time as directed in the recipe. Punch down and knead the dough a few times. Divide it into 24 pieces and roll each piece into a 12" to 15" long rope. Place the ropes on oiled baking sheets and shape them into pretzel (open knot) shapes. Sprinkle them with salt and allow them to rise for about 20 minutes. Bake at 350° for 20 to 25 minutes, or until they are lightly browned. Remove them from the baking sheet immediately with a metal spatula and cool them on a wire rack. Makes 24 3-inch pretzels.

This recipe is free of wheat, milk, eggs, corn, soy, and refined sugar.

English Muffins

These are delicious split, toasted, and spread with a little all-fruit jam.

> 1 c. warm (115°) water
> 1 tbsp. apple juice concentrate, thawed
> 1 package quick-rise yeast
> 2 1/2 to 2 3/4 c. spelt flour, divided
> 1/4 c. oil
> 1/2 tsp. salt

Combine the water, juice, and yeast in a large electric mixer bowl and let it stand for about 10 minutes or until it is foamy. Mix in 1 1/2 c. of the flour and beat on medium speed for 3 to 5 minutes, or until the gluten is developed and the dough climbs up the beaters. Beat in the oil and salt. Knead in enough of the remaining flour to make a soft dough. Roll the dough out to about 3/8" thickness on a thoroughly floured board. Thoroughly flour the top of the dough before and after rolling it. Cut it into 3" rounds using a mug or widemouthed glass. Sprinkle flour on a baking sheet. Transfer the rounds to the baking sheet and allow them ro rise in a warm (85° to 90°) place for about 45 minutes, or until they double in volume. Heat an ungreased griddle or skillet over medium heat, or an electric griddle or skillet to 375°. Carefully transfer the rounds to the griddle and bake them for 6 to 7 minutes on each side, or until each side is brown. Cool them on a wire rack. To split thcm, make a shallow cut with a knife all around the center of the outside edge of each muffin, then gently pull the top and bottom of the muffins apart. The muffins split more easily when cool. Makes about 16 muffins.

This recipe is free of wheat, milk, eggs, corn, soy, and refined sugar.

Cinnamon Swirl Bread

This is a great breakfast bread, especially when toasted.

> 1 batch "Rye Yeast Bread" dough (page 58) OR 1/3 batch "Spelt Yeast Bread" dough (page 60)
> 2 tbsp. honey OR 2 tbsp. grape juice sweetener OR 1/4 c. apple juice concentrate that has been boiled down to 2 tbsp. OR 2 to 4 tbsp. sugar
> 2 tsp. cinnamon
> 2 tsp. oil (only if sugar is used for the sweetener)
> 1/2 c. raisins (optional)

Make the bread dough as directed in the recipe and let it rise once. Punch it down and roll it into an 18" by 8" rectangle. If sugar is used for the sweetener, brush the rectangle with the oil. Spread the rectangle with the sweetener, cinnamon, and raisins. Roll it up tightly, starting with the short edge, and pinch the final edge onto the outside of the roll. Place the roll into an oiled 8" by 4" loaf pan with the seam side down. Allow it to rise again and bake it as directed in the bread recipe. Makes one loaf.

This recipe is free of wheat, milk, eggs, corn, and soy. It is free of refined sugar if one of the fruit sweeteners is used rather than the sugar or honey.

Spelt Sweet Roll Dough

You can use this dough to make several yeast bread treats - cinnamon rolls, doughnuts, or "Tea Ring," below. If you use sugar or honey as the sweetener, the dough is lighter than if you use apple juice.

1 c. apple juice concentrate, thawed and warmed to 115°
OR 1 c. warm (115°) water plus 1/3 c. sugar OR
3/4 c. warm (115°) water plus 1/3 c. honey
1 package quick-rise yeast
3 tbsp. oil
1/2 tsp. cinnamon (optional)
1/4 tsp. salt
3 to 3 1/2 c. spelt flour, divided

In a large electric mixer bowl, stir the yeast into the warm apple juice concentrate or warm water and sweetener. Let the mixture stand for 10 minutes or until it is foamy. Add the oil, cinnamon, salt, and 2 1/4 c. of the spelt flour and beat the dough on medium speed for 4 to 6 minutes, or until it becomes cohesive and climbs up the beaters. Knead in enough of the rest of the flour to make a firm and elastic dough. Then knead it for another 10 minutes. Let the dough rise in a warm (85° to 90°) place for about 45 minutes to 1 hour, or until it has doubled in volume. Shape and bake it as directed in the individual recipe. The number of rolls, doughnuts, etc. this recipe makes is given in the individual recipes.

This recipe is free of wheat, milk, eggs, corn, and soy. It is free of refined sugar if it is sweetened with the juice.

Tea Ring

Serve this for an old-fashioned tea party or as a not-too-sweet but elegant dessert.

1 batch of "Rye Yeast Bread" dough (page 58) OR
1/4 batch "Spelt Yeast Bread" dough (page 60) OR
1 batch "Spelt Sweet Roll Dough" made using
apple juice (page 64) OR 2/3 batch "Spelt Sweet
Roll Dough" made using sugar or honey (page 64)
1/3 c. all-fruit (unsweetened) blueberry preserves,
or other all-fruit preserves
1/3 c. chopped nuts
1 1/2 tsp. cinnamon

Prepare the dough as directed in the individual recipe and allow it to rise the first time. Punch it down and knead it a few times, then roll it into a 12" by 12" square. Spread all but a 1" margin on one edge of the square with the preserves; sprinkle the preserves with the nuts and cinnamon. Roll the square up, beginning with the edge opposite the edge with no toppings. Pinch the edge without toppings to the outside of the roll. Place the roll, seam side down, on a oiled baking sheet. Using a sharp knife, make eleven cuts at one-inch intervals that extend 3/4 of the way through the roll from one side. Form the roll into a circle, using the uncut side as the center of the ring. Turn the slices down on their sides all facing the same way. Allow the ring to rise about 30 minutes to one hour, or until it is doubled in volume. Bake at 350° for 20 to 30 minutes, or until it is lightly browned. Remove it from the baking sheet to a serving dish immediately. Makes one tea ring.

This recipe is free of wheat, milk, eggs, corn, and soy. It is free of refined sugar if it is sweetened with the juice.

Cinnamon Rolls

These not-too-sweet rolls are a great treat any time of the day - for breakfast, for an after school snack, or for dessert.

> 1 batch "Rye Yeast Bread" dough (page 58) OR 1/3 batch "Spelt Yeast Bread" dough (page 60) OR 1 batch "Spelt Sweet Roll Dough" made with apple juice (page 64) OR 2/3 batch "Spelt Sweet Roll Dough" made with sugar or honey (page 64)
> 2 tbsp. grape juice sweetener OR 1/4 c. apple juice concentrate boiled down to 2 tbsp. volume OR 2 tbsp. honey OR 2 tbsp. sugar
> 1 tbsp. oil (only if sugar is used above)
> 1 1/2 tsp. cinnamon
> 1/3 c. raisins (optional)

Prepare the dough and allow it to rise the first time as directed in the individual recipe. Punch it down and roll it out on an oiled board with an oiled rolling pin into a 12" by 12" square. Spread the square with oil only if sugar is used for the sweetener. Spread it with the sweetener and sprinkle it with the cinnamon and raisins. Roll the square up starting from one side. Cut the roll into 9 slices and place them cut side down into an oiled 8" by 8" or 9" by 9" baking pan. Allow the rolls to rise in a warm (85° to 90°) place for about 20 to 30 minutes, or until they double in volume and fill the pan. Bake at 375° for 20 to 30 minutes, or until they are lightly browned. Makes 9 cinnamon rolls. If you wish to use a whole batch of "Spelt Sweet Roll Dough" made with sugar or honey in this recipe, roll the dough out to a 12" by 18" rectangle, spread it with 1 1/2 times the given amounts of toppings, roll it up starting on the long side, cut the roll into 12 slices, and bake in a 13" by 9" pan to make 12 rolls.

This recipe is free of wheat, milk, eggs, corn, and soy. It is free of refined sugar if it is sweetened with the fruit juice.

No-fry Doughnuts

These are a delightful dessert for kids of all ages as well as being relatively easy to make.

Quinoa-Cinnamon:

> 1 c. apple juice concentrate, thawed
> 1 package quick-rise yeast
> 2 1/2 c. quinoa flour
> 1 3/4 tsp. guar gum
> 1 tsp. cinnamon
> 1/8 tsp. salt (optional)
> 3 tbsp. oil
> Additional oil
> Optional coating: 1/4 c. sugar plus 1 tsp. cinnamon

Rye:

> 1 c. water plus 1/3 c. maple syrup OR 2 2/3 c. white
>   grape juice boiled down to 1 1/3 c.
> 1 package quick-rise yeast
> 3 1/4 to 3 3/4 c. rye flour

1/4 tsp salt (optional)
3 tbsp. oil
Additional oil
Optional coating: 1/4 c. maple sugar

Carob:

1 1/3 c. apple juice concentrate, thawed
1 package quick rise yeast
3 c. rye flour
1/3 c. carob powder
1/4 tsp. salt (optional)
3 tbsp. oil
Additional oil
Optional coating: 1/2 c. carob powder

Spelt:

1 batch of "Spelt Sweet Roll Dough," page 64
Additional oil
Optional coating: 1/3 c. sugar plus 1 1/2 tsp. cinnamon
   (only 2/3 this amount will be needed if the dough is
   sweetened with apple juice)

If you are making spelt doughnuts, prepare the "Spelt Sweet
Roll Dough" as directed in the recipe, allow it to rise the first time,
punch it down, and begin following the directions in this recipe
in the last paragraph. If you are making another type of doughnuts, choose one set of ingredients above. Heat the juice or syrup
and water to 115°. Stir in the yeast and let the mixture stand about
10 minutes, or until it is foamy. Stir the dry ingredients and 3
tbsp. oil into the yeast mixture in a large mixer bowl. (For the
rye doughnuts, start with 3 1/4 c. flour, and add more if needed
to make a soft dough.)

For the quinoa dough, beat the dough for 3 minutes at medium
speed. The rye dough and carob doughs may be kneaded by hand
for a few minutes instead if they are too stiff for your mixer.
Scrape the dough from the beaters and sides of the bowl. Oil the
top of the dough and the sides of the bowl and cover the bowl with

a towel. Put the dough in a warm (85° to 90°) place and let it rise for 45 minutes to 1 hour, or until it has doubled in volume. Beat the quinoa dough for 3 more minutes on medium speed; punch the rye and carob doughs down.

Roll out the dough to about 1/2" thickness on a floured board and cut it with a floured doughnut cutter. Transfer the doughnuts to an oiled cookie sheet with a spatula. Brush the tops of them with oil. Let them rise again until they have doubled in volume, about 20 minutes. Bake at 400° for 10-15 minutes, or until they are golden brown. Immediately brush them with oil and sprinkle them with or shake them in a bag with the coating, if desired. Makes about 11 to 12 quinoa, carob, or apple-juice-sweetened spelt doughnuts, 12 to 13 rye doughnuts, or 15 to 16 spelt doughnuts if the dough is made with sugar or honey.

This recipe is free of wheat, milk, eggs, corn, and soy. It is free of refined sugar if it is sweetened with fruit juice rather than sugar or honey. The quinoa doughnuts are also free of gluten and all grains.

5

Main Dishes

Main dishes do not pose the same degree of difficulty for the person with food allergies that breads and breakfast foods do. There are many recipes in ordinary cookbooks for broiling, roasting, or baking plain fish, meat, or poultry. However, if you want to make a casserole or one-dish meal, it is more difficult to find a suitable recipe. This chapter provides such recipes, as well as recipes for those who cannot use ordinary meats. It contains vegetarian recipes and recipes using goat, rabbit, duck, fish, buffalo, and wild game. To obtain buffalo and wild game, see "Sources of Special Foods," ch. 16.

Wild game sometimes has a gamey taste or is tough. To reduce the gamey taste, rub or sprinkle the frozen meat liberally with salt before placing it in the refrigerator to thaw. A crockpot is ideal for cooking game because the long, slow cooking tenderizes the meat.

Stuffed Zucchini

This is a tasty way to use the larger zucchinis from summer gardens.

4 large (about 10" long) zucchini squash
1 c. cracker crumbs, from "Quinoa Crackers," page 35
  or "Canola Seed Crackers," page 38
8 oz. goat cheese, shredded
1/4 tsp. salt (optional)
1/8 to 1/4 tsp. pepper (optional)
3 tsp. oil

Wash the zucchinis, cut off the stems, and cut them in half lengthwise. Scoop out the seeded part of the pulp and chop about half of it to make 1 1/2 c. chopped pulp. Mix this with the cracker crumbs, cheese, salt, and pepper. Oil one 9" by 13" and one 9" by 9" baking pan with the oil. Put the zucchini halves in the pans cut side up and fill them with the pulp mixture. Bake them uncovered at 350° for 45 minutes, or until the zucchini part is tender. This may be made ahead and refrigerated and then baked about 1 hour at 350°. Makes 6 to 8 servings.

This recipe is free of wheat, cow's milk, eggs, corn, soy, and refined sugar. If it is made with amaranth or quinoa crackers, it is also free of gluten and all grains.

Stuffed Acorn Squash

This is a delicious winter squash one-dish meal.

3 medium acorn squash, about 4 1/2 to 5 lbs. total weight
3 medium apples, about 1 lb. total weight, OR 1 to 1 1/2 c.
  fresh or canned pineapple (optional)
1/4 c. raisins (optional)
2 c. crumbled goat's or sheep's milk feta cheese, about
  12 oz. drained weight
1/2 tsp. cinnamon (optional)
1 tbsp. oil

Cut the squash in half lengthwise and remove the seeds. Place them cut side down in an oiled baking dish and bake them at 350° for 30 minutes. Peel, core, and finely chop the apples, or chop the pineapple into small pieces. Mix the raisins, cheese, cinnamon, and oil with the fruit. Turn the squash cut side up and heap the fruit and cheese mixture into the centers of the squash halves. Bake them for an additional 30 to 45 minutes, or until the squash part is tender. Makes six servings.

This recipe is free of all grains (including wheat and corn), gluten, cow's milk, eggs, soy, yeast, and refined sugar. It is suitable for use on a low-yeast diet if feta cheese is tolerated and the fruit is omitted.

NOTE ON FETA CHEESE: Feta cheese is produced from milk by a rapid process involving rennet and salt rather than fermentation. Therefore, some doctors allow it on their low-yeast diets. As with any food, what determines if you can eat it is your individual tolerance for it.

Quinoa Stuffed Peppers

Because quinoa contains high-quality protein, this is a very satisfying vegetarian dish.

> 1 1/2 c. quinoa
> 3 c. water
> 1 lb. frozen chopped spinach
> 2 tbsp. oil
> 2 tsp. salt
> 3/4 tsp. pepper
> 3 tbsp. chopped fresh or 3 tsp. dry sweet basil
> 2 tbsp. paprika (optional - for color)
> 6 green bell peppers, seeded
> Additional oil

Wash the quinoa thoroughly and combine it with the water in a saucepan. Bring it to a boil, reduce the heat, and simmer it for 15 to 20 minutes. Cook the spinach in the 2 tbsp. of oil, adding no water, for 5 to 10 minutes, or until it is barely tender. Mix the quinoa and spinach with the seasonings and stuff the mixture into the peppers. To cook the peppers in the traditional Italian way, put a little oil into a heavy frying pan, lay the peppers in the pan on their sides, cover the pan, and fry the peppers slowly, turning them to brown all sides, for 30 to 45 minutes. Or, if you would rather bake the peppers, parboil them for 5 minutes before stuffing them, stuff them, and bake them in an oiled casserole dish at 350° for 45 minutes. Makes 4 to 6 servings.

This recipe is free of all grains (including wheat and corn), gluten, milk, eggs, soy, yeast, refined sugar, meat, and tomatoes.

No Meat Or Tomato Chili

The paprika and Vitamin C crystals add the color and tang of tomatoes to this vegetarian chili.

> 1/2 c. cold water or bean liquid
> 1 tsp. tapioca starch or arrowroot
> 1/16 to 1/8 tsp. chili powder, or to taste
> 1 tsp. paprika (optional - for color)
> 1/8 tsp. salt, or to taste (optional)
> 1 1/2 to 2 c. cooked pinto or kidney beans
> 1/2 to 5/8 tsp. tart-tasting unbuffered Vitamin C crystals, such as Vital Life brand

Combine the water or bean liquid and tapioca starch or arrowroot in a saucepan. Add the chili powder, paprika, and salt and bring the mixture to a boil, stirring it often. Add the beans, crushing a few of them against the side of the pan, and simmer the chili for a few minutes. Stir in the Vitamin C crystals. Serve the chili alone or over cooked rice, quinoa, or baked potatoes. Makes one to two servings.

This recipe is free of all grains (including wheat and corn), gluten, milk, eggs, soy, yeast, refined sugar, meat, and tomatoes.

Two-Food-Family Vegetarian Chili

The textured vegetable protein in this recipe, which is derived from soy beans, seems to be meat, but is not.

> 3/4 c. textured vegetable protein (optional)
> 3/4 c. boiling water (needed only if you are using the textured vegetable protein)

5 c. cooked kidney or other type of beans, drained
3 c. tomato sauce or fresh peeled and chopped or pureed
    tomatoes
1/2 c. water
1/2 tsp. salt (optional)
1/8 to 1/4 c. canned diced green chiles OR 1/4 to
    3/4 tsp. chili powder, or to taste (Use the chiles for
    two food families.)

Combine the textured vegetable protein and boiling water in a large saucepan and allow them to stand for 5 to 10 minutes, or until the water is all absorbed. Add the beans, tomato sauce or tomatoes, water, salt, and chiles or chili powder and bring the chili to a boil. Reduce the heat and simmer it for 15 to 30 minutes. Makes 4 to 6 servings.

This recipe is free of all grains (including wheat and corn), gluten, milk, eggs, yeast, refined sugar, and meat. It is also free of soy if the textured vegetable protein is omitted.

Italian Rice Meal In A Bowl

This makes an easy and satisfying hot lunch.

1 c. peeled and pureed fresh tomatoes OR 1
    8-oz. can tomato sauce
1 c. water
1/2 tsp. salt (optional)
1 1/2 c. uncooked brown rice
1 c. shredded goat cheese, divided
1/2 c. sliced pitted black olives

Combine the tomatoes or tomato sauce, water, salt, and rice in a large saucepan and bring them to a boil. Reduce the heat and simmer them, covered, for 40 minutes. Remove the pan from the heat, fluff the rice with a fork, and fold in the olives and 3/4 c. of the cheese. Let the rice stand in the pan for a few minutes. Sprinkle it with the remaining cheese before serving it. Makes 4 servings.

This recipe is free of wheat, gluten, cow's milk, eggs, corn, soy, and refined sugar.

Turkey Pot Pie

Turn that leftover turkey into meals in your freezer using this recipe.

1 batch of any kind of pie crust, page 199-201
2 c. cooked, cubed turkey
2 c. cooked, cubed vegetables, such as potatoes, carrots,
   celery, green beans, peas, or a combination of vegetables
1 1/4 to 1 1/2 c. turkey gravy, white sauce, or clear sauce,
   below

Make one of the following binders for the pie filling:

TURKEY GRAVY: Add 3 tbsp. rye, spelt, or barley flour to about 3 to 4 tbsp. of turkey drippings and cook the mixture over medium heat, stirring it, for a few minutes. Gradually add 1 c. water while stirring the mixture, and cook it for a few minutes more, or until it is thick and smooth. Season it to taste with salt, if desired.

WHITE SAUCE: Combine 1 1/4 c. cold water and 4 tbsp. rye or barley flour in a jar and shake it until the lumps are gone. Cook the mixture over medium heat, stirring, until it becomes thick and bubbly. Simmer it for a few minutes more and season it to taste with salt, if desired.

CLEAR SAUCE: Combine 1 1/2 c. cold water and 2 tbsp. arrowroot or tapioca starch in a saucepan. Cook the mixture over medium heat, stirring it often, until it boils and thickens. Season it to taste with salt, if desired.

Make the pie crust as directed in the recipe. If you are using a rye or spelt crust, roll out half of it on a floured pastry cloth and put it into a pie dish. For any other kind of crust, press half of it into a pie dish. Combine the turkey, vegetables, and gravy or sauce and put them into the bottom crust of the pie. Roll out the top crust of a spelt or rye pie and put it over the filling; crimp the edges together and prick the top of the crust. If you are using any other kind of crust, sprinkle crumbs of the crust evenly over the pie filling. Bake at 350° for 45 minutes or until the crust begins to brown. This pie can be frozen before baking and baked without thawing at 350° for about one hour. Serves 4 to 6.

This recipe is free of wheat, milk, eggs, corn, soy, yeast, and refined sugar. If made with clear sauce and an amaranth or quinoa crust, it is also free of gluten and all grains.

Pasties

This is a great meal to have in the freezer for the days when you can have yeast.

>   1/3 batch "Spelt Yeast Bread" dough (page 60) OR
>   1 batch "Rye Yeast Bread" dough (page 58)
>   1 tbsp. spelt or rye flour (the same type as used in
>   the dough)
>   2 tsp. oil
>   1/2 c. water
>   1/8 tsp. salt (optional)
>   2 c. chopped leftover meat or cooked ground meat of
>   any kind (10 to 12 oz. weight of ground meat before
>   cooking)
>   2 c. cooked vegetables, any kind or combination

Prepare the yeast bread dough and allow it to rise the first time. Combine the flour and oil in a saucepan and heat the mixture over medium heat until it begins to bubble. Then cook it for 1 to 2 minutes, stirring it constantly. Add the water and salt and cook it until it boils and thickens. Stir in the meat and vegetables. Divide the dough into 12 pieces. Roll each piece out into a 6-inch circle on a lightly floured board. Put one-twelfth of the meat and vegetable filling on each circle. Fold the circles in half over the filling, press the edges together, and prick the tops of the pasties with a fork. Put them on two oiled baking sheets. Let them rise for about 15 minutes. Bake them at 375° for 15 to 20 minutes, or until they are lightly browned. Makes 12 pasties.

This recipe is free of wheat, milk, eggs, corn, soy, and refined sugar.

Biscuit Topping For Casseroles

Use these toppings for the buffalo, duck, or bean casseroles, to follow, or for a casserole filling of your own creation.

Barley:

> 7/8 c. barley flour (3/4 c. plus 2 tbsp.)
> 3/4 tsp. baking soda
> 1/4 tsp. unbuffered Vitamin C crystals
> 1/4 tsp. salt (optional)
> 3/8 c. water (1/4 c. plus 2 tbsp.)
> 2 tbsp. oil

Rye:

> 3/4 c. rye flour
> 3/4 tsp. baking soda
> 1/4 tsp. unbuffered Vitamin C crystals
> 1/4 tsp. salt (optional)
> 3/8 c. water (1/4 c. plus 2 tbsp.)
> 2 tbsp. oil

Spelt:

> 7/8 c. spelt flour (3/4 c. plus 2 tbsp.)
> 3/4 tsp. baking soda
> 1/4 tsp. unbuffered Vitamin C crystals
> 1/4 tsp. salt (optional)
> 3/8 c. water (1/4 c. plus 2 tbsp.)
> 2 tbsp. oil

Amaranth:

> 3/4 c. amaranth flour
> 1/4 c. arrowroot
> 3/4 tsp. baking soda

1/4 tsp. unbuffered Vitamin C crystals
1/4 tsp. salt (optional)
3/8 c. water (1/4 c. plus 2 tbsp.)
2 tbsp. oil

Quinoa:

5/8 c. quinoa flour (1/2 c. plus 2 tbsp.)
2 tbsp. tapioca flour
3/4 tsp. baking soda
1/4 tsp. unbuffered Vitamin C crystals
1/4 tsp. salt (optional)
3/8 c. water (1/4 c. plus 2 tbsp.)
2 tbsp. oil

Choose one set of ingredients, above. Combine the flour(s), baking soda, Vitamin C crystals, and salt in a bowl. Mix together the water and oil and stir them into the flour mixture until just mixed. Spread the batter over the casserole filling of your choice and bake it at 350° for 35 to 45 minutes, or until the topping browns. Makes enough topping for a casserole serving 4 to 6 people.

This recipe is free of wheat, milk, eggs, corn, soy, yeast, and refined sugar. If the amaranth or quinoa versions are made, it is also free of gluten and all grains.

Buff-n-Biscuit

Meat, vegetables, and bread - this casserole has everything you could want for a meal in one dish.

5 to 6 stalks celery (about 1/2 lb.)
1/2 onion
2 tsp. oil
1 lb. ground buffalo
3/4 to 1 tsp. salt, or to taste (optional)
1/4 tsp. pepper (optional)
2 tsp. paprika (optional - for color)
1 1/4 c. water, divided

2 tbsp. arrowroot or tapioca starch
1 batch of "Biscuit Topping For Casseroles," page 77

Slice the celery into 1/4" slices and chop the onion. Saute them in a skillet with the oil until they begin to brown. Remove them to a 3-quart casserole dish. Put the buffalo in the remaining oil in the skillet and cook it, stirring it occasionally, until it is well browned. Drain the fat from the pan, and add the salt, pepper, paprika, and 1 c. of the water. Simmer the mixture for 30 minutes, adding more water while it is cooking, if necessary, to bring it back to its original level. Combine the arrowroot or tapioca starch with the remaining 1/4 c. cold water and add the mixture to the pan. Return the meat mixture to a boil and simmer it until it thickens. Put the meat into the casserole dish with the celery and onion and stir them together. Top them with the biscuit topping of your choice, and bake at 350° for 35 to 45 minutes, or until the topping browns. Makes 4 to 6 servings.

This recipe is free of wheat, milk, eggs, corn, soy, yeast, and refined sugar. If it is made with amaranth or quinoa biscuit topping, it is also free of gluten and all grains.

Duck-n-Biscuit

Here is a way to use up that leftover duck.

3/4 lb. cooked duck, skinned and cut into 3/4" cubes
    (about 2 1/2 c. cubes)
3/4 lb. butternut squash, pared, seeded, and cut into
    3/4" to 1" cubes (about 3 c. cubes)
1/2 lb. small zucchini, sliced into 1/2" slices
    (about 3 c. slices)
1/2 to 3/4 tsp. salt, or to taste (optional)
1/4 tsp. pepper (optional)
1 1/2 c. water
2 tbsp. arrowroot or tapioca flour
1 batch of "Biscuit Topping For Casseroles," page 77

Combine the water and arrowroot or tapioca flour in a sauce-pan. Cook it over medium heat until it thickens and boils. Stir in the duck, vegetables, and seasonings, return it to a simmer, and heat it through for a few minutes. Pour the mixture into a 3-quart casserole dish, top it with the biscuit topping of your choice, and bake it at 350° for 35 to 45 minutes, or until the topping browns. Makes 4 to 6 servings.

This recipe is free of wheat, milk, eggs, corn, soy, yeast, and refined sugar. If it is made with amaranth or quinoa biscuit topping, it is also free of gluten and all grains.

Bean-n-Biscuit

In this vegetarian casserole, the protein in the beans and the protein in the grain combine to give you a complete protein.

> 1/4 small onion, chopped (optional)
> 1 tbsp. oil (optional - only needed if you are using the onion)
> 1 1/2 c. water OR 1 1/2 c. tomato sauce OR 1 lb. Italian plum tomatoes plus 1 c. water
> 2 tbsp. arrowroot or tapioca starch
> 1 10-oz. package frozen green lima beans (about 1 1/2 c. beans)
> 1 1/2 c. cooked kidney beans, drained
> 1 1/2 c. cooked white beans, such as canellini or navy beans, drained
> 1/2 tsp. salt, or to taste (optional)
> 1/4 tsp. pepper (optional)
> 1/8 tsp. chili powder, or to taste (optional)
> 1 batch of "Biscuit Topping For Casseroles," page 77

If you are using the onion, saute it in the oil until it begins to brown. If you are using the fresh tomatoes, remove the stem ends from them and cut them into eighths. Combine the water or tomato sauce with the arrowroot or tapioca flour in a saucepan. Cook them over medium heat, stirring often, until the mixture thickens and boils. Stir in the beans, tomatoes (if you are using them), onion, and seasonings. Return the mixture to a boil and pour it into a 3-quart casserole dish. Top it with the biscuit topping of your choice, and bake it at 350° for 35 to 45 minutes, or until the topping browns. Makes 4 to 6 servings.

This recipe is free of wheat, milk, eggs, corn, soy, yeast, refined sugar, and meat. If it is made with amaranth or quinoa biscuit topping, it is also free of gluten and all grains.

Macaroni and Cheese

Children love this traditional favorite. It is best to make it right before serving time with most types of pasta, but you can make it ahead of time and freeze it if you use spelt pasta.

>   10 to 12 oz. uncooked pasta, any type and shape
>   1 batch of either "Cheese Sauce I" OR "Cheese Sauce II,"
>   below

Prepare the cheese sauce while bringing the water to a boil for the pasta. When the cheese sauce is almost finished, cook the pasta according to the directions for cooking pasta on pages 95-96 and the cooking time for the type of pasta you are using given on the package or on pages 98 or 100. Do not overcook the pasta, or it will get mushy standing in the cheese sauce. When the pasta has finished cooking, drain it, combine it with the hot cheese sauce, and serve it immediately. Makes 4 servings.

CHEESE SAUCE I:
>   5 oz. goat's or sheep's milk feta cheese, crumbled
>   (about 1 c. crumbled cheese)
>   3/4 c. water
>   4 1/2 tsp. arrowroot or tapioca flour

Blend all of the ingredients in a blender until they are smooth. Pour the mixture into a saucepan and heat it over medium heat until it thickens slightly and barely boils. Use it with pasta for "Macaroni and Cheese" or as a sauce for vegetables.

CHEESE SAUCE II:
>   3 tbsp. arrowroot OR 2 tbsp. rye or barley flour
>   plus 2 tbsp. oil

1/4 tsp. salt (optional)
Dash of pepper (optional)
2 c. goat milk
8 to 10 oz. goat jack or cheddar cheese, shredded

To thicken the sauce with the arrowroot, combine the arrowroot, seasonings, and milk in a saucepan. Cook the mixture over medium heat, stirring it occasionally, until it thickens and just begins to boil.

To thicken the sauce with the rye or barley flour, combine the flour, oil, and seasonings in a saucepan. Cook the mixture over medium heat, stirring constantly, until it begins to bubble. Add the milk very gradually while stirring it and cook it until it thickens and just begins to boil.

After the sauce has thickened, remove the pan from the burner and add the cheese. Stir it until the cheese has melted, and then combine it with cooked pasta for "Macaroni and Cheese" or serve it with cooked vegetables.

This recipe is free of wheat, cow's milk, eggs, corn, soy, and refined sugar. If the sauce is made with arrowroot or tapioca flour and a non-grain pasta is used, this recipe is free of gluten and all grains. If the feta cheese is used, it is suitable for a low-yeast diet. (See "Note on Feta Cheese," page 72.)

Game Stroganoff

This is an elegant way to prepare game.

1 to 1 1/2 lbs. elk, antelope, or venison steak, cut into
    thin strips about 2" long
3/4 lb. mushrooms, sliced (optional)
1 small onion, minced (optional)
3 tbsp. oil
1 1/2 c. water
1 to 1 1/2 tsp. salt, or to taste (optional)
2 tbsp. arrowroot
3/4 c. wine or additional water
4 c cooked noodles

Saute the vegetables in the oil until they are tender and remove them from the pan. Brown the meat in the oil remaining in the pan. Add the 1 1/2 c. water and the salt and simmer the meat, covered, for 45 minutes. Add the vegetables, return the mixture to a boil, and simmer it for a few minutes. Combine the arrowroot with the wine or additional water and stir them into the meat and vegetable mixture. Simmer the mixture until it thickens. Serve it over hot cooked noodles. Makes 4 servings.

This recipe is free of wheat, milk, eggs, corn, soy, and refined sugar. If non-grain noodles are used, it is also free of gluten and all grains. If the wine and mushrooms are omitted, it is suitable for a low-yeast diet.

Crockpot Game Roast

The long, slow cooking of the crockpot gives this roast a delicious flavor while tenderizing it.

    1 2-3lb. antelope, elk, or venison roast
    1/2 to 3/4 tsp. salt
    3 1/2 c. water, or enough to barely cover the roast

The day before cooking this dish, rub the frozen roast with the salt and allow it to thaw overnight in the refrigerator. In the morning, place the roast in a 3-quart crockpot and add enough water to barely cover the roast. Cook it on low for 8 to 10 hours. Serves 4 to 6.

This recipe is free of all grains (including wheat and corn), gluten, milk, eggs, soy, yeast, and refined sugar.

Game Roast Dinner

If you start this in the crockpot in the morning, you will have a delicious complete dinner ready for you at the end of the day.

    1 2-3lb. antelope, elk, or venison roast
    1/2 to 3/4 tsp. salt
    2 to 3 lbs. sweet potatoes, or a combination of

sweet potatoes, carrots, and/or parsnips
6 1/2 c. water, or enough to barely cover the roast
  and vegetables

The day before cooking this dish, rub the frozen roast with the salt and allow it to thaw overnight in the refrigerator. In the morning, place the vegetables in a 3-quart crockpot, put the roast on top of them, and add enough water to barely cover the roast. Cook it on low for 8 to 10 hours. Serves 4 to 6.

This recipe is free of all grains (including wheat and corn), gluten, milk, eggs, soy, yeast, and refined sugar.

Game Stew

To decrease the number of food families in this recipe to three, omit the bay leaf and black pepper and either use 3 seeded and chopped green peppers instead of the carrots and celery or omit the potatoes.

2 to 3 lbs. of elk, antelope, or venison round steak, cut
  into cubes
5 carrots (about 1 lb.), peeled and cut into 1" pieces
5 stalks of celery, cut into 1" pieces
2 to 3 potatoes, peeled and cut into 1" cubes (optional)
1/2 c. tapioca
1 bay leaf (optional)
2 tsp. salt, divided
1/4 tsp. pepper (optional)
3 c. water

The day before you plan to serve this stew, rub the frozen meat with 1 tsp. of the salt and allow it to thaw overnight in the refrigerator. In the morning, cut the meat into cubes, trimming off all of the fat, and combine it with the vegetables, tapioca, bay leaf, remaining 1 tsp. salt, pepper, and water in a 3-quart crock-pot. Stir the mixture well to evenly distribute the tapioca and cook it on low for 8 to 10 hours or on high for 6 hours. Any leftover stew freezes well. Makes 8 servings.

This recipe is free of all grains (including wheat and corn), gluten, milk, eggs, soy, yeast, and refined sugar.

Zucchini Stew

Zucchini does not get mushy when it is frozen in this stew, so this is a perfect dish to make in the summer when zucchini is abundant and eat in the middle of the winter. It can be made with game or buffalo, or even beef, if you can tolerate it.

1 to 1 1/4 lbs. ground antelope, elk, venison, or buffalo
2 tbsp. finely chopped onion, or to taste (optional)
1 tbsp. oil
1 1/4 lbs. Italian plum tomatoes, stemmed and cut into
    quarters OR 1 1-lb. can peeled tomatoes
6 tbsp. tomato paste (optional) OR 1 8-oz. can tomato
    sauce (optional - omit the water, below, if the
    sauce is used)
1 tsp. salt
1/4 tsp. pepper (optional)
1/4 to 1/2 c. water
2 to 2 1/2 lbs. zucchini, sliced about 3/8" thick

In a large saucepan, brown the meat and onion in the oil. Drain off all of the fat. Add the tomatoes, tomato paste or sauce, salt, pepper, and 1/4 c. of water (omit it if tomato sauce was used) and simmer the stew for about 15 minutes. Add the zucchini and simmer it for about an additional 15 minutes, or until the zucchini is just tender. (For very large zucchini, the simmering time will be longer.) Add the additional 1/4 c. water if the stew begins to dry out during cooking. Makes 4 to 6 servings.

This recipe is free of all grains (including wheat and corn), gluten, milk, eggs, soy, yeast, and refined sugar. If fresh tomatoes are used rather than canned and neither the tomato paste nor tomato sauce is used, it is suitable for use on a low-yeast diet.

Golden Game Stew

The sweetness of the vegetables used in this stew is a perfect complement to the game.

> 1 1/2 lbs. antelope, elk, or venison round steak
> 1 1/2 lbs. (about 2 to 3 large) sweet potatoes, peeled and
>   cut into 1" cubes (about 4 c. cubes)
> 1 1/2 lbs. carrots, cut into 3/4" to 1" slices (optional)
> 1/2 c. tapioca
> 2 tsp. salt, divided
> 1/4 tsp. pepper (optional)
> 2 whole cloves (optional)
> 1 bay leaf (optional)
> 1 c. water
> 1 1/2 lbs. butternut squash, pared, seeded, and cut
>   into 1" cubes (about 4 c. cubes) (optional)

The day before you plan to serve this stew, rub the frozen meat with 1 tsp. of the salt and allow it to thaw in the refrigerator overnight. Cut it into 1" cubes and combine it with the sweet potatoes, tapioca, remaining 1 tsp. salt, pepper, clove, bay leaf, and water in a 3-quart crockpot. Cook the stew on high for 6 hours or on low for 8 to 10 hours. If you are using the squash, add it 2 hours before the end of the cooking time. Leftovers from this recipe freeze well. Makes 6 to 8 servings.

This recipe is free of all grains (including wheat and corn), gluten, milk, eggs, soy, yeast, and refined sugar.

Game Chili

The game is so well disguised in this recipe that it will please even a fussy eater.

> 1 1/2 lbs. ground antelope, elk, venison, or buffalo
> 1 tbsp. oil (optional)
> 3 c. tomato sauce or pureed fresh tomatoes
> 1/2 to 3/4 tsp. chili powder, or to taste
> 1/4 tsp. salt

1/2 c. water
5 c. kidney or other cooked beans, drained

In a large saucepan, brown the meat in the oil or without the oil. Pour off as much of the fat as possible. Add the rest of the ingredients, adding more water if you prefer a juicier chili. Simmer the chili for 30 minutes. Makes 4 to 6 servings.

This recipe is free of all grains (including wheat and corn), gluten, milk, eggs, soy, yeast (if the fresh tomatoes are used), and refined sugar.

Crispy Broiled Fish

This is a grain-free change from plain broiled fish. To obtain cassava meal by mail order, see "Sources of Special Foods," ch. 16.

1 lb. cod, halibut, haddock, turbot, or other
   fish fillets or steaks
Oil
Salt (optional)
1 to 2 tbsp. cassava meal or crumbs from
   "Cassava Crackers," page 40

Brush oil on both sides of the fish and sprinkle it lightly with salt. Pat the cassava meal or cracker crumbs onto both sides of the fish. Broil it at 450° for 10 minutes per inch of thickness of the fish, turning the fish over halfway through the broiling time. Makes 2 servings.

This recipe is free of all grains (including wheat and corn), gluten, milk, eggs, soy, yeast, and refined sugar.

Salmon Loaf or Patties

When made as patties, this recipe is delicious served on any type of sandwich buns with "Pine Nut Dressing," page 131, and fresh vegetables.

1 15-oz can salmon
1/2 c. finely crushed cracker crumbs, made from
    "Quinoa Crackers," page 35, "Saltines," page 36,
    or "Canola Seed Crackers," page 38
Oil

Drain the salmon, reserving the liquid. Remove the skin from the meat, if desired. Knead together the fish and the cracker crumbs, adding a little of the reserved fish liquid if necessary to help the mixture stick together. Press it into an oiled 7" by 7" glass baking dish. Bake it uncovered at 350° for 25 to 30 minutes, or until it begins to brown on top. Or, form the mixture into four patties and fry them on both sides in a little oil. (The patties are fragile.) Makes 4 servings.

This recipe is free of wheat, milk, eggs, corn, soy, yeast, and refined sugar. If it is made with "Quinoa Crackers" or the amaranth version of "Canola Seed Crackers," it is also free of gluten and all grains.

Roast Duck With Cherry Sauce

This makes an elegant dinner while avoiding the citrus fruits and cornstarch that many are allergic to.

1 duck, weighing about 5 lbs.
Salt (optional)
1 16-oz. can tart cherries, packed in water
1 c. apple juice concentrate
4 tsp. arrowroot or tapioca flour

Clean the duck and cut off the excess skin and fat. Rub the inside of the cavity with salt. Place it on a rack in an uncovered roasting pan and bake it at 325° for 3 to 3 1/2 hours, or until it is brown. Up to 2 days ahead, or at least 1/2 hour before the end of the roasting time, drain the cherries, reserving the liquid. Combine 1/2 c. of the cherry liquid with the apple juice concentrate and arrowroot or tapioca flour in a saucepan. Cook this mixture over medium heat until it thickens and begins to boil. Stir in the cherries and return it to a boil. Serve the sauce warm over or along side of the duck. The cherry sauce is best made 1 to 2 days ahead so the sweetness of the apple juice can permeate the cherries, and then reheated right before serving time. Makes 2 to 4 servings.

This recipe is free of all grains (including wheat and corn), gluten, milk, eggs, soy, yeast, refined sugar, and citrus fruits.

Crispy Oven-Fried Chicken

Chicken does not have to be laden with wheat, eggs, and fat to be delicious, as this recipe proves.

1 chicken, weighing about 3 to 4 lbs.
1/2 c. rye, barley, spelt, or oat flour, or cassava meal
1/4 tsp. salt (optional)
1/8 tsp. pepper (optional)
3 tbsp. oil (optional)

Wash and clean the chicken and cut it into serving-size pieces. Combine the flour or meal, salt, and pepper in a bag. If you are using the oil, put it in a shallow bowl, dip each piece of chicken in it, turning it to coat all of the sides, and allow the excess oil to drip off. Put each chicken piece into the bag and shake it to coat it with flour or meal. Place the chicken pieces in a baking dish and bake them, uncovered, at 350° for 1 1/2 to 2 hours, or until nicely browned. Makes 4 servings.

This recipe is free of wheat, milk, eggs, corn, soy, yeast, and refined sugar. If it is made with the cassava meal, it is also free of gluten and all grains.

Italian-Style Baked Rabbit

This is an old family recipe when made with the wine, but is also delicious made with water or juice.

1 rabbit, weighing about 2 to 2 1/2 lbs.
1 clove garlic (optional)

> 1/4 to 1/2 tsp. salt, or to taste (optional)
> 1/8 tsp. pepper (optional)
> 2 tsp. dry sweet basil, or 1 tbsp. finely chopped fresh
>   sweet basil
> 3/4 c. white wine, white grape juice, apple juice, or water

Cut the rabbit into serving-size pieces and place them in a 13" by 9" baking dish. Cut the garlic into quarters and put the pieces of garlic between the pieces of rabbit in the dish. Pour the wine, juice, or water over the rabbit. Sprinkle it with the salt, pepper, and sweet basil. Cover it with foil or a glass baking dish lid and bake it at 350° for 1 hour. Uncover it and bake it 1/2 to 1 hour longer, or until it is brown and the liquid has evaporated. Serves 4 to 6.

This recipe is free of all grains (including wheat and corn), gluten, milk, eggs, soy, yeast (if the wine is not used), and refined sugar.

Tender Goat Chops or Steak

Broiled goat can be tough if well-done. Long cooking with water makes it tender.

> 1 to 1 1/2 lbs. goat chops, round steak, shoulder steak,
>   or other cut of meat
> Salt
> Pepper (optional)
> Water

Place the chops or steak in a glass baking dish that has a lid and add water to a depth of about 3/4 of the thickness of the meat. Sprinkle the meat with salt and pepper. Bake it covered at 350° for 2 hours, uncovering it the last half hour, if necessary, to allow most of the water to evaporate. Makes 4 servings.

This recipe is free of all grains (including wheat and corn), gluten, milk, eggs, soy, yeast, and refined sugar.

Goat Ribs

These ribs are delicious, either plain, for those who cannot eat tomatoes, or barbecue-style.

Rib (center) section of a small goat (about 3 1/2 lbs.)
About 6 to 8 c. water
Salt
2 c. catsup (optional) - about 2 batches of "Easy Catsup," page 220, or 1 batch of "Fresh Tomato Catsup," page 221

Flatten out the center section of a small goat, breaking a few ribs, if necessary, to flatten it. Place it in a large roaster and add water to 1/2 to 3/4 the depth of the meat. Salt the meat. Cover it and bake it at 350° for 1 1/2 hours. Uncover it and bake it 1 hour longer, or until the top of the meat has browned nicely. For plain ribs, serve it at this point. For barbecue-style ribs, pour off as much of the liquid as possible from the roaster. Pour the catsup over the meat and bake it, uncovered, for another 1/2 to 1 hour, basting it often. Makes 6 servings.

This recipe is free of all grains (including wheat and corn), gluten, milk, eggs, soy, and refined sugar. If made with "Fresh Tomato Catsup" made with stevia, it is also suitable for a low-yeast diet.

Braised Goat

This is a traditional way to prepare young goat for Easter.

1 quarter of a young goat (about 4 lbs.)
Oil
Salt (optional)
Pepper (optional)
Rosemary (optional)

Rub the goat with oil. Sprinkle all sides of the meat generously with the salt, pepper, and rosemary. Place it on a rack in a roasting pan and bake it, uncovered, at 400° for 30 to 45 minutes, or until it begins to brown. Add 1" of boiling water to the bottom of the roaster, cover it, and bake it at 350° for an additional 2 hours. Makes 6 to 8 servings.

This recipe is free of all grains (including wheat and corn), gluten, milk, eggs, soy, yeast, and refined sugar.

Sloppy Goat Sandwiches

This is a delicious way to use leftover "Braised Goat," above.

> 6 oz. scraps of cooked goat
> 1/2 c. catsup, either "Easy Catsup," page 220, or
>   "Fresh Tomato Catsup," page 221
> Bread or sandwich buns (see the preceding two chapters
>   for recipes)

Mix the meat and catsup in a saucepan and heat them over medium heat until the mixture begins to boil. Reduce the heat and simmer them for a few minutes to heat the meat through thoroughly. Serve it on bread or sandwich buns. Makes 2 servings.

This recipe is free of wheat, milk, eggs, corn, soy, and refined sugar. If amaranth or quinoa bread or buns are used, it is free of gluten and all grains. If "Fresh Tomato Catsup" made with stevia and a baking-soda-raised bread are used, it is also suitable for a low-yeast diet.

Buffalo Loaf

The fresh vegetables added to this meatloaf give it such an excellent flavor that it doesn't really need the optional catsup.

> 1 lb. ground buffalo
> 1/4 small onion, finely chopped (optional)
> 1/2 small green pepper, finely chopped (about
>   1/3 c. chopped)
> 1 c. grated carrots
> 1/4 c. arrowroot or tapioca flour
> 3/4 tsp. salt, or to taste (optional)

1/4 tsp. pepper (optional)
1/4 tsp. dry mustard (optional)
1/2 c. water, divided
1/4 c. catsup, (optional - "Easy Catsup," page 220, or
    "Fresh Tomato Catsup," page 221)

Mix together the buffalo, vegetables, arrowroot or tapioca flour, seasonings, and 1/4 c. of the water, and shape the mixture into a loaf. Place it into a 2-3 quart covered casserole dish with the remaining 1/4 c. water. Cover the casserole dish with its lid and bake the meatloaf at 350° for 45 minutes. Then uncover it and bake it for another 30 minutes. Top it with the catsup during the last 15 minutes of baking, if desired. Makes 6 servings.

This recipe is free of all grains (including wheat and corn), gluten, milk, eggs, soy, yeast, and refined sugar. If the catsup is omitted or "Fresh Tomato Catsup" made with stevia is used, it is suitable for use on a low-yeast diet.

Braised Buffalo Burgers

This recipe is for those who like their burgers well-done, but find thoroughly broiled buffalo too tough.

1 lb. ground buffalo
1/2 tsp. salt, or to taste (optional)
1/8 to 1/4 tsp. pepper (optional)
2 tbsp. tapioca starch or arrowroot
2 tbsp. water

Mix all the ingredients together thoroughly. Shape the mixture into four patties. Place the patties in a covered casserole and add water to a depth of 1/4" to 1/2." Cover the casserole with its lid and bake the burgers at 350° for 30 minutes. Uncover them and bake them an additional 15 minutes. Turn the burgers over and bake them for another 15 minutes, or until the second side is browned on the top. Makes 4 servings.

This recipe is free of all grains (including wheat and corn), gluten, milk, eggs, soy, yeast, and refined sugar.

Lentil Burgers

These vegetarian hamburgers are excellent with any type of bread or sandwich buns and fresh vegetables or homemade condiments (pages 220 to 223.)

> 1 lb. dry lentils
> Water
> 2 tbsp. chopped onion (optional)
> 2 tsp. salt, or to taste (optional)
> 1/4 tsp. pepper (optional)
> 1/2 c. tapioca flour, arrowroot, or water chestnut flour
> Oil

Wash the lentils and soak them overnight in about 2 quarts of water. In the morning, drain and rinse them 2 to 3 times, and drain them again. Add the onion, if you are using it, and enough water to the lentils to barely cover them (about 4 c. water), and bring them to a boil. Reduce the heat, and simmer them, covered, for 1 1/2 to 2 hours, or until they are tender and the water is almost completely absorbed. Mash them with a potato masher, mashing in the starch, salt, and pepper. Return the mixture to the heat and cook it over low heat, stirring it often, for about 30 minutes, or until it is very thick and the whiteness of the starch has disappeared. (The mixture may be refrigerated at this point, if you wish to.) Form the mixture into patties and fry them in a small amount of oil on both sides. These patties freeze well and may be reheated in the oven. Makes 8 to 10 patties.

This recipe is free of all grains (including wheat and corn), gluten, milk, eggs, soy, yeast, refined sugar, and meat.

6

Pasta and Ethnic Dishes

When I was diagnosed as being allergic to all of the major ingredients in most Italian dishes, my husband's comment was that my "Italian license" was going to be revoked. But being allergic to wheat (or even all grains), milk, eggs, tomatoes, and beef does not mean that one can no longer enjoy Italian or other ethnic foods. There are non-wheat and non-grain commercial pastas available (See "Sources of Special Foods," ch. 16), and this chapter also provides recipes for making pasta. You can make pasta sauces with ingredients other than tomatoes. (See "Pesto," page 100, and "Garlic, Pepper, and Oil Sauce," page 101.) You can use meat other than beef or pork in these recipes or omit it altogether. You can use goat or sheep cheese, if you tolerate it, or simply omit the cheese. Don't give up your Italian license! It is worth a little extra effort to make and enjoy these foods.

To Cook Pasta:

Bring at least 4 quarts of water to a rolling boil for each pound of pasta to be cooked. Add 1 to 2 tsp. of salt, if it is allowed on your diet, to make the water boil even faster. Add the pasta, stir it to keep it from sticking together, and rapidly return it to a boil. Begin timing the cooking of the pasta when the water returns to a boil. Reduce the heat enough to keep it from boiling over and boil it until the pasta is *al dente,* or offers some resistance "to the tooth." In The <u>Romagnoli's Table</u>, Margaret and G. Franco Romagnoli describe *al dente* as being "bitable but not raw, can be felt under the teeth but is neither crunchy nor rubbery; it means that each piece of pasta retains its individuality and texture, yet is just tender enough to please." The only foolproof way to determine when pasta is *al dente* is to remove a piece of it from the boiling water and bite it. The length of time it will take to cook the pasta varies with the type and size of the pasta, the altitude, etc. It ranges from 2 to 4 minutes for some homemade pastas to 12 minutes for some commercial pastas. Approximate cooking times are given in the following recipes. Begin testing the pasta a few minutes before the time should be up until you become familiar with each type of pasta. When the pasta is *al dente,* pour it and the water through a large colander set in the sink. Then immediately pour the pasta into a bowl containing a generous amount of sauce or oil and toss it to coat the pasta thoroughly. You do not have to let it stand in the colander long enough to be drained until it is dry; a little water left on it keeps the strands from sticking together. Serve it immediately with oil, salt (optional), and pepper (optional) or with the sauce of your choice.

Pasta For Rolling By Hand

It is not difficult to roll and cut pasta by hand, or you can roll and cut the spelt and rye varieties of this recipe with a crank-type pasta machine.

Spelt:

> 4 c. spelt flour
> 1 1/4 c. water

Rye:

> 4 c. rye flour
> 1/2 tsp. salt (optional)
> 1 c. water

Barley:

    4 c. barley flour
    1 1/2 c. water

Quinoa:

    2 c. quinoa flour
    2 c. tapioca flour
    1/2 tsp. salt (optional)
    1 c. plus 2 tbsp. water

Amaranth:

    3 c. amaranth flour
    1/2 c. arrowroot
    3/4 c. water

Chestnut:

    4 1/2 c. chestnut flour
    3/4 c. water

Measure the flour(s) onto a large board or into a large bowl. Make a crater in the center of the flour and gently pour the water into it. Begin stirring the water and flour together in the center of the crater with a fork. If you are using a board rather than a bowl, shore up the walls of the crater with your other hand as you stir. When the dough in the center of the crater becomes very thick, set aside the fork and mix the dough with your hand until all, or almost all, of the flour is mixed in. The dough will be very stiff. Knead the dough on a lightly floured board for 10 minutes. Then lightly oil the board and the ball of dough. Place the dough on the board, cover it with an inverted bowl, and let it rest for at least 30 minutes.

Roll the dough out as thinly as possible with a rolling pin on a floured board, or, for the more fragile doughs, on a floured pastry cloth. For lasagne, layer the dough in the pan with the other ingredients at this point. For manicotti, cut the dough into squares with a sharp knife at this point. For noodles, flour the dough well and either fold the dough (for less breakable ones like rye and spelt), roll it up like a jelly roll, or for very fragile doughs, like chestnut, leave it flat. Cut the dough into noodles of the desired width.

If you have a crank-type pasta machine, after the dough has rested, the rye or spelt doughs may be rolled to about 1/4" thickness and then cut into 4 to 6 pieces for rolling through the machine. Flour each piece well and roll it through the rollers several times, starting with the widest spacing and working down to the desired thickness of the dough. Use the sheets of dough for lasagne or manicotti at this point, or flour them well and roll them through the cutters for noodles.

Spread the noodles on a lightly floured cloth, separating the strands, and allow them to dry, or cook them immediately. (See "To Cook Pasta," pages 95-96.) The amaranth pasta is not suitable for cutting into noodles and boiling (it turns to mush in any type of sauce), but only for use in lasagne or manicotti. For egg-containing amaranth noodles that can be boiled, see The Allergy Self-Help Cookbook, page 140. (See "References," page 271.) The cooking time for pasta is affected by many factors including the thickness of the noodles, the altitude, etc. Pasta should be tested for being *al dente* as described on page 96, but approximate cooking times are:

Spelt	— 10 to 13 minutes
Rye	— 6 1/2 to 8 minutes
Barley	— 2 to 3 minutes
Quinoa	— 3 1/2 to 4 minutes
Chestnut	— 2 1/2 to 3 minutes.

This recipe is free of wheat, milk, eggs, corn, soy, yeast, and refined sugar. If made with quinoa, amaranth, or chestnut flour, this recipe is also free of gluten and all grains.

Pasta Made With An Extrusion Machine

If you enjoy pasta often or wish to make a variety of shapes, an extrusion machine is a good investment.

Spelt:

> 4 c. plus 1 to 2 tbsp. spelt flour
> 200 ml. water

Rye:

> 3 1/2 c. rye flour
> 185 ml. water

Barley:

> 4 c. plus 1 to 2 tbsp. barley flour
> 250 ml. water

Quinoa:

> 3 1/2 c. quinoa flour
> 212 ml. water

Stir the flour, gently spoon it into the measuring cup, level it off with a knife, and put it in the mixing chamber of the machine. Carefully measure the water. (Most measuring cups have milliliter markings, which give a more precise measurement, as well as cup markings.) Turn on the machine and add the water to the flour as directed in the machine's instructions. After a few minutes of mixing, take a few crumbs of the dough between your thumb and index finger and pinch them together. (This is called the "pinch test.") They should stick together, but the dough should be dry rather than sticky. If the dough is sticky, add 1 tbsp. of flour to the machine, allow it to mix a few more minutes, and do the pinch test again. If it is still sticky, continue to add flour 1 tbsp. at a time, mixing and doing a pinch test after each addition, until the proper consistency is reached. If the crumbs of dough do not stick together when the pinch test is performed, add 1 tsp. of water to the machine, allow it to mix for a few minutes, and do another pinch test. If it is still too dry, add water 1 tsp. at a time, mixing and performing a pinch test between each addition, until the proper consistency is reached. Make a note of the final amount of water and flour you used for future reference. Allow the pasta to extrude according to the machine's instructions. Lay the strands of pasta on a lightly floured cloth to dry, separating the strands as you lay them down, or cook them immediately. For macaroni, extrude pasta with a hole in the middle of it, let the strands dry for a few hours, cut them into the desired lengths, and allow them to finish drying or cook them immediately. The cooking time is affected by many factors, including the size and shape of the pasta, with macaroni tending to cook more quickly than spaghetti. Cook the pasta according to the directions given in "To Cook Pasta," pages 95-96, testing it often to avoid overcooking it. Note the cooking times for each type and shape of pasta for future reference. The approximate cooking times given below are for spaghetti:

Spelt	— 12 to 14 minutes
Rye	— 6 1/2 to 8 minutes
Barley	— 2 1/2 to 3 minutes
Quinoa	— 3 to 3 1/2 minutes.

This recipe is free of wheat, milk, eggs, corn, soy, yeast, and refined sugar. If it is made with quinoa flour it is free of gluten and all grains.

Pesto

Because of the protein supplied by the nuts, pasta served with this tomato-free sauce is a complete main dish.

3 1/2 c. parsley, spinach, or sweet basil leaves, washed, stemmed, and dried (about 1/4 lb. as purchased)
1 to 2 cloves of garlic (optional)
1/2 c. pine nuts
1/2 c. olive or other oil
1/4 to 1/2 tsp. salt, or to taste
1/8 tsp. pepper (optional)

Chop the garlic in a food processor or blender using a pulsing action. Add the parsley, spinach, or sweet basil and pulse to chop the leaves as finely as possible. Add the nuts and process continually until they are ground. Add the oil gradually while processing. Add the seasonings and process until they are blended in. Serve the sauce over warm cooked pasta. This sauce is very rich, so a little goes a long way. Makes about 1 c. of sauce.

This recipe is free of all grains (including wheat and corn), gluten, milk, eggs, soy, yeast, refined sugar, tomatoes, and meat.

Garlic, Pepper, And Oil Sauce

This is a very simple yet flavorful way to serve pasta without using tomatoes.

    5 tbsp. oil, preferably olive oil
    1 to 2 cloves of garlic, peeled (optional)
    3 tbsp. finely chopped Italian (flat-leaf) parsley
       (if necessary, substitute 2 tbsp. dry parsley)
    1 tsp. pepper, or to taste
    1/8 tsp. salt (optional)
    1 lb. pasta

Saute the garlic in the olive oil until it is lightly browned, then remove and discard the garlic. Cook and drain the pasta. (See "To Cook Pasta," pages 95-96.) Pour the warm olive oil over the pasta, sprinkle it with the parsley, pepper, and salt, and toss it thoroughly to mix all the ingredients. Makes 4 to 6 servings.

This recipe is free of wheat, milk, eggs, corn, soy, yeast, refined sugar, meat, and tomatoes. If a non-grain pasta is used, it is also free of gluten and all grains.

Easy Vegetarian Spaghetti Sauce

If you can tolerate canned tomato products but wish to avoid meat, this is the sauce for you.

2 tbsp. olive or other oil
1 clove of garlic, peeled and cut into quarters (optional)
1 18-oz. can tomato paste
1 28-oz. can tomato puree
2 c. water
1 tbsp. fresh chopped or 1 tsp. dry oregano
1 tsp. fresh chopped or 1/2 tsp. dry sweet basil
1 tsp. salt (optional)
1/8 tsp. pepper (optional)

Saute the garlic in the olive oil in a large kettle until it begins to brown. Then remove and discard the garlic. Add the tomato paste and cook it slowly, stirring it frequently, for about 10 minutes, or until it begins to darken slightly. Add the tomato puree, water, and seasonings and simmer the sauce for about 2 hours, stirring it frequently. Freeze any leftover sauce in meal-size portions. Makes 6 to 7 cups of sauce.

This recipe is free of all grains (including wheat and corn), gluten, milk, eggs, soy, refined sugar, and meat.

Fresh Tomato Sauce

If you can tolerate tomatoes but not canned tomato products, this multipurpose recipe is the one to use.

4 lbs. ripe Italian plum tomatoes
4 tbsp. olive or other oil
1 clove of garlic, minced (optional)
1/8 tsp. pepper OR 1/4 dried red pepper pod, seeded
    and crumbled (about 1/2" of a pod) (optional)
1/2 to 1 tsp. salt, or to taste (optional)
1 tbsp. chopped fresh or 1 tsp. dry sweet basil, or to taste
    (optional)

Scald the tomatoes in boiling water for 2 minutes, then slip the skins off. Puree them in a food processor or blender. Saute the garlic in the olive oil in a large saucepot. When the garlic is brown, it may be removed, if desired. Add the pureed tomatoes and seasonings and, if desired, partially cover the pan with its lid. Simmer the sauce, stirring it frequently, for 45 minutes to 1 hour or until it is very thick. If you wish to serve meatballs with this sauce, make and brown them as directed in "Easy Spaghetti Sauce With Meatballs," below, and add them to a double batch of this sauce for its simmering time. To use this sauce on pizza, omit the pepper and 1 tbsp. fresh or 1 tsp. dry sweet basil and instead add 1 tbsp. chopped fresh or 1 tsp. dry oregano, 1 tsp. chopped fresh or 1/2 tsp. dry thyme, and 1 tsp. chopped fresh or 1/2 tsp. dry sweet basil. A single batch of this recipe makes about 2 1/2 c. of sauce.

This recipe is free of all grains (including wheat and corn), gluten, milk, eggs, soy, yeast, refined sugar, and meat.

Easy Spaghetti Sauce With Meatballs

The meatballs for this sauce are delicious when made with alternative meats.

> 2 lbs. lean ground beef, pork, buffalo, turkey, or game meat
> 1 tbsp. chopped fresh or 1 tsp. dry parsley (optional)
> 1 1/2 tsp. salt, divided (optional)
> 1/2 tsp. pepper, divided (optional)
> 2 tbsp. olive or other oil
> 1 clove of garlic, peeled (optional)
> 1 28-oz. can tomato puree
> 1 12-oz. can tomato paste
> 1 c. water
> 1 tsp. chopped fresh or 1/4 tsp. dry oregano (optional)
> 1 tsp. chopped fresh or 1/4 tsp. dry sweet basil (optional)

Mix together the meat, 1/2 tsp. salt, 1/4 tsp. pepper, and the parsley and press them firmly into about 10 meatballs. Put the oil, meatballs, and garlic in a large kettle, and cook the meatballs slowly, uncovered, turning them to brown all the sides. Remove the clove of garlic and drain off all of the fat. Add the tomato puree, tomato paste, water, 1 tsp. salt, 1/4 tsp. pepper, oregano, and sweet basil and simmer the sauce, stirring it frequently, for 1 1/2 to 2 hours. Remove the meatballs after the first hour of simmering to keep them from falling apart. Any sauce and meatballs that you do not use immediately freeze very well. Makes about 5 c. sauce and 10 meatballs.

This recipe is free of all grains (including wheat and corn), gluten, milk, eggs, soy, and refined sugar.

Easy Meat Sauce For Lasagne

Use this sauce for meat-containing lasagne or if you prefer ground meat in your spaghetti sauce.

> 1 1/2 lbs. lean ground beef, pork, buffalo, turkey, or
>   game meat
> 1 12-oz. can tomato paste
> 1 16-oz. can tomato puree
> 3 c. water
> 1 tsp. salt (optional)
> 1/8 tsp. pepper (optional)

Brown the meat in a large saucepot. Drain off all of the fat. Add the tomato paste, tomato puree, water, and seasonings and simmer the sauce, stirring it frequently, for 1 1/2 to 2 hours. If you wish to, you can allow the sauce to settle after cooking and skim off 1 c. of relatively meat-free sauce from the top of the pan to serve on the side with the lasagne. Makes 8 to 9 cups of sauce, or enough for one batch of "Lasagne," page 106.

This recipe is free of all grains (including wheat and corn), gluten, milk, eggs, soy, and refined sugar.

Easy Pizza Sauce

If can tolerate canned tomatoes and want your pizza in a jiffy, use this sauce.

> 1 6-oz. can tomato paste
> 1 8-oz. can tomato sauce
> 1/2 c. water
> 2 tbsp. olive or other oil (optional)

1 tbsp. chopped fresh or 1 tsp. dry oregano
1 tsp. chopped fresh or 1/2 tsp. dry thyme
1 tsp. chopped fresh or 1/2 tsp. dry sweet basil

Combine all of the ingredients in a saucepan and simmer them for 30 to 45 minutes, stirring frequently. Makes enough sauce for 2 pizzas.

This recipe is free of all grains (including wheat and corn), gluten, milk, eggs, soy, and refined sugar.

Manicotti

This delicious meat-free dish is nice to prepare ahead and freeze.

> 2 c. of "Easy Vegetarian Spaghetti Sauce," page 101, or
>   "Fresh Tomato Sauce," page 102
> 1 lb. goat or sheep feta cheese or goat or cow ricotta,
>   drained
> 1/4 c. goat or cow Romano cheese (optional)
> 1/4 tsp. salt (optional - with cow ricotta only)
> 1/8 tsp. pepper (optional)
> 2 tsp. chopped fresh or dry parsley (optional)
> 1 batch of "Pasta For Rolling By Hand," page 96

Using a potato masher, mash together the cheese(s), salt, pepper, and parsley. Prepare the pasta, roll it out into thin sheets as directed in the pasta recipe, and cut it into 4" to 5" squares. Place 2 to 3 tbsp. of the cheese filling on each square and roll them up diagonally. Put about 1/2 c. of the sauce in the bottom of a 9" by 12" baking dish. Lay the manicotti in the dish with the seam side of the pasta down. Put another 1/2 c. of the sauce on top of the manicotti. Bake them, covered, at 350° for 30 minutes. Serve the manicotti with the remaining sauce on the side. Any leftover pasta dough may be cut into noodles and dried for future use. Makes 4 to 6 servings.

This recipe is free of wheat, cow's milk (if the cow ricotta and Romano are not used), eggs, corn, soy, refined sugar and meat. If

*it is made with quinoa, amaranth, or chestnut pasta it is also free
of gluten and all grains. If the feta cheese is the only cheese used
and it is made with "Fresh Tomato Sauce," it is also suitable for
a low-yeast diet. (See "Note on Feta Cheese," page 72.)*

Polenta

*This northern Italian dish is traditionally made with cornmeal
flour (not grits), but may also be made with cassava meal. Its
flavor comes from the sauce.*

> 2 c. cornmeal flour OR 1 1/3 c. cassava meal (See
>   "Sources of Special Foods," ch. 16.)
> 4 c. water
> 1 to 1 1/2 tsp. salt, or to taste
> Any tomato-based pasta sauce, pages 101 to 104, OR
>   "Pesto," page 100
> Grated goat cheese or crumbled goat or sheep feta cheese
>   (optional)

Combine the cornmeal flour or cassava meal with 2 c. of cold
water. Bring the rest of the water and the salt to a boil in a large
saucepot. Add the wet meal a little at a time, stirring constantly.
Return the mixture to a boil and cook it over very low heat for 1
hour for the cornmeal flour or for 30 minutes for the cassava meal,
stirrring it frequently. It will become very stiff. Spread it on a
platter and top it with the sauce and optional cheese, serving
more sauce and cheese on the side. Any leftovers that do not have
sauce on them may be packed into an oiled loaf pan, refrigerated
overnight, sliced 1/2" thick, and fried in a small amount of oil for
breakfast. Makes 4 servings.

*This recipe is free of wheat, gluten, milk, eggs, soy, and refined
sugar. If it is made with the cassava meal, it is free of all grains,
including corn. If "Fresh Tomato Sauce" or "Pesto" and feta cheese
are used, it also may be suitable for a low-yeast diet. (See "Note
on Feta Cheese," page 72.)*

Lasagne

This dish may be prepared a day ahead to serve to a large crowd of guests for a dinner party.

1 batch of "Pasta For Rolling By Hand," page 96
1 1/2 lbs. goat ricotta cheese OR sheep or goat feta cheese
1/2 tsp. salt (optional - omit with feta cheese)
1/4 tsp. pepper (optional)
1 tbsp. finely chopped fresh or dried parsley
1 1/2 lbs. goat jack cheese (optional)
1 tbsp oil
1 batch of "Easy Meat Sauce For Lasagne," page 104,
    OR 1 1/2 batches of "Fresh Tomato Sauce," page 102,
    OR 1/2 batch of "Easy Vegetarian Spaghetti Sauce,"
    page 101

Prepare the pasta as directed in the recipe. While the dough is resting, mash together the ricotta or feta cheese, salt, pepper, and parsley with a potato masher. Thinly slice the jack cheese if you are using it. Use the oil to grease the sides and bottom of a 9" by 13" baking dish. Divide the pasta dough into three pieces. Roll one piece out to the size of the pan on a floured pastry cloth, invert the cloth into the pan, and peel the cloth off of the pasta. (If you are using spelt or rye pasta you can just pick it up to put it in the pan.) Cover the pasta with about 3/4 c. of tomato sauce without meat or 1 1/2 to 2 c. of sauce with meat. Top this with half of the ricotta or feta mixture and half of the sliced jack cheese. Roll out another piece of pasta and add it to the pan and repeat the layers of sauce and cheese. Roll out the final piece of pasta and add it to the pan. Top it with about 1 c. of sauce. Cover the pan with foil and bake it at 350° for 1 hour, or until it is bubbly and hot all the way through. If you make the lasagne ahead and refrigerate it, increase the baking time to 1 1/2 hours. Cut any leftovers into meal-size portions and freeze them. Makes 8 to 10 servings.

This recipe is free of wheat, cow's milk, eggs, corn, soy, and refined sugar. If a non-grain pasta is used, it is free of gluten and all grains. If feta cheese is the only cheese used and it is made with

"Fresh Tomato Sauce," it is suitable for a low-yeast diet. (See "Note on Feta Cheese," page 72.)

Pizza

This is very satisfying to both body and soul even if it is made without the meat and cheese.

> 1/2 batch of "Easy Pizza Sauce," page 104, OR
> > 1/2 batch of "Fresh Tomato Sauce," page 102,
> > made with the spices listed for pizza
>
> 1 to 1 1/2 c grated goat jack cheese, about 4 to 6 ounces (optional)
> 1/4 to 1/2 lb. ground meat of any kind, cooked, crumbled, and drained of fat (optional)
> 1/2 to 1 c. total amount of assorted vegetable toppings, such as sliced black olives, chopped green peppers, etc.
> Pizza dough - choose one of the following:

Yeast doughs:

> 1/3 batch of "Spelt Yeast Bread," page 60
> 1 batch of "Rye Yeast Bread," page 58
> 1/2 batch of "Quick Barley Yeast Bread," page 59

Non-yeast doughs:

Spelt:

> 3 1/2 c. spelt flour
> 2 tsp. baking soda
> 1/2 tsp. unbuffered Vitamin C crystals
> 1/2 tsp. salt (optional)
> 1/2 c. oil
> 1 1/4 c. water

Rye:

> 3 c. rye flour
> 1 1/2 tsp. baking soda

1/2 tsp. unbuffered Vitamin C crystals
1/2 tsp. salt (optional)
3/8 c. oil
1 1/4 c. water

Barley:

2 1/2 c. barley flour
1/2 c. arrowroot
1 1/2 tsp. baking soda
1/2 tsp. unbuffered Vitamin C crystals
1/2 tsp. salt (optional)
3/8 c. oil
1 1/4 c. water

Amaranth:

3 c. amaranth flour
1 1/2 c. arrowroot
2 1/4 tsp. baking soda
3/4 tsp. unbuffered Vitamin C crystals
3/4 tsp. salt (optional)
1/2 c. oil
1 1/2 c. water

Quinoa:

3 c. quinoa flour
1 1/2 c. tapioca flour
2 1/4 tsp. baking soda
3/4 tsp. unbuffered Vitamin C crystals
3/4 tsp. salt (optional)
1/2 c. oil
1 1/2 c. water

Chestnut:

2 1/2 c. chestnut flour
1 1/2 c. arrowroot

1 tsp. baking soda
1/2 tsp. unbuffered Vitamin C crystals
1/2 tsp. salt (optional)
3/8 c. oil
1 1/4 c. water

If you are making a yeast dough pizza, prepare the dough as directed in the bread recipe and set it in a warm place to rise the first time. Prepare the tomato sauce as directed in the recipe, grate the cheese if you are using it, cook and drain the meat if you are using it, and chop the vegetables. If you are using a non-yeast pizza dough, begin making it at this point, after all of the toppings are ready. Combine the flour(s), baking soda, Vitamin C crystals, and salt in a large bowl. Combine the water and oil and stir them into the flour mixture until just mixed. Pat the dough into an oiled and floured 12" pizza pan with a floured hand, or if you are using a yeast dough, pat it into an oiled 12" pizza pan with an oiled hand. Top the dough with the sauce, cheese, meat and vegetables. Bake at 400° for 25 to 30 minutes, or until the edge of the pizza is brown. Makes one 12" pizza.

This recipe is free of wheat, cow's milk, eggs, corn, soy, and refined sugar. If the amaranth, quinoa, or chesnut dough is used, it is free of gluten and all grains. If the meat is omitted, it is free of meat. If it is made with "Fresh Tomato Sauce," a non-yeast dough, and the cheese is omitted, it is suitable for a low-yeast diet.

Pesto Pizza

This is just as delicious as the usual type of pizza, but avoids tomatoes for those who are sensitive to them.

1 recipe of any pizza dough, above
3/4 c. pesto made with sweet basil, page 100
1 to 1 1/2 c. shredded goat jack cheese, about 4 to 6
    ounces (optional)
1/2 c. sliced black olives (optional)

Prepare the pizza dough and pat it into a prepared pan as directed above. Spread the pesto on the dough, sprinkle it with the cheese, and top it with the olives, if desired. Bake at 400° for 25 to 30 minutes, or until the edge of the pizza begins to brown. Makes one 12" pizza.

This recipe is free of wheat, cow's milk, eggs, corn, soy, and refined sugar. If the amaranth, quinoa, or chesnut dough is used, it is free of gluten and all grains. If a non-yeast dough is used and the cheese is omitted, it is suitable for a low-yeast diet.

Pasta e Fagioli

This traditional Italian soup is quite easy to make.

> 1 to 2 large stalks of celery (use 2 if you are omitting the onion and garlic)
> 2 slices nitrate-free bacon or salt pork (optional)
> 1 small onion (optional)
> 1 clove of garlic (optional)
> 3 tbsp. olive or other oil
> 3 to 4 Italian plum tomatoes, peeled and coarsely chopped (about 4 to 6 oz.)
> 6 c. hot water
> 1 1/2 tsp. salt
> 1/8 tsp. pepper (optional)
> 2 c. cooked cannelini beans or other white beans, drained
> 2 c. small pasta or spaghetti broken into 1" to 2" pieces

Place the celery, pork, onion, and garlic on a chopping board and chop them together until they are almost the consistency of a paste. Saute this mixture in the oil in a large saucepot until it begins to brown. Add the tomatoes and cook them for a few minutes. Add the water, salt, and beans, and boil the soup for 5 minutes. Add the pasta and boil the soup for an additional 2 to 12 minutes, or until the pasta is *al dente*. (The cooking time depends on what type of pasta is used. See "To Cook Pasta," pages 95-96.) Serve the soup immediately since, except for spelt and rye pasta, most alternative pastas become mushy upon standing in liquid. Makes 4 to 6 servings, or about 8 c. of soup.

This recipe is free of wheat, milk, eggs, corn, soy, yeast, and refined sugar. If the pork is omitted it is free of meat. If it is made with a non-grain pasta, it is free of gluten and all grains.

Tortillas

These are not just for Mexican food. Eat them with breakfast or dinner, or make a sandwich using them in place of the bread for lunch.

Garbanzo:

> 2 c. garbanzo flour
> 1/2 tsp. salt
> 1/2 c. water

Quinoa:

> 2 c. quinoa flour
> 1/2 tsp. salt
> 3/4 c. water

Amaranth:

> 2 1/4 c. amaranth flour
> 1/2 tsp. salt
> 3/4 c. water

Rye:

> 2 c. rye flour
> 1/2 tsp. salt
> 3/4 c. water

Spelt:

> 2 c. spelt flour
> 1/2 tsp. salt
> 1/2 c. plus 2 tbsp. water

Stir together the flour and salt. Add the water and stir and knead to form a stiff dough. Divide the dough into portions - 4 for large (8" to 9") tortillas, or 6 for small (6" to 7") tortillas. Flour each portion well and roll it out to about 1/8" thickness on a well floured board, turning the dough over and flouring it on both sides while rolling it.

For soft tortillas, such as for the "Enchilada Casserole," page 116, heat a heavy frying pan over medium heat. One at a time, put each tortilla into the pan and cook it for about 3 minutes on the first side. or until it begins to brown in spots on the underside. Turn it with a spatula and cook it for about 3 minutes on the second side also. Cool them on a dish towel or a wire rack.

For crisp tortillas, such as for "Tostadas," page 115, heat about 1/2" of oil in a frying pan until a small piece of dough sizzles when put into the oil. One at a time, put each tortilla into the oil and cook it until the edges turn brown. Carefully turn it with a large slotted spatula and cook it until the second side browns. Cool them on dishtowels to absorb the oil. Makes 4 large or 6 small tortillas.

This recipe is free of wheat, milk, eggs, corn, soy, yeast, and refined sugar. If it is made with garbanzo, quinoa, or amaranth flour, it is free of gluten and all grains.

Quick Refried Beans

If these beans are fried with soy or peanut oil and served on top of "Garbanzo Tortillas," above, you have a one-food-family meal.

1 lb. Anasazi or pink, red, or speckled beans
Water
2 tsp. salt, or to taste
3 tbsp. oil

Wash the beans and cover them with 3 to 4 times their volume of cold water. Soak them overnight OR bring them to a boil, boil them for 2 minutes, turn off the heat, and let them stand for 1 hour. Drain the water and rinse them two or three times until the rinse water is clear. (This removes some of the hard-to-digest carbohydrates.) Cover them with water, add the salt, bring them to a boil, and then cook them over medium heat until they are very soft, about 2 to 2 1/2 hours for anasazi beans. (The cooking time may vary for other types of beans.) Drain almost all of the water and mash the beans with a potato masher. Put the oil in a large frying pan, add the beans, and cook them until they are dry, turning them with a spatula as they are cooking. This recipe makes about 4 c. of refried beans.

This recipe is free of all grains (including wheat and corn), gluten, milk, eggs, soy, yeast, and refined sugar.

Mexican Sauce

This spicy sauce may be made with canned tomato puree or, for those who can tolerate tomatoes but not canned tomato products, with fresh tomatoes.

        4 1/2 lbs. Italian plum tomatoes OR 1 28-oz. can
            tomato puree
        1/4 onion, finely chopped (optional)
        1 tbsp. oil (needed only if you are using the onion)
        1/2 clove garlic, finely chopped (optional)
        1/8 tsp. ground cumin
        1/4 tsp. oregano
        2 tsp. chili powder, or more to taste
        1 tsp. salt (optional)

If you are using the fresh tomatoes, quarter them, remove the seeds, and puree them in a blender or food processor. If you are using the onion, saute it in the oil until it is soft. Combine the tomato puree, onion, garlic, cumin, oregano, chili powder, and salt in a saucepan and cook the sauce over medium heat, stirring it about every 10 minutes, until it is thickened. For the fresh tomatoes, cook the sauce uncovered for about 1 hour. For the canned tomato puree, cook it covered for 30 to 40 minutes. This recipe makes about 3 c. of sauce.

This recipe is free of all grains (including wheat and corn), gluten, milk, eggs, soy, and refined sugar. If it is made with the fresh tomatoes, it is suitable for a low-yeast diet.

Avocado Sauce

Use this sauce with "Enchilada Casserole," page 116, "To-stadas," page 115, or as a dip for fresh vegetables.

    1 large (about 1/2 lb. in weight) ripe avocado
    1/8 tsp. tart-tasting unbuffered Vitamin C crystals,
        such as Vital Life brand
    1 tbsp. finely chopped onion (optional)
    1/4 tsp. salt (optional)
    1/8 tsp. pepper (optional)

Thoroughly mash the avocado with the Vitamin C crystals, onion, salt, and pepper. Makes about 2/3 c. of sauce.

This recipe is free of all grains (including wheat and corn), gluten, milk, eggs, soy, yeast, and refined sugar.

Tostadas

These make a delicious and nutritious vegetarian lunch. If they are made with garbanzo tortillas and bean sprouts, you can keep the number of food families used down to one plus the number of toppings used.

    1 batch of 6 large crisp "Tortillas," page 112
    1 batch of "Quick Refried Beans," page 113, OR 2 16-oz
        cans of vegetarian refried beans, warmed
    3 to 5 c. of bean sprouts or shredded lettuce
    Shredded goat jack cheese (optional)
    Sliced black olives (optional)
    Chopped tomatoes (optional)
    Sliced avocado or "Avocado Sauce," page 115 (optional)
    "Mexican Sauce," page 114 (optional)

While the tortillas are still warm from being fried as in the "Tortilla" recipe, spread them with the warmed beans and top them with the desired toppings listed above. This recipe makes 6 tostadas.

This recipe is free of wheat, cow's milk, eggs, corn, soy, refined sugar, and meat. If it is made with garbanzo, amaramth, or quinoa tortillas, it is free of gluten and all grains. If the cheese is omitted and the "Mexican Sauce" is either made with fresh toma- toes or omitted, it is suitable for a low-yeast diet.

Enchilada Casserole

This vegetarian casserole is great for a make-ahead meal.

> 1 batch of soft "Tortillas," page 112
> 3 c. "Quick Refried Beans," page 113, OR 1 1/2 16-oz cans of vegetarian refried beans
> 1 batch of "Mexican Sauce," page 114
> 1 c. shredded goat jack cheese (optional)
> Sliced avocado or "Avocado Sauce," page 115 (optional)
> Sliced black olives (optional)

Make four soft tortillas about the same size as an 8" or 9" round baking dish as directed in the tortilla recipe. Put one of the tortillas in the baking dish, spread it with 1 c. of the beans, and top the beans with 1/3 c. of the "Mexican Sauce" and 1/4 c. of the cheese. Repeat the layers two more times. Top the casserole with the last tortilla, 1/3 c. sauce, and 1/4 c. cheese. Bake it at 350° for 30 minutes, or until it is bubbly. Cut the casserole into wedges and serve it with more "Mexican Sauce," avocado slices or "Avo- cado Sauce," and sliced olives, if desired. Makes 6 servings.

This recipe is free of wheat, cow's milk, eggs, corn, soy, refined sugar, and meat. If it is made with garbanzo, amaranth, or quinoa tortillas, it is also free of gluten and all grains. If the "Mexican Sauce" is made with fresh tomatoes and the cheese is omitted, it is suitable for a low-yeast diet.

Oriental Game or Chicken

This is a healthy way to prepare game or chicken.

1 to 1/2 lbs. antelope, elk or venison steak OR 2 whole
   boned and skinned chicken breasts
2 tbsp. oil
2 1/2 to 3 c. water, divided
1 c. celery, sliced diagonally
1 5-oz. can sliced water chestnuts, drained
1 green pepper, seeded and cut into 1/2" pieces
3/4 tsp. salt, or to taste
1/4 tsp. pepper, or to taste
1/4 c. arrowroot, tapioca flour, or water chestnut starch
1/2 c. bean sprouts (optional)
1/2 lb. fresh mushrooms plus 1 tbsp. oil OR 1 4-oz can
   sliced mushrooms, drained (optional)
3 to 4 c. cooked rice, quinoa, or noodles, or puffed
   amaranth cereal

Cut the meat into thin strips about 1 1/2" to 2" long. Brown them in the 2 tbsp. oil in a frying pan. Add 2 c. of the water and the celery, water chestnuts, green pepper, salt, and pepper, and simmer the mixture for 30 minutes. While it is simmering, if you plan to use the fresh mushrooms, saute them in the 1 tbsp. oil in another pan. At the end of the simmering time, add the bean sprouts and mushrooms to the large pan, if you are using them. Mix the starch and 1/2 c. cold water and add them to the pan. Return the mixture to a boil and simmer it until it is thick, adding an additional 1/2 c. hot water if it is too thick. Serve it over cooked rice, quinoa, or noodles, or puffed amaranth cereal. Makes 4 to 6 servings.

This recipe is free of wheat, milk, eggs, corn, soy, yeast, and refined sugar. If it is served with quinoa, non-grain noodles, or puffed amaranth cereal, it is also free of all grains. If is is served with rice, quinoa, noodles that do not contain gluten, or puffed amaranth cereal, it is free of gluten.

7

Vegetables, Side Dishes, and Soups

Vegetables, side dishes, and soups round out any meal. Some of them can be a meal all by themselves. Most commonly on an allergy diet, vegetables are eaten either plain or with a little oil and salt, so this chapter does not include a lot of vegetable recipes. For a complete discussion on how to prepare both common and unusual vegetables, see The Yeast Connection Cookbook, pages 229 to 269. (See "References," page 271.)

Harvard Beets

This recipe eliminates both the sugar and the cornstarch found in most Harvard Beets.

> 1/2 c. apple juice concentrate, thawed, OR 1/2 c. water
>   plus 1/4 tsp. stevia working solution, page 226
> 2 tsp. arrowroot or tapioca flour
> 1/4 tsp. salt (optional)
> 2 whole cloves
> 3/4 tsp. tart-tasting unbuffered Vitamin C crystals,
>   such as Vital Life brand
> 2 c. sliced cooked beets

Combine the juice or water and stevia with the starch, salt, and cloves in a saucepan. Bring the mixture to a boil and simmer it until it is thick and clear. Stir in the Vitamin C crystals and beets, return the mixture to a boil, and then reduce the heat and simmer it until the beets are heated through. Makes 2 to 4 servings.

This recipe is free of all grains (including wheat and corn), gluten, milk, eggs, soy, yeast, and refined sugar.

Vegetables With Cheese Sauce

When served with bread or crackers, this dish is satisfying enough to make a meal.

> 1 lb. broccoli, cauliflower, spinach, or the vegetable
>   of your choice, fresh or frozen
> 1 recipe of either "Cheese Sauce I" or "Cheese Sauce II,"
>   page 81

If you are using frozen vegetables, cook them according to the package directions. If you are using fresh broccoli or cauliflower, steam or boil it for 10 to 15 minutes. (The cooking time depends on many factors, including the size of the pieces.) If you are using fresh spinach, put it in a pan with the water that clings to the leaves after washing it and cook it, stirring it often, for 3 to 10 minutes. Prepare the cheese sauce as directed in the recipe. Pour the cheese sauce over the vegetables and serve them. Makes 4 to 6 servings.

This recipe is free of wheat, cow's milk, eggs, corn, soy, and refined sugar. If the cheese sauce is thickened with arrowroot or tapioca flour, it is free of gluten and all grains. If "Cheese Sauce I," made with feta cheese, is used, it is suitable for use on a low-yeast diet. (See "Note on Feta Cheese," page 72.)

Dried Beans

Cooked dried beans may be eaten as a vegetable, either plain or with a little oil and salt, or used in other recipes, such as several in the main dish, ethnic dish, and salad sections of this book. Do not hesitate to cook a large batch - they freeze well for future use.

Wash the beans to remove any sand or dirt, and pick out and discard any bad-looking beans. Soak them in about 3 times their volume of water overnight. In the morning, rinse the beans 2 to 3 times with fresh water to remove some of the hard-to-digest substances that may cause intestinal gas.

Cover them with about twice their volume of water and bring them to a boil. Reduce the heat and simmer them until they are tender to soft. (From the standpoint of digestability, it is better to cook beans to the point of softness rather than just cook them until they are tender.) The cooking time varies with the hardness of the water, type and age of the beans, altitude, etc., but some general guidelines are:

Anasazi beans	—2 to 2 1/2 hours
Black beans	—2 to 3 hours
Garbanzo beans	—2 to 3 hours
Kidney beans	—2 1/2 to 3 hours
Lentils	—1 to 2 hours
Lima beans	—1 to 1 1/2 hours
Navy beans	—3 to 3 1/2 hours
Pinto beans	—2 hours
Small white beans	—2 to 3 hours
Split peas	—1 1/2 to 2 1/2 hours

It is best to salt the beans after cooking them. When trying to determine how many dried beans you need to cook for a recipe, a rule of thumb is that 1 cup of dried beans will yield 2 to 2 1/2 cups of cooked beans.

This recipe is free of all grains (including wheat and corn), gluten, milk, eggs, soy, yeast, and refined sugar.

Sugar- and Tomato-Free Baked Beans

From the flavor of these beans, one would never guess that they contain no sugar, tomatoes, or meat. They are easy to make in a crockpot.

    2 lbs. small white or small navy beans
    Water
    6 c. white grape, apple, or pineapple juice OR 6 c.
        water plus 1/8 tsp. white stevia powder
    1 tbsp. salt
    1/2 tsp. pepper
    3 tbsp. finely chopped onion, or 2 tsp. dried onion
        flakes (optional)
    2 tbsp. finely chopped fresh sweet basil OR 1 tbsp.
        dried sweet basil
    1 tbsp. paprika

Sort over and wash the beans. Soak them in 2 to 3 times their volume of water overnight. In the morning, rinse them 2 to 3 times with fresh water, and then simmer them in about 2 times their volume of fresh water for 1/2 to 1 hour, or until they begin to soften. Drain them and place them in a roaster with the juice or water and stevia and the seasonings. Bake them at 250° for about 8 hours, stirring them often and adding more water as needed.

To cook the beans in a crockpot, after they have soaked and been rinsed, place them in a 3-quart crockpot with the juice or water and stevia and the seasonings. Cook them on high for 6 to 7 hours or on low for 8 to 10 hours, or until they are tender. Stir them every few hours, and while stirring them, smash a few beans against the side of the pot to thicken the sauce. Makes 12 to 14 servings. This recipe may be halved, but will take less time to cook. Any leftover beans freeze well.

This recipe is free of all grains (including wheat and corn), gluten, milk, eggs, soy, yeast, refined sugar, tomatoes, and meat.

Quinoa Poultry Stuffing or Side Dish

This grain-free poultry stuffing is also excellent served as a side dish with meat, poultry, or fish and vegetables. Be sure to wash the soap-like coating off of the quinoa before using it.

2 c. sliced celery
1/4 small onion, chopped (optional)
4 tbsp. oil
1 c. quinoa, thoroughly washed
2 c. water
1/2 to 1 tsp. salt, or to taste
1/4 tsp. pepper
3 tbsp. finely chopped fresh parsley OR 1 tbsp. dried
    parsley
1 tbsp. finely chopped fresh sweet basil OR 1 tsp. dried
    sweet basil
1 tsp. finely chopped fresh rosemary OR 1/4 tsp. ground
    dried rosemary (optional)

Using a saucepan, saute the celery and onion in the oil until they just begin to brown. Add the quinoa and water, bring the mixture to a boil, and simmer it for 15 to 20 minutes, or until the quinoa is translucent. Stir in the seasonings thoroughly and allow the quinoa to stand for a few minutes so that the flavors can blend. Serve it as a side dish or stuff it into a large chicken and then roast the chicken. If you use this stuffing for a turkey, double the recipe for a 12-lb. turkey or triple it for a 24-lb. turkey. Makes 4 to 6 servings.

This recipe is free of all grains (including wheat and corn), gluten, milk, eggs, soy, yeast, and refined sugar.

Two-Food-Family Lentil Soup

The lentils in this easy and delicious vegetarian soup are one of the most easily tolerated legumes.

1 lb. lentils
Water

    3 to 5 carrots, peeled and sliced
    3 stalks of celery, sliced
    2 tsp. salt
    1/4 tsp. pepper (optional—omit it for only two food
        families)

Sort over and wash the lentils. In a 3-quart crockpot, soak them in about three times their volume of water overnight. Drain and rinse them two or three times in the morning. Add 5 c. of water and the carrots, celery, salt, and pepper to the drained lentils in the crockpot. Cook the soup on high for about 6 hours or on low for 8 to 10 hours. Add more boiling water before serving it if you like your soup thinner. Makes about 2 1/2 quarts of soup, or 5 to 8 servings. If you want to make a larger batch to freeze, use a 5-quart crockpot, double the amounts of all of the ingredients, and cook the soup on high for 8 to 10 hours. A double batch makes about 5 quarts of soup, or 10 to 16 servings.

This recipe is free of all grains (including wheat and corn), gluten, milk, eggs, soy, yeast, refined sugar, tomatoes, and meat.

Split Pea Soup

For the nonallergic members of your household, add a little warmed cubed ham to their serving bowls before ladling in this soup.

    1 lb. split peas
    Water
    2 to 3 carrots, peeled and sliced
    2 to 3 stalks of celery, sliced
    2 tsp. salt
    1/4 tsp. pepper (optional)
    1 bay leaf (optional)

Sort over and wash the peas. Soak them in about three times their volume of water overnight in a 3-quart crockpot. Drain and rinse them two or three times in the morning. To the drained peas, add 5 c. of water and the carrots, celery, salt, pepper, and bay leaf. Cook the soup on high for about 6 hours or on low for 8 to 10 hours. Add more boiling water before serving it if you like your soup thinner. Makes about 2 1/2 quarts of soup, or 5 to 8 servings. If you want to make a larger batch to freeze, use a 5-quart crockpot, double the amounts of all of the ingredients, and cook the soup on high for 8 to 10 hours. A double batch makes about 5 quarts of soup, or 10 to 16 servings.

This recipe is free of all grains (including wheat and corn), gluten, milk, eggs, soy, yeast, refined sugar, and meat.

Two-Food-Family Black Bean Soup

This is a very spicy soup. If you do not like spicy food, omit the black or red pepper or decrease the amount you use.

1 lb. of black beans
Water
1 large or two small green peppers, seeded and cut
    into 1/2" square pieces
1 small onion, diced (optional - Omit it if you want to use
    only two food families.)
1 tbsp. any type of oil (Use soy or peanut oil if you
    want to use only two food families.)
1 1/4 to 1 1/2 lbs. tomatoes OR 1 15-oz. can tomato sauce
2 tsp. salt
1/4 to 1/2 tsp. black pepper OR 1/2 to 1 2" chili pepper,
    seeded and crumbled (optional - Use the chili pepper
    rather than the black pepper if you want to use only
    two food families.)

Sort through and wash the bean. Soak them in about three times their volume of water overnight. In the morning, rinse and drain them two or three times. Saute the green pepper and onion in the oil until they are soft and slightly browned. If you are using the fresh tomatoes, peel and chop them to make about 2 c. of chopped tomatoes. Combine the drained beans, green pepper, onion, tomatoes or tomato sauce, seasonings and 2 to 3 c. of water in a saucepan, cover it, and heat it to boiling. Reduce the heat and simmer the soup for 2 to 3 hours, or until the beans are tender. Stir it occasionally while it is cooking, adding more water if necessary. Makes about 2 1/2 quarts of soup, or about 8 servings.

This recipe is free of all grains (including wheat and corn), gluten, milk, eggs, soy, yeast, and refined sugar.

"Cream" of Vegetable Soup

This recipe is a good way to use the excess zucchini from summer gardens as well as any leftover vegetables you may have on hand.

> 3 lbs. zucchini
> 5 large carrots (about 1 1/4 lbs.)
> 4 large stalks of celery
> 1/4 onion, chopped (optional)
> Water or broth (4 to 5 cups)
> 2 tsp. salt, or to taste
> 1/8 to 1/4 tsp. pepper (optional)
> 1 c. cooked vegetables, any kind (optional)

Peel the zucchini and carrots. Cut the zucchini, two of the carrots, and two of the stalks of celery into chunks. Combine the chunks of vegetables, enough water or broth to barely cover them (about 4 c.), salt, and pepper in a large saucepan, bring them to a boil, reduce the heat, and simmer them for about 30 minutes, or until the vegetables are soft. While they are simmering, dice the remaining 3 carrots and 2 stalks of celery and simmer them until they are just tender in a little more water in a separate pan. When the chunks of vegetables are very soft, puree them and their cooking liquid in small batches in a food processor or blender. Return the puree to the pan and add the diced carrots and celery and optional cooked vegetables. If the soup is too thick, you may also add some of the cooking water from the diced carrots and celery. Reheat the soup to boiling and serve it. Makes 6 servings.

This recipe is free of all grains (including wheat and corn), gluten, milk, eggs, soy, yeast, and refined sugar.

Duck Soup

Here is a poultry soup for people who are allergic to chicken. You can make it from the leftovers from a roasted duck.

Bones, meat scraps, and skin with most of the fat
    removed from a roasted duck which weighed
    about 5 lbs. before roasting
3 quarts (12 c.) water
2 stalks of celery with leaves, cut into chunks
1 carrot, cut into chunks
1/2 small onion, sliced (optional)
2 tbsp. chopped fresh parsley OR 1 tbsp. dried parsley
2 tsp. salt, or to taste
3 peppercorns OR 1/4 tsp. pepper (optional)
1 1/2 to 2 c. chopped cooked duck
1 1/2 c. sliced celery (about 3 stalks)
2 c. peeled and sliced carrots (about 3 to 4)
One or more of the following extra ingredients (optional):
    2 potatoes, peeled and diced
    1 c. peas
    1 c. shredded cabbage

Combine the bones, meat scraps and skin from the duck with the water, celery and carrot chunks, onion, parsley, salt, and pepper in a large kettle. Bring the soup to a boil and skim the foam from the top of it. Reduce the heat and simmer the soup for about 2 hours. Strain the broth. If you wish to remove all of the fat from it, refrigerate it overnight and skim off the fat in the morning. Add the chopped duck, sliced celery, sliced carrots, and optional potatoes to the broth and bring it to a boil. Reduce the heat and simmer it until the vegetables are barely tender. Add the optional peas or cabbage if you wish to use them and simmer the soup until they are tender. Makes 6 servings.

This recipe is free of all grains (including wheat and corn), gluten, milk, eggs, soy, yeast, and refined sugar.

Two-Food-Family Chicken Soup

This is old fashioned chicken soup just like Mom used to make. It can be easily limited to two food families if the optional ingredients are omitted.

1 3 1/2 to 4 lb. chicken, cleaned
3 quarts of water
1 to 1 1/2 lbs. carrots, peeled and sliced
3 stalks of celery, sliced
1/2 medium-sized onion, chopped (optional)
4 tsp. salt
1/4 tsp. pepper (optional)
2 to 3 c. total of the following extra ingredients (optional):
　　Cooked pasta
　　Cooked rice
　　Cooked barley
　　Cooked peas
　　Cooked beans

Put the chicken and water into a large kettle, bring them to a boil, and simmer them for about 1/2 hour. Skim off the foam from the top of the soup a few times while it is simmering. Add the carrots, celery, onion, salt, and pepper, return the soup to a boil, and simmer it for about another 2 hours. Refrigerate the soup overnight or until it is cool enough to handle. Skim off the fat and remove the chicken bones and skin from the meat, returning the meat to the pot. Add the optional extra cooked ingredients and reheat the soup. If not all family members can eat the optional ingredients, warm them separately and add them to the individual serving bowls as the soup is served. If you are using alternative pasta other than spelt pasta, do not allow it to stand in the soup too long before serving time, or it will become mushy. Any leftover soup without pasta freezes well. Makes 8 servings.

This recipe is free of wheat, milk, eggs, corn, soy, yeast, and refined sugar. If the rice, barley, or any grain-containing pasta is omitted, it is free of all grains. If the barley or any gluten-containing pasta is omitted, it is free of gluten.

8

Salads and Dressings

If you have to avoid lettuce and vinegar, making salads can pose a problem. But you can make salads with other leafy vegetables besides lettuce, such as cabbage and spinach, or with shredded vegetables, such as jicama, carrots, or zucchini. You can also use fruit salads, meat salads, or fish salads. Some individuals who are allergic to lettuce may even tolerate other members of the composite family to which lettuce belongs. For example, I still react to lettuce after avoiding it for over ten years, but can eat belgian endive as often as every fifth day with no problems.

If you cannot have yeast-containing foods such as vinegar and also cannot substitute citrus fruit juices for vinegar in salads, it may seem impossible for you to eat most salads. But there are two possible substitutes for vinegar in salads besides citrus fruit juices. The first is unbuffered Vitamin C crystals. Different brands differ in how they taste. Experiment with whatever brands you can find in your area, or order Vital Life brand, which is tart and tasty, by mail. (See "Sources of Special Foods," ch. 16.) Because of its purity, most doctors allow their patients to have Vitamin C crystals on every day of their rotation cycle.

The other substitute for vinegar is dehydrated acetic acid, which you can also obtain by mail order. (See "Sources of Special Foods," ch. 16.) It is not made by fermentation, so should not cause problems due to yeast allergies. However, it is extracted from wood, so it may pose problems for some individuals who are sensitive to petrochemicals. If you wish to use dehydrated acetic acid crystals instead of Vitamin C crystals in the following recipes, replace the Vitamin C called for by twice as much acetic acid. You may also wish to increase the amount of liquid used to dissolve it slightly.

Italian Dressing

This classic dressing is delicious on almost any kind of vegetables. Try it on shredded zucchini.

  3/4 c. oil
  1 1/2 tsp. finely chopped fresh oregano OR 1/2 tsp.
      dried oregano (optional)
  1/4 tsp. finely chopped fresh thyme OR 1/8 tsp.
      dried thyme (optional)
  1 clove of garlic, crushed (optional)
  1 tsp. salt
  2 tsp. tart-tasting unbuffered Vitamin C crystals, such as
      Vital Life brand
  1 1/2 tsp. water

Combine the oil, spices, and crushed garlic in a glass jar and refrigerate them at least overnight. Remove and discard the garlic. Mix the salt and Vitamin C crystals with the water until they dissolve and add them to the oil just before serving time. Shake the jar well before pouring the dressing on the salad. Makes about 3/4 c. of dressing.

This recipe is free of all grains (including wheat and corn), gluten, milk, eggs, soy, yeast, and refined sugar.

Fruity Salad Dressing

This is the dressing to use when you want something slightly sweet.

1/2 c. oil

1/4 c. apple, orange, or pineapple juice concentrate,
    thawed 1 tbsp. tart-tasting unbuffered Vitamin C
    crystals, such as Vital Life brand

1/4 tsp. salt (optional)

Dash of pepper (optional)

Combine all of the ingredients in a glass jar and shake until they are uniformly dissolved. Serve this dressing over salad greens, sliced fruit, or avocado halves. Makes about 3/4 c. of dressing.

This recipe is free of all grains (including wheat and corn), gluten, milk, eggs, soy, yeast, and refined sugar.

Avocado-Canola Seed Dressing

This rich dressing may be served with salad greens, sliced cucumbers (See "Cucumber-Avocado Salad," page 132), or as a dip for fresh vegetables.

1 large ripe avocado

Water (about 1/3 c.)

1 tsp. tart-tasting unbuffered Vitamin C crystals, such as
    Vital Life brand, or to taste

1/8 tsp. salt, or to taste (optional)

Dash of pepper, or to taste (optional)

1 tbsp. canola seeds (optional)

Peel the avocado and mash the pulp in a glass measuring cup. There should be about 2/3 c. of mashed avocado. Add water to the 1 c. mark. Transfer the avocado and water to a blender or food processor. Add the Vitamin C crystals, salt, and pepper and puree the mixture until it is smooth. Stir in the canola seeds and serve the dressing immediately. Makes about 1 c. of dressing.

This recipe is free of all grains (including wheat and corn), gluten, milk, eggs, soy, yeast, and refined sugar.

Pine Nut Dressing

This dressing may be used in many of the foods where you would use mayonaise. If you make it without the stevia, it is an excellent dip for artichokes.

> 1/2 c. pine nuts
> 1/4 c. water
> 1/4 c. oil
> 1 tsp. tart-tasting unbuffered Vitamin C crystals, such as Vital Life brand
> 1/16 tsp. or a dash of salt
> Dash of pepper (optional)
> 1/4 tsp. stevia working solution, page 226
> (optional - Use it only if you want a sweet dressing.)

Grind the nuts to a fine powder in a blender or food processor. Add the water and blend the mixture until it is smooth. Add the oil in the slowest stream possible while the blender or processor is running. Add the seasonings and blend briefly. If this dressing loses its tartness after being refrigerated for a while, mix 1/2 to 1 tsp. Vitamin C crystals with 1/2 to 1 tsp. of water and stir it into the dressing. Makes about 3/4 c. of dressing.

This recipe is free of all grains (including wheat and corn), gluten, milk, eggs, soy, yeast, and refined sugar.

Waldorf Salad

This classic salad is excellent when made with "Pine Nut Dressing," above. The stevia-sweetened version of the dressing is especially good with this salad.

> 2 c. diced apple (about 2 small or 1 1/2 large apples)
> 3/4 c. diced celery (2 to 3 stalks)
> 1/4 c. pine nuts or chopped larger nuts
> 1/4 c. raisins (optional)
> 1/2 c. "Pine Nut Dressing," above

Combine the apple, celery, nuts, and raisins in a bowl. Stir in the dressing. Makes 2 to 4 servings.

This recipe is free of all grains (including wheat and corn), gluten, milk, eggs, soy, yeast, and refined sugar.

Cucumber-Avocado Salad

This is a delicious way to use "Avocado-Canola Seed Dressing," page 130.

> 1 recipe of "Avocado-Canola Seed Dressing," page 130
> 2 large or 3 small (about 1 1/2 lbs. total weight)
>   cucumbers

Peel and slice the cucumbers. Toss them with the dressing and serve. Makes 2 to 4 servings.

This recipe is free of all grains (including wheat and corn), gluten, milk, eggs, soy, yeast, and refined sugar.

Coleslaw

This old favorite is more nutritious and satisfying when you make it with "Pine Nut Dressing" than when it is made with mayonaise.

> 1 lb. cabbage, finely shredded (This is about 4 c.
>   shredded, or 1/2 of a large head.)
> 1 medium-sized carrot, grated (optional)
> 1/2 c. "Pine Nut Dressing," page 142
> 1/8 to 1/4 tsp. tart-tasting unbuffered Vitamin C crystals,
>   such as Vital Life Brand, or to taste (optional)

Combine the cabbage and carrot in a large bowl. If more tartness is desired in the dressing, thoroughly mix the Vitamin C crystals into it in a separate bowl. Toss the vegetables with the dressing and serve the salad. Makes 2 to 4 servings.

This recipe is free of all grains (including wheat and corn), gluten, milk, eggs, soy, yeast, and refined sugar.

Cucumber Salad

This is an old-country Italian salad when you make it with the tomatoes. The juice in the bottom of your bowl is delicious sopped up with bread.

> 2 medium-sized cucumbers, peeled and sliced
> 1 large ripe avocado, cut into cubes, OR 2 regular
>   tomatoes, sliced, with the slices quartered, OR 4
>   to 6 Italian plum tomatoes, sliced
> 1/4 to 1/2 tsp. tart-tasting unbuffered Vitamin C crystals,
>   such as Vital Life brand
> 1/8 tsp. pepper
> 1/16 to 1/8 tsp. salt (optional)
> 1/2 tsp. water
> 2 tbsp. oil

Combine the cucumbers with the avocado or tomatoes in a large bowl. In a small bowl or a glass jar, mix the Vitamin C crystals, pepper, and salt with the water until the Vitamin C and salt are dissolved. Stir or shake the oil into the solution thoroughly. Pour the dressing over the vegetables and toss the salad. Makes 2 to 4 servings.

This recipe is free of all grains (including wheat and corn), gluten, milk, eggs, soy, yeast, and refined sugar.

Carrot and Olive Salad

This tasty salad uses only two food families.

> 1 1/2 c. grated carrots (about 2 small or 1 1/2
>   medium sized carrots)
> 1/2 c. sliced black olives
> 2 tbsp. olive oil
> 2 tbsp. juice from the olives

Combine the carrots and olives in a bowl. Stir together the olive oil and olive juice in another bowl, pour them over the vegetables, and toss the salad. Makes 2 to 4 servings.

This recipe is free of all grains (including wheat and corn), gluten, milk, eggs, soy, yeast, and refined sugar.

Beet Salad

This is a delicious way to serve cold leftover beets.

> 3/4 tsp. tart-tasting unbuffered Vitamin C crystals,
>   such as Vital Life brand
> 1/8 tsp. pepper
> 1/16 to 1/8 tsp. salt (optional)
> 1/2 tsp. water
> 2 tbsp. oil
> 3 to 4 c. cooked, sliced beets

In a small bowl or a glass jar, mix the Vitamin C crystals, pepper, and salt with the water until the Vitamin C and salt are dissolved. Stir or shake the oil into the solution thoroughly. Pour the dressing over the beets and toss. Makes 2 to 4 servings.

This recipe is free of all grains (including wheat and corn), gluten, milk, eggs, soy, yeast, and refined sugar.

One-Food-Family Crunch Salad

If you make this salad with the nuts, it is almost satisfying enough to be a whole meal.

> 1/4 to 3/8 tsp. tart-tasting unbuffered Vitamin C crystals,
>   such as Vital Life Brand
> Dash of salt (optional)
> Dash of pepper (optional - Omit it for one food family.)
> 1/2 tsp. water
> 1 tbsp. canola or other oil (Use canola oil for one
>   food family.)
> 2 c. shredded cabbage

1 tbsp. canola seeds
1/4 c. pine nuts or other nuts (optional - Omit them for
    one food family.)

Mix the Vitamin C crystals, salt, and pepper with the water in a small bowl or glass jar until the Vitamin C crystals and salt are dissolved. Add the oil and mix or shake it until it is thoroughly combined. Pour the dressing over the cabbage and toss the salad. Stir in the canola seeds and nuts. Serves one as a main dish or two as a side dish.

This recipe is free of all grains (including wheat and corn), gluten, milk, eggs, soy, yeast, and refined sugar.

Garbanzo Bean Salad

Here is a simple and tasty way to use leftover cooked garbanzo beans.

1/4 tsp. tart-tasting unbuffered Vitamin C crystals,
    such as Vital Life brand
Dash of pepper
Dash of salt
1/2 tsp. water
1 tbsp. oil
1 1/2 c. cooked garbanzo beans, drained

In a small bowl or a glass jar, mix the Vitamin C crystals, pepper, and salt with the water until the Vitamin C and salt are dissolved. Stir or shake the oil into the solution thoroughly. Pour the dressing over the beans and toss. Makes 1 to 2 servings.

This recipe is free of all grains (including wheat and corn), gluten, milk, eggs, soy, yeast, and refined sugar.

Spinach Salad

This salad contains everything you could want for a light meal —vegetables in the spinach and beets, some starch in the crackers, and protein in the feta cheese, garbanzo beans, or sunflower seeds.

1/8 to 1/4 tsp. tart-tasting unbuffered Vitamin C crystals,
  such as Vital Life Brand
Dash of salt (optional)
Dash of pepper (optional)
1/2 tsp. water
1 tbsp. oil
4 c. spinach leaves, washed, dried, and torn into
  bite-sized pieces 1/4 c. crumbled "Cassava Crackers,"
  page 40, or other crackers (optional)
1/4 c. crumbled goat or sheep feta cheese (about 1 1/2 oz.
  drained weight) OR 1/4 c. cooked garbanzo beans,
  drained (optional)
1 c. diced or sliced cooked beets (optional)
1/4 c. sunflower seeds (optional)

Combine the Vitamin C crystals, salt, and pepper with the
water in a small bowl or glass jar. Add the oil and mix or shake
it until it is thoroughly combined. Pour the dressing over the
spinach and toss. Stir in the rest of the ingredients. Serves one
as a main dish or two as a side dish.

*This recipe is free of wheat, cow's milk, eggs, corn, soy, yeast,
and refined sugar. If the crackers used are cassava crackers or
other non-grain crackers, it is free of gluten and all grains. If the
garbanzo beans are not used, it is suitable for use on a low-yeast
diet. (See "Note on Feta Cheese," page 72.)*

Belgian Endive Salad

*Belgian endive is not as bitter as some types of endive. With the
addition of cheese or nuts and crumbled crackers, this salad is
satisfying enough to be a light meal all by itself.*

3/8 tsp. tart-tasting unbuffered Vitamin C crystals,
  such as Vital Life Brand
Dash of salt (optional)
Dash of pepper (optional)
1/2 tsp. water
2 tbsp. oil
6 to 8 oz. belgian endive, cut into bite-size pieces

(about 2 1/2 c. pieces)
1/3 c. crumbled "Quinoa Crackers," page 35,
   "Canola Seed Crackers," page 38,
   "Cassava Crackers," page 40, or other crackers
1/2 c. grated goat jack cheese OR 1/4 c. sunflower seeds
   or chopped nuts

Combine the Vitamin C crystals, salt, and pepper with the water in a small bowl or glass jar. Add the oil and mix or shake it until it is thoroughly combined. Pour the dressing over the endive and toss. Stir in the crackers and cheese or nuts. Serves one as a main dish or two as a side dish.

This recipe is free of wheat, cow's milk, eggs, corn, soy, and refined sugar. If the crackers used are "Quinoa Crackers," the amaranth version of "Canola Seed Crackers," or "Cassava Crackers," it is free of gluten and all grains. If the cheese is omitted, it is suitable for use on a low yeast diet.

Christmas Salad

This salad is as delightful to look at as it is to eat. It makes any meal special even when it is not Christmas.

2 lbs. jicama
Red dressing:
   1/4 c. fresh or frozen unsweetened raspberries
   1/3 c. oil
   1/4 to 1/2 tsp. tart-tasting unbuffered Vitamin C
      crystals, uch as Vital Life brand (Use the smaller
      amount if the raspberries are tart.)
   1/3 c. water OR apple or pineapple juice concentrate,
      thawed (Use the fruit juice if the raspberries
      are tart.)
   Dash of salt (optional)
Green dressing:
   1/2 c. diced green pepper
   1/3 c. oil
   3/4 tsp. tart-tasting unbuffered Vitamin C crystals,
      such as Vital Life brand

1/4 c. water
Dash of salt (optional)
Dash of pepper (optional)

Peel the jicama and shred it with a grater or a food processor. Make each dressing separately by the following method: Puree the raspberries or green pepper with the oil in a blender or food processor until there are no longer any visible chunks. Add the Vitamin C crystals, water or juice, and seasoning(s) and blend again briefly. Divide the shredded jicama between 8 serving plates. Drizzle each plate with a little of both dressings - one dressing on each half of the plate, one in the center and the other around the edge, or whatever pattern you choose. Makes 8 servings.

This recipe is free of all grains (including wheat and corn), gluten, milk, eggs, soy, yeast, and refined sugar.

Avocado and Almond Salad

This salad is slightly sweet and very satisfying.

1 1/2 tsp. tart-tasting unbuffered Vitamin C crystals, such as Vital Life Brand, or to taste
1/8 tsp. salt (optional)
Dash of pepper (optional)
2 tbsp. apple, orange, or pineapple juice concentrate, thawed
4 tbsp. oil
8 c. spinach or other salad greens, washed, dried, and torn into bite-size pieces
1/4 c. sliced almonds
1 large ripe avocado, peeled and cut into cubes

Mix the Vitamin C crystals, salt, and pepper with the juice in a small bowl or glass jar until the Vitamin C crystals and salt are dissolved. Add the oil and mix or shake it until it is thoroughly combined. Place the salad greens, almonds, and avocado cubes in a large bowl. Pour the dressing over them and toss the salad. Makes 4 servings.

This recipe is free of all grains (including wheat and corn), gluten, milk, eggs, soy, yeast, and refined sugar.

Pasta Salad

This is great as a side dish or as a summertime lunch or dinner, as well as being a good way to use up leftover vegetables and pasta.

> 2 to 3 oz. dry pasta OR 1 to 1 1/2 c. cooked pasta
>   (If you are using spaghetti, break or cut it into 1" to 2"
>   pieces.)
> 2 tbsp. oil
> 1 1/4 c. assorted cooked dried beans, thawed frozen
>   vegetables or lightly cooked fresh vegetables,
>   cut into small pieces (such as carrots, peas,
>   green beans, broccoli, etc.)
> 3/4 to 1 tsp. tart-tasting unbuffered Vitamin C crystals,
>   such as Vital Life brand, to taste or as tolerated
>   (See the comment on tolerance in this recipe.)
> 1/8 tsp. salt (optional)
> 1/8 tsp. pepper (optional)
> 2 tsp. water

Cook and drain the pasta. (See "To Cook Pasta," pages 95-96.) Immediately toss it with the oil. Refrigerate the cooked pasta and vegetables until they are thoroughly chilled. Add the vegetables to the pasta and mix them gently. Combine the Vitamin C crystals, salt, and pepper with the water in a small bowl or glass jar. Pour this mixture over the pasta and vegetables and toss the salad thoroughly. Serve it immediately, as this salad tends to lose its tartness upon standing. If is loses its tang, you may mix 1/2 tsp. Vitamin C crystals with 2 tsp. water and thoroughly stir it into the salad. However, some individuals do not have bowel tolerance for this great of an amount of Vitamin C taken at one time. Makes 2 to 3 servings.

This recipe is free of wheat, milk, eggs, corn, soy, yeast, and refined sugar. If the pasta used is a non-grain pasta, it is free of gluten and all grains.

Three Bean Salad

This is an incredibly easy salad to make from leftover cooked dried beans. Or, if you can tolerate canned beans, the salt-free ones often do not contain sugar or additives and make the preparation of this salad even easier.

> 1 1/4 c. cut green beans, cooked, drained, and chilled
> 1 1/4 c. cooked kidney beans, drained and chilled
> 1 1/4 c. cooked garbanzo beans, drained and chilled
> 2 tbsp. finely chopped onion (optional)
> 1/2 c. finely chopped green pepper (optional)
> 2 tbsp. apple juice concentrate, thawed, OR 2 tbsp. water
>   plus 1/4 tsp. stevia working solution, page 226
> 1/4 tsp. salt
> 1/8 to 1/4 tsp. pepper (optional)
> 2 tsp. tart-tasting unbuffered Vitamin C crystals, such as
>   Vital Life brand, or more to taste as tolerated (See the
>   comment on tolerance in this recipe.)
> 1/4 c. oil

Combine the beans, onion, and green pepper in a large bowl. In a separate small bowl, stir together the juice or water plus stevia, salt, and pepper until the stevia and salt are dissolved. Stir in the Vitamin C crystals last. (They will not dissolve completely.) Pour this mixture and the oil over the beans, toss them thoroughly, and serve the salad immediately. This salad loses its tartness rapidly if made very far ahead of serving time. To restore its tang, you may mix an additional 1/2 tsp. Vitamin C with 2 tsp. of water and thoroughly stir it into the salad. However, some individuals do not have bowel tolerance for this great of an amount of Vitamin C taken at one time, or even the amount originally in the recipe if a large serving is eaten. Makes 4 to 6 servings.

This recipe is free of all grains (including wheat and corn), gluten, milk, eggs, soy, yeast, and refined sugar.

Pita or Tortilla Salad

This vegetarian salad or sandwich is packed with nutrition.

> 2 c. coarsely chopped spinach, lightly packed into the
>   measuring cup
> 1 medium-sized cucumber, peeled and cut into 1/2" cubes
>   (about 1 1/2 c. cubes)
> 1 large carrot, grated (about 1 c. grated)
> 1 large ripe avocado, cut into 1/2" cubes
> 1 c. goat jack cheese, cubed (about 4 oz.) OR 2/3 c
>   crumbled goat or sheep feta cheese (about 3 oz.)
>   (optional)
> 1/4 c. sunflower seeds OR 1/2 c. coarsely chopped almonds
>   or other nuts (optional)
> 1 1/2 tsp. tart-tasting unbuffered Vitamin C crystals,
>   such as Vital Life Brand
> Dash of salt (optional)
> Dash of pepper (optional)
> 2 tsp. water
> 2 tbsp. oil
> 4 to 6 pitas, page 61, OR 4 large or 6 small tortillas,
>   page 112 (optional)

Combine the spinach, cucumber, carrot, avocado cubes, cheese, and seeds or nuts in a large bowl. In a separate small bowl or glass jar, mix the Vitamin C crystals, salt, and pepper with the water. Add the oil and mix or shake it until it is thoroughly combined. Pour the dressing over the vegetable mixture and toss it until all the ingredients are coated with the dressing. Serve the salad as is, stuff it into halved pita bread, or serve it on top of tortillas. Makes 4 to 6 servings.

This recipe is free of wheat, cow's milk, eggs, corn, soy, and refined sugar. If it is served without bread or with amaranth, quinoa, or garbanzo tortillas it is free of gluten and all grains. If the cheese is omitted or feta cheese is used and it is served without bread or with the tortillas, it is suitable for use on a low-yeast diet. (See "Note on Feta Cheese," page 72.)

Rabbit Salad

Serve this salad alone, over salad greens, or in a sandwich made with tortillas (page 112) or bread or buns (pages 46-49, 52 and 56-62).

2 c. cubed cooked rabbit, page 89
1/2 c. diced celery
1/3 c. "Pine Nut Dressing," page 131
1/8 to 1/4 tsp. salt, or to taste (optional)
Dash of pepper (optional)

Combine the rabbit and celery in a bowl. Stir the seasonings into the dressing and mix it into the rabbit thoroughly. Makes 2 to 4 servings.

This recipe is free of all grains (including wheat and corn), gluten, milk, eggs, soy, yeast, and refined sugar.

9

Cookies

Nutritious fruit-sweetened cookies are a mother's best friend. They round out a brown-bagged lunch, are a good between-meal snack that will not ruin you child's appetite for the next meal and, best of all, your child will enjoy them. Cookies are easy to make, easy to store, and come in serving-size portions. They can make a restricted allergy diet seem more tolerable. They are truly a treat for kids of all ages.

This chapter contains many fruit-sweetened cookie recipes. It also contains some recipes minimally sweetened with refined sugars as a concession to the problem of "what the other kids are eating." If your children do not have yeast problems, it may not be practical to restrict them completely in regard to sugar. If you do, they may swap their sandwiches for another child's Oreos.™

If you must avoid even fruit sweeteners, you will enjoy stevia-sweetened "Quinoa Brownies," page 144, stevia-sweetened "Carrot Cookies," page 146, stevia-sweetened "Quinoa Carob Chip Cookies," page 148, stevia-sweetened "Sugar Cookies," page 156, and stevia-sweetened "Carob Wafers," page 161. For tips on measuring small amounts of stevia powder, see page 227. Being on a strict low yeast diet does not mean that you cannot enjoy cookies.

Quinoa Brownies

These brownies are delicious and nutritious when made with apple juice or, if you must avoid fruit sweeteners, you can enjoy them made with stevia.

        1 c. quinoa flour
        1/4 c. tapioca flour
        1/3 c. carob powder, sifted to remove any lumps
        1 tsp. baking soda
        1/4 tsp. unbuffered Vitamin C crystals
        1/4 c. oil
        3/4 c. apple juice concentrate, thawed, OR 3/4 c. water
            plus 1/8 tsp. white stevia powder
        1/4 c. chopped nuts (optional)

In a large mixing bowl combine the quinoa flour, tapioca flour, carob powder, baking soda, Vitamin C crystals, stevia (if you are using it rather than the apple juice), and optional nuts. Mix the oil with the water or apple juice and stir them into the dry ingredients until they are just mixed. Put the batter into an oiled and floured 9" by 5" pan and bake it at 350° for 18 to 20 minutes. Cut it into squares. Makes 10 brownies.

This recipe is free of all grains (including wheat and corn), gluten, milk, eggs, soy, yeast, and refined sugar.

Rye Brownies

You would never know these are sweetened with grape juice— the carob hides the color.

        2 1/2 c. rye flour
        3/8 c. (1/4 c. plus 2 tbsp.) carob powder, sifted to
            remove any lumps
        1 1/2 tsp. baking soda
        1 c. grape juice concentrate, thawed
        1/2 c. oil
        3/4 c. chopped nuts (optional)

Stir together the flour, carob powder, baking soda, and optional nuts in a large bowl. Mix the juice and oil together and stir them into the dry ingredients until they are just mixed in. Spread the batter in an oiled and floured 13" by 9" pan. Bake at 350° for 18 to 20 minutes. (Do not overbake these brownies -they should still be moist inside.) Cool and frost them, if desired, with "Very Carob Frosting," page 181, or "Party Carob Frosting," page 182. Cut them into 1 3/4" squares. Makes about 3 dozen brownies.

This recipe is free of wheat, milk, eggs, corn, soy, yeast, and refined sugar.

Pineapple-Coconut Cookies

These fruit-sweetened cookies are a tropical delight.

> 1 c. unsweetened canned pineapple with its juice
>   or fresh pineapple with juice to cover
> 3/4 c. pineapple juice, concentrate, thawed
> 1/2 c. oil
> 2 c. rye flour
> 1/2 tsp. baking soda
> 1 c. shredded unsweetened coconut

Puree the pineapple with its juice in a blender or food processor. Add the pineapple juice concentrate and oil and blend again briefly. In a mixing bowl, combine the flour, baking soda, and coconut. Stir the pineapple mixture into the dry ingredients until they are just mixed. Drop heaping teaspoonfuls of the dough onto an oiled cookie sheet. Bake at 350° for 15 to 20 minutes, or until the cookies begin to brown. Makes about 3 1/2 dozen cookies.

This recipe is free of wheat, milk, eggs, corn, soy, yeast, and refined sugar.

Oatmeal Raisin Cookies

These taste just like Mom used to make but contain no sugar.
They are also an excellent source of fiber.

> 2 c. white raisins
> 2 c. white grape juice
> 1/2 c. oil
> 2 c. oat flour
> 2 c. oatmeal
> 1 tsp. baking soda
> 1 1/2 tsp. cinnamon
> 1 c. brown raisins
> 1/2 c. chopped nuts (optional)

Soak the white raisins in the grape juice overnight, then puree them together in a blender or food processor. Add the oil and blend again briefly. Combine the oat flour, oatmeal, baking soda, cinnamon, brown raisins, and nuts in a mixing bowl. Stir in the raisin puree until it is just mixed into the flour mixture. Drop the batter by heaping teaspoonfuls onto an ungreased baking sheet and bake at 375° for 15 to 18 minutes, or until the cookies are lightly browned. Makes about 6 dozen cookies.

This recipe is free of wheat, milk, eggs, corn, soy, yeast, and refined sugar.

Carrot Cookies

These cookies are packed with nutrition, and can be sweetened with either fruit juice or stevia. If you are just getting used to stevia, use the smaller amount.

> 3 c. quinoa or spelt flour
> 1 c. tapioca flour or arrowroot
> 1 1/2 tsp. baking soda
> 3/8 tsp. unbuffered Vitamin C crystals if you are using
>   the apple juice OR 1/2 tsp. unbuffered Vitamin C
>   crystals if you are using the stevia and water
> 1 1/2 tsp. cinnamon

2 1/4 c. grated carrots

1 c. raisins or chopped dates (optional)

1 3/8 c. (1 1/4 c. plus 2 tbsp.) apple juice concentrate,
    thawed OR 3/4 to 1 tsp. white stevia powder
    plus 1 3/8 c. (1 1/4 c. plus 2 tbsp.) water

1/2 c. oil

Mix together the flours, baking soda, Vitamin C crystals, cinnamon, and stevia, if you are using it, in a large bowl. Stir in the carrots and raisins or dates. Combine the juice or water and oil and stir them into the flour mixture until they are just mixed in. Drop the batter by heaping teaspoonfuls onto an ungreased cookie sheet and bake at 350° for 12 to 15 minutes. The stevia-sweetened cookies will not brown very much, but will feel dry when they are touched. Makes 4 to 5 dozen cookies.

This recipe is free of wheat, corn, milk, eggs, soy, yeast, and refined sugar. If it is made with the quinoa flour, it is free of gluten and all grains. If you sweeten these cookies with stevia and omit the raisins or dates they are suitable for use on a low-yeast diet.

Millet or Teff Apple Cookies

These fruit-sweetened cookies are fragile but delicious, especially when made with the carob chips.

2 c. millet or teff flour

1/2 tsp. baking soda

1/2 c. unsweetened applesauce

3/4 c. apple juice concentrate, thawed

1/2 c. oil

3/4 c. chopped nuts OR milk-free unsweetened carob
    chips (optional)

Combine the flour and baking soda in a large bowl. Mix together the applesauce, juice, and oil in a small bowl, and then stir them into the flour until they are just mixed in. Quickly fold in the nuts or carob chips. Drop the batter by heaping teaspoonfuls onto an ungreased baking sheet. Bake at 350° for 15 to 20 minutes, or until the cookies begin to brown. Makes about 3 1/2 dozen 1 1/2" cookies.

This recipe is free of wheat, gluten, milk, eggs, corn, soy, yeast, and refined sugar.

Quinoa Carob Chip Cookies

The quinoa flour makes these cookies very satisfying. If you make them with the stevia they are also excellent for low yeast diets.

> 3 c quinoa flour
> 1 c. tapioca flour
> 1 1/2 tsp. baking soda
> 3/8 tsp. unbuffered Vitamin C crystals if you are using
>   the apple juice OR 1/2 tsp. unbuffered Vitamin C
>   crystals if you are using the stevia and water
> 2 c. apple juice concentrate OR 1 3/8 c. water plus 3/4
>   to 1 tsp. white stevia powder
> 1/2 c. oil
> 1 1/4 c. milk-free unsweetened carob chips

If you are using the apple juice, boil it down to 1 3/8 c. (1 1/4 c. plus 2 tbsp.) and allow it to cool. In a large bowl, combine the quinoa flour, tapioca flour, baking soda, Vitamin C crystals, and stevia, if you are using it. In a separate bowl, stir together the juice or water and the oil, then stir them into the dry ingredients until they are just mixed in. Fold in the carob chips. Drop the dough by tablespoonfuls onto an ungreased baking sheet and flatten them to about 1/4" thickness with your fingers held together. Bake at 350° for 10 to 15 minutes, or until the cookies are lightly browned. The stevia-sweetened cookies will not brown, but will feel dry to the touch. Makes about 5 dozen cookies.

This recipe is free of all grains (including wheat and corn), gluten, milk, eggs, soy, yeast, and refined sugar. It is suitable for use on a low-yeast diet if it is sweetened with the stevia.

Spelt Carob Chip Cookies

You can vary the sweetness of these fruit-sweetened cookies to suit your preference.

    2 1/3 c. spelt flour
    1/2 tsp. baking soda
    3/4 c. apple juice concentrate, thawed, OR 1 1/4 c.
        apple juice concentrate, depending on the degree
        of sweetness desired
    1/2 c. oil
    3/4 c. milk-free unsweetened carob chips (optional)

If you like your cookies fairly sweet, boil 1 1/4 c. apple juice concentrate down to 3/4 c. in volume and allow it to cool. For minimally sweetened cookies, use 3/4 c. apple juice concentrate. Stir together the spelt flour and baking soda in a large bowl. Mix the oil and apple juice concentrate and stir them into the flour mixture until they are just mixed in. Fold in the carob chips. Drop the dough by heaping teaspoonfuls onto a lightly oiled baking sheet and bake them at 350° for 10 to 14 minutes, or until they begin to brown. Makes 3 dozen cookies.

This recipe is free of wheat, milk, eggs, corn, soy, yeast, and refined sugar.

Shortbread

This cookie is very easy to make. Take your choice of several different varieties.

Amaranth:

    1 1/4 c. amaranth flour
    1 c. arrowroot
    1/2 tsp. baking soda
    3/8 c. (1/4 c. plus 2 tbsp.) oil
    1/2 c. pineapple juice concentrate, thawed

Pineapple-Oat:

    2 1/2 c. oat flour
    1/2 tsp. baking soda
    3/8 c. (1/4 c. plus 2 tbsp.) oil
    1/2 c. pineapple juice concentrate, thawed

Date-Oat:

    2 1/4 c. oat flour
    1/2 c. date sugar, pressed through a strainer to remove
        any lumps
    1/2 tsp. baking soda
    1/8 tsp. unbuffered Vitamin C crystals
    3/8 c. (1/4 c. plus 2 tbsp.) oil
    1/2 c. water

Barley:

    2 c. barley flour
    1/2 tsp. baking soda
    3/8 c. (1/4 c. plus 2 tbsp.) oil
    1/2 c. apple juice concentrate, thawed

Spelt:

    1 1/2 c. spelt flour
    1 c. arrowroot or tapioca flour
    1/2 tsp. baking soda
    1/8 tsp. unbuffered Vitamin C crystals (omit them if you
        are using the apple juice)
    3/8 c. (1/4 c. plus 2 tbsp.) oil
    1/2 c. water plus 1/4 c. cane or beet sugar OR 1/2 c.
        apple juice concentrate, thawed

Choose one set of ingredients above. Combine the flour(s), baking soda, Vitamin C crystals (if the recipe calls for them), and date, cane, or beet sugar (if you are using it) in a large bowl. Stir together the oil and juice or water and add them to the dry ingredients, mixing with a spoon and your hands until the dough sticks together. If necessary, add another 1 to 2 tablespoons of water or juice to help it stick together. Roll the dough out to 1/4" thickness on an ungreased baking sheet and cut it into 1" by 2" to 3" bars. Bake at 350° until the cookies begin to brown; 15 to 20 minutes for the amaranth, oat, and spelt varieties, and 20 to 25 minutes for the barley. Makes 2 1/2 to 3 dozen bars.

This recipe is free of wheat, milk, eggs, corn, soy, and yeast. If any variety except the spelt with cane or beet sugar is made, it is also free of refined sugar. If the amaranth variety is made, it is free of gluten and all grains.

Carob Sandwich Cookies

These are a lot like what the rest of the kids are eating but do not contain any sugar.

1 2/3 c. rye flour
1/3 c. carob powder
1/2 tsp. baking soda
1/8 tsp. unbuffered Vitamin C crystals
2/3 c. grape juice concentrate, thawed
1/3 c. oil
3/4 c. milk-free unsweetened carob chips (optional)

Combine the flour, carob powder, baking soda, and Vitamin C crystals in a large bowl. Mix together the juice and oil and stir them into the dry ingredients until they are just mixed in. Drop the dough by heaping teaspoonfuls onto an ungreased baking sheet and flatten them into 2" rounds that are about 1/8" to 1/4" thick with your hand. Bake at 350° for 7 to 9 minutes, or until the cookies are set and begin to feel dry. Using a spatula, immediately remove the cookies from the baking sheet and allow them to cool completely. Melt the carob chips in a double boiler over water that is just below the boiling point, stirring them frequently. Put the bottoms of the cookies together in pairs with the melted carob chips to make sandwiches. Makes about 1 1/2 dozen sandwiches. If the carob chips are not used, this recipe makes about 3 dozen single cookies.

This recipe is free of wheat, milk, eggs, corn, soy, yeast, and refined sugar.

Fig Newtons

This old favorite is quite rich, even when you make it without the butter.

Filling:

> 8 oz. dried figs
> 1 c. water
> 2 tsp. corn-free natural vanilla flavoring (optional)

Amaranth Dough:

> 3 c. amaranth flour
> 1 c. arrowroot
> 3/4 c. oil
> 3/8 c. (1/4 c. plus 2 tbsp.) to 1/2 c. cold water

Rye Dough:

> 3 c. rye flour
> 1 c. soft butter
> 1/2 c. cold water

Choose one set of dough ingredients, above. Mix together the flour(s) and butter or oil with a pastry cutter until the mixture is crumbly. Gradually add enough of the water to make a soft dough. Divide the dough in half and flatten each half unto a small square. Refrigerate the rye dough. (You do not need to refrigerate the amaranth dough; you can even make it while the figs for the filling are cooling, below.)

To make the filling, remove the stems from the figs. Combine the figs and water in a saucepan, bring them to a boil, reduce the heat, and simmer them on low heat for 30 minutes. Cool the figs, stir in the optional vanilla, and puree them in a blender or food processor until they are smooth.

Roll one half of the dough out into an 8" by 12" rectangle on an ungreased cookie sheet and spread it with the filling. Roll the other half of the dough out into an 8" by 12" rectangle on a well-floured pastry cloth. (If you are not sensitive to waxed paper chemically or to the traces of corn it may contain, you can roll the second piece of dough out between two pieces of waxed paper and peel off the top piece.) Invert the pastry cloth or waxed paper with the dough on it onto the top of the fig filling and dough on the baking sheet. Bake at 400° for 25 to 30 minutes for the amaranth dough or 30 to 35 minutes for the rye dough, or until it begins to brown. Cool it for 10 minutes, then carefully cut it into 1 1/2" squares with a sharp knife. Makes about 3 dozen cookies.

This recipe is free of wheat, eggs, corn, soy, yeast, and refined sugar. The amaranth version is also free of milk, gluten, and all grains.

Pizzelles

These traditional Italian Christmas cookies can be made with or without the anise flavoring.

Make any variety of "Ice Cream Cones," page 193, as directed in the recipe. If you wish, add 1 1/2 tsp. anise flavoring to the batter before adding the flour. Bake the cookies in a pizzelle iron until they are lightly browned and lay them flat to cool. Makes about 12 to 15 8" pizzelles that each break into four smaller cookies, or 2 to 3 dozen 6" cookies.

This recipe is free of wheat, milk, eggs, corn, soy, and yeast. If the amaranth or quinoa varieties are made, it is free of gluten and all grains. If any variety except the amaranth one is made, it is free of refined sugar.

Cookie Press Cookies

No one needs to feel deprived at Christmas time if you have some of these made in the shape of Christmas trees around.

Oat:

2 c. oat flour
1 c. date sugar
1 tsp. baking soda
1/4 tsp. unbuffered Vitamin C crystals
1/2 c. coconut oil
5/8 c. (1/2 c. plus 2 tbsp.) water
1 tsp. corn-free natural vanilla or other flavoring
   (optional)

Spelt:

2 1/2 c. spelt flour
1 c. date sugar OR 1/2 c. beet or cane sugar
1 tsp. baking soda
1/4 tsp. unbuffered Vitamin C crystals
1/2 c. coconut oil
3/4 c. water with the date sugar OR 1/2 c. water with the
   beet or cane sugar
1 tsp. corn-free natural vanilla or other flavoring
   (optional)

Barley:

2 1/2 c. barley flour
1/2 c. beet or cane sugar
1 tsp. baking soda
1/2 tsp. unbuffered Vitamin C crystals
1/2 c. coconut oil
5/8 c. (1/2 c. plus 2 tbsp.) water
1 tsp. corn-free natural vanilla or other flavoring
   (optional)

Amaranth:

2 c. amaranth flour
1/2 c. arrowroot
1/2 c. beet or cane sugar

1 tsp. baking soda

1/4 tsp. unbuffered Vitamin C crystals

1/2 c. coconut oil

1/2 c. water

1 tsp. corn-free natural vanilla or other flavoring
(optional)

Quinoa:

2 c. quinoa flour

1/2 c. beet or cane sugar (beet is in the same food family
as quinoa)

1 tsp. baking soda

1/4 tsp. unbuffered Vitamin C crystals

1/2 c. coconut oil

1/2 c. water

1 tsp. corn-free natural vanilla or other flavoring
(optional)

Choose one set of ingredients above. Melt the coconut oil and allow it to cool until it is just very slightly warm. If you are using date sugar, press it through a wire mesh strainer with the back of a spoon to remove any small lumps, or they will clog the cookie press. Combine the flour(s), sugar, baking soda, and Vitamin C crystals in a large bowl. Mix together the oil, water, and flavoring and stir them into the dry ingredients. Put the dough into a cookie press and press out the cookies onto an ungreased baking sheet. Bake at 375° until the bottoms of the cookies begin to brown. If you make them as trees, hearts, etc. this takes about 10 to 12 minutes for the oat and amaranth cookies and about 11 to 15 minutes for the spelt, barley, and quinoa cookies. If you make them as spritz strips, which are thinner, reduce the baking time by 2 to 4 minutes for each type of cookie. Remove the cookies from the baking sheet immediately. Makes 4 to 5 dozen cookies.

This recipe is free of wheat, milk, eggs, corn, soy, and yeast. If made with date sugar, it is also free of refined sugar. The amaranth and quinoa versions are free of gluten and, if they are made with beet sugar, are free of all grains.

Gingerbread Men

These are crisp, crunchy, and flavorful.

3 c. spelt flour
3/4 tsp. baking soda
1/4 tsp. unbuffered Vitamin C crystals
1/2 tsp. ginger
1/4 tsp. nutmeg
3/4 c. molasses
1/2 c. oil
Raisins or dried fruit (optional)

Combine the spelt flour, baking soda, Vitamin C crystals, and spices in a large bowl. Stir together the molasses and oil and mix them into the dry ingredients using a spoon and then your hands to make a stiff dough. Roll the dough out to between 1/8" and 1/4" thickness on a floured board. Cut it into gingerbread men and transfer them to an ungreased baking sheet with a spatula. Decorate them with raisins or small pieces of dried fruit, if desired. Bake them at 350° for 11 to 15 minutes. Makes about 1 1/2 dozen 6" tall gingerbread men.

This recipe is free of wheat, milk, eggs, corn, and soy. If the dried fruit is not used, it is also free of yeast.

Sugar Cookies

You can make these light and flaky cookies with a minimal amount of sugar or with stevia. Use the smaller amount of the stevia if you are just getting used to it.

3 c. barley flour OR 3 1/8 c. (3 c. plus 2 tbsp.) spelt flour
1/2 c. sugar OR 3/8 to 1/2 tsp. white stevia powder
1/2 tsp. baking soda
1/8 tsp. unbuffered Vitamin C crystals
1/2 c. oil
1/2 c. water

Combine the flour, sugar or stevia, baking soda, and Vitamin C crystals in a large bowl. Stir together the water and oil thoroughly and add them to the flour mixture quickly before they have a chance to separate. Mix the dough together with a spoon and then your hands until all of the flour is worked in. If the dough is too stiff, you may add an additional tablespoon or two of water. Roll the dough out on a well floured board to just under 1/4" thickness. Cut it into shapes and sprinkle the cookies with additional sugar if desired. Bake them at 350° for 15 to 20 minutes for the barley version or 10 to 15 minutes for the spelt version, or until the cookies begin to brown. The stevia-sweetened cookies will not brown very much, but will feel dry to your touch. Makes 2 1/2 to 3 dozen 3" cookies.

This recipe is free of wheat, milk, eggs, corn, soy, and yeast. If it is made with the stevia, it is also free of refined sugar.

Sandwich Cookies

If these cookies are made in shapes other than round, they are actually "better" than what the other kids have in their lunch boxes.

1 batch of "Sugar Cookies," above
1 to 1 1/2 c. of milk-free unsweetened carob chips

Melt the carob chips in a double boiler over water that is just under the boiling point, stirring them frequently. When they are just melted, remove the top of the double boiler from the pan. Spread the melted carob on the bottoms of half of the cookies. Immediately after each cookie is spread, top it with another cookie, putting their bottoms together. Cool them completely. Makes 1 1/2 dozen sandwich cookies.

This recipe is free of wheat, milk, eggs, corn, soy, and yeast. If it is made with the stevia, it is also free of refined sugar.

Gingersnaps

These are delicious and easy to make.

> 1 1/2 c. barley flour
> 1/2 tsp. baking soda
> 1/8 tsp. unbuffered Vitamin C crystals
> 1/4 tsp. ginger
> 1/2 c. light molasses
> 1/4 c. oil

Combine the flour, baking soda, Vitamin C crystals, and ginger in a large bowl. Mix together the molasses and oil and stir them into the dry ingredients until they are just blended in. Drop the dough by tablespoonfuls onto an ungreased baking sheet and flatten the cookies to about 1/4" thickness with your fingers held together. Bake them at 350° for 10 to 15 minutes, or until they begin to brown. Makes 1 1/2 to 2 dozen cookies.

This recipe is free of wheat, milk, eggs, corn, soy, and yeast.

Sugar and Spice Cookies

These grain-free cookies contain foods from just two food families if you make them with beet sugar and avocado oil. If you use beet sugar and a different oil, they contain foods from just three food families.

> 2 c. quinoa flour
> 1/2 c. beet or cane sugar (beet is in the same food
>   family as quinoa)
> 1 tsp. baking soda
> 1/4 tsp. unbuffered Vitamin C crystals
> 1 1/2 tsp. cinnamon
> 1/4 c. oil
> 3/8 c. plus 1 tbsp. (or 1/4 c. plus 3 tbsp.) water

Combine the flour, sugar, baking soda, Vitamin C crystals and cinnamon in a large bowl. Mix together the oil and water and stir them into the dry ingredients until they are just mixed in. Form the dough into 1" balls and flatten them with your hand to about 1/4" thickness on a lightly oiled baking sheet. Bake them at 375° for 10 to 15 minutes, or until they begin to brown. Makes 2 to 2 1/2 dozen cookies.

This recipe is free of wheat, gluten, corn, milk, eggs, soy, and yeast. If it is made with the beet sugar, it is free of all grains.

Maple Cookies

These cookies are sturdy enough to take some rough handling of the lunch box.

> 5 c. rye flour
> 1 1/4 tsp. baking soda
> 1 tsp. cream of tartar OR 1/2 tsp. unbuffered Vitamin C
>   crystals
> 1 1/2 c. maple syrup
> 1 c. oil
> 1 1/2 c. raisins or milk-free unsweetened carob chips
>   (optional)

Combine the flour, baking soda, and cream of tartar or Vitamin C crystals in a large bowl. Mix together the maple syrup and oil and stir them into the dry ingredients. Stir in the raisins or carob chips if you are using them. Drop the dough by tablespoonfuls onto a lightly oiled baking sheet and flatten the cookies to 1/4" to 3/8" thickness with your fingers held together. Bake them at 375° for 10 to 15 minutes, or until they begin to brown. Makes about 4 dozen cookies.

For easy-to-make diamond-shaped cookies, make the cookie dough as above, but omit the raisins or carob chips. Divide the dough into two parts and roll or pat each half out to 1/4" thickness on a lightly oiled baking sheet. Cut it into 1 1/2" to 2" diamonds with a sharp knife. Bake them at 350° for 15 to 20 minutes, or until the cookies begin to brown. Cut them again through the previous cuts. Remove them from the baking sheet. Makes about 5 dozen cookies.

This recipe is free of wheat, milk, eggs, corn, and soy.

Gingerbread Cutout Cookies

These cookies are strictly grain-free if you make them with the beet sugar and apple juice.

> 2 c. quinoa flour
> 1/3 c. cane or beet sugar
> 1 tsp. baking soda
> 1/4 tsp. unbuffered Vitamin C crystals
> 1/2 tsp. ginger
> 1/2 tsp. nutmeg
> 1/4 c. oil
> 1/4 c. light molasses plus 1/4 c. water OR 1/2 c.
>   apple juice concentrate, thawed
> Raisins or dried fruit (optional)

Mix together the flour, sugar, baking soda, Vitamin C crystals, and spices in a large bowl. Combine the oil with the molasses and water or juice, add them to the dry ingredients, and stir until they are just mixed in. Roll the dough out to between 1/8" and 1/4" thickness on a well-floured pastry cloth. Or, if you are not sensitive to waxed paper chemically or to the traces of corn it may contain, you can roll the dough out between two pieces of waxed paper and peel off the top piece. Cut the dough with cookie cutters. Carefully transfer the cookies to an ungreased baking sheet with a spatula. Decorate the cookies with raisins or cut-up dried fruit if desired. Bake them at 350° for 10 to 12 minutes, or until they begin to brown. Remove them from the cookie sheet immediately with a spatula. Makes about 1 1/2 dozen 6" gingerbread men or about 3 dozen 3" cookies.

This recipe is free of wheat, gluten, milk, eggs, corn, and soy. If it is made with the beet sugar and apple juice, it is free of all grains. If the dried fruit is not used, it is free of yeast.

Cashew Butter Cookies

This is a variation on traditional peanut butter cookies, but without the peanut butter, which many people are allergic to.

2 c. rye flour
1/2 tsp. baking soda
1/8 tsp. unbuffered Vitamin C crystals
2/3 c. cashew butter
1/4 c. oil
3/4 c. maple syrup

Combine the flour, baking soda, and Vitamin C crystals in a large bowl. In a small bowl, thoroughly mix together the cashew butter, oil and maple syrup. Stir this mixture into the dry ingredients. Drop the dough by heaping teaspoonfuls onto an ungreased baking sheet. Use an oiled fork to flatten the balls of dough, making an "X" on the top of them with the fork tines. Bake the cookies at 400° for 8 to 10 minutes, or until they are golden brown. Makes 3 dozen cookies.

This recipe is free of wheat, milk, eggs, corn, soy, yeast, and peanuts.

No-Grain Carob Sandwich Cookies or Carob Wafers

You can put these sandwich cookies together with sugar-free jam or carob chips or eat them plain, as "Carob Wafers," for everyday use. For a special occasion, fill them with "White Stuff," page 162, and they will remind your kids of Oreos.™

1 1/2 c. carob powder
1 1/2 c. tapioca flour
1 tsp. baking soda
1/4 tsp. unbuffered Vitamin C crystals
1 c. apple juice concentrate, thawed OR 3/4 tsp.
   white stevia powder plus 1 c. water
1/2 c. oil

About 2/3 c. all-fruit (sugarless) jam or jelly OR 2/3 c.
of "White Stuff," page 162, OR 1 c. milk-free
unsweetened carob chips (optional)

Combine the carob powder, tapioca flour, baking soda, vitamin
C crystals and stevia (if you are using it) in a large bowl. Mix
together the juice or water and oil and stir them into the dry
ingredients until they are thoroughly mixed in. Roll the dough
into 1" balls and place them on an ungreased baking sheet.
Flatten each ball to 1/8" to 1/4" thickness with an oiled glass
bottom or your fingers held together. Or, for more perfectly
shaped cookies, roll the dough directly onto an ungreased baking
sheet to 1/8" to 1/4" thickness, cut circles with a 2" round cookie
cutter, and carefully remove the dough between the circles with
a fork and your fingers. Bake the cookies at 350° for 10 to 12
minutes or until they are firm. Remove them from the baking
sheet with a spatula and cool them completely. If you are using
the carob chips, melt them in the top of a double boiler over water
that is just below the boiling point, stirring them frequently. As
soon as they are melted, remove the top of the double boiler from
the pan. Put the cookies together in pairs, with their bottoms
together, using the melted carob chips, jelly or jam, or "White
Stuff," below, if desired. Makes about 2 dozen sandwich cookies
or 4 dozen plain carob wafers.

WHITE STUFF:
1 c. water
3 c. cane or beet sugar
1/16 tsp. cream of tartar

Bring the water to a boil in a large saucepan. Remove it from
the heat and stir in the sugar until it dissolves. Return it to the
heat and bring it to a boil, stirring in the cream of tartar just as
it starts boiling. Wash down any crystals from the side of the pan
with hot water and a brush. Place a candy thermometer in the
boiling liquid, but not touching the bottom of the pan. Cook the
solution without stirring it to 238° at sea level or to 26° more than
the boiling temperature of water in your area. (See "The Effect
of Altitude on Candy Making," page 228.) When it reaches the

right temperature, immediately pour it onto a wet marble slab or wet large stoneware platter. Cool it for a few minutes. Then, using a candy scraper or metal knife-type spatula, lift the edges of the mixture to the center. Continue working it this way until the mixture becomes opaque and creamy. Then knead it with your hands briefly. This white fondant stores well in a covered container at room temperature. Makes about 1 1/2 c. of "White Stuff."

This recipe is free of wheat, gluten, milk, eggs, corn, soy, and yeast. If the cane sugar is not used, it is free of all grains. If the jam, jelly, or carob chips are used to put the cookies together or if they are left as wafers, it is also free of refined sugar. If the cookies are made with the stevia and put together with carob chips or eaten as wafers, they are suitable for a low-yeast diet.

Mix and Match Cookies

These rich cookies can be varied in so many ways that children will not recognize them (or get tired of them) from one batch to the next.

> 3 1/2 c. oat flour OR 3 1/4 c. barley flour
> 1 tsp. baking soda
> 1/4 tsp. unbuffered Vitamin C crystals
> 1/2 tsp. salt (optional)
> 1 c. oil
> 1 c. honey
> 1 tsp. corn-free natural vanilla flavoring (optional)
> 1 to 1 1/2 c. of any combination of raisins, milk-free
>   unsweetened carob chips, chopped nuts, chopped dates,
>   or other chopped dried fruit (optional)

Combine the flour, baking soda, Vitamin C crystals, and salt in a large bowl. Mix together the oil, honey, and vanilla and stir them into the dry ingredients. Fold in the raisins, carob chips, nuts, or fruit, if desired. Drop the dough by heaping teaspoonfuls at least 2" apart on an ungreased baking sheet. Bake at 375° for 8 to 10 minutes. Cool the cookies for about 5 minutes on the baking sheet before removing them to a dishcloth or paper towel to cool completely. Makes 3 1/2 dozen cookies.

This recipe is free of wheat, milk, eggs, corn, and soy. If dried fruit is not used, it is also free of yeast.

Quinoa Almond Cookies

These cookies can be made crisp or soft. If you would like to save time on chopping the nuts, Ener-G Foods' "NutQuik," which is finely chopped almonds, can be used in place of the chopped nuts.

> 1 1/2 c. quinoa flour
> 3/4 tsp. baking soda
> 1/4 tsp. unbuffered Vitamin C crystals
> 1/2 c. very finely chopped almonds (1/8" pieces)
> 1/2 c. oil
> 1/2 c. honey (for crisp cookies) OR 1/2 c. honey plus
>   1/2 c.water (for soft cookies) OR 1 c. apple juice
>   concentrate, thawed (for fruit-sweetened
>   soft cookies)

Combine the flour, baking soda, Vitamin C crystals, and almonds in a large bowl. Thoroughly mix the oil with the honey, honey and water, or juice in a small bowl, and then immediately pour it into the dry ingredients. Stir the dough until it is just mixed. Drop it by teaspoonfuls onto an ungreased baking sheet and flatten the cookies with an oiled glass bottom or your fingers held together. Bake the cookies at 375°for 5 to 7 minutes for crisp cookies or for 7 to 9 minutes for soft cookies. Makes about 2 dozen crisp or 3 dozen soft cookies.

This recipe is free of all grains (including wheat and corn), gluten, milk, eggs, soy, and yeast. If it is made with the apple juice, it is also free of refined sugar.

Frazelle

This recipe is adapted from an old family recipe that was one of my favorites when my aunt, Louise Giardino, made it when I was a child.

2 3/4 c. spelt flour OR 2 c. amaranth flour plus 1 c.
    arrowroot
1/2 c. beet or cane sugar
1/4 tsp. salt (optional)
1/2 tsp. baking soda
1/4 tsp. unbuffered Vitamin C crystals
1/3 c. sliced almonds
2/3 c. water
1/3 c. oil
1 tsp. corn-free natural almond flavor
1 tsp. corn-free natural vanilla

Stir together the flour(s), sugar, salt, baking soda, Vitamin C crystals, and almonds in a large bowl. In a small bowl, mix the water, oil, and flavorings; then stir them into the dry ingredients. Transfer the dough to a generously floured board and knead it about 30 times. On a lightly oiled baking sheet, form the dough into a flat-topped loaf about 14" long, 3" wide, and 1" high. Bake it at 350° for 30 to 35 minutes, or until it is set and barely beginning to brown. Remove it from the oven and, using a serrated knife, cut it down the middle lengthwise and slice it crosswise into 3/4" to 1" slices. Lay the slices down on their cut sides on the cookie sheet. Bake the slices and additional 20 to 25 minutes, or until they are hard and lightly browned. Makes 2 1/2 dozen cookies.

This recipe is free of wheat, milk, eggs, corn, soy, and yeast. If the spelt flour is not used it is free of gluten. If it is made with the amaranth flour and beet sugar, it is free of all grains.

Maple Bars

These easy-to-make cookies are especially chewy when they are fresh.

2 2/3 c. rye flour
1/3 c. uncooked rye flakes or cream of rye cereal
1/2 tsp. baking soda
1/4 tsp. unbuffered Vitamin C crystals
1/4 tsp. salt (optional)

1 tsp. cinnamon (optional)
1 1/4 c. maple syrup
1/3 c. oil
1 c. raisins, currants, or milk-free unsweetened carob
    chips (optional)

Combine the flour, rye flakes, baking soda, Vitamin C crystals, salt, and cinnamon in a large bowl. Thoroughly mix together the maple syrup and oil and stir them into the dry ingredients until they are just mixed in. Stir in the raisins, currants, or carob chips. Spread the dough in a oiled and floured 13" by 9" baking dish. Bake at 350° for 30 to 35 minutes. Immediately cut it into 1 1/2" square. Cool the cookies completely before you remove them from the pan. Makes about 3 dozen cookies.

This recipe is free of wheat, milk, eggs, corn, soy, and yeast.

10

Cakes and Frostings

What is a birthday without a cake? For certain occasions in life, a cake is an integral part of the celebration. Cakes are especially important to children. On their birthdays, they want a cake like the other kids have. And if they attend a friend's birthday party, Mom would do well to find out what is going to be served, try to duplicate it as nearly as possible, and send it along to the party. This chapter provides recipes for cakes rich with fruits and vegetables, spice cakes, gingerbread, carob cakes, and frostings. Most of the cakes are fruit-sweetened. If you want to avoid fruit sweeteners as well as avoiding sugar, there are two recipes that are sweetened with stevia (pages 174 and 178). And there are some recipes for cakes and frostings minimally sweetened with sugar so mothers can make their allergic children birthday cakes much like what other children have. Cakes made with alternative flours are not as light or as sturdy as cakes made with refined wheat flour, but what they lack in lightness they make up for in flavor. Try one of these carrot cakes, and you will wonder why you ever liked bakery-type cakes. There are several ways to cope with the fragility of cakes made with alternative flours. The simplest is to serve the cake from the pan instead of trying to remove it in one piece. If you wish to make a layer cake, it can be removed from the pan most successfully in the following way: After oiling and flouring the baking pan, cut a piece of parchment paper (See "Sources of Special Foods and Products," ch. 16) or waxed paper (if you can tolerate it chemically and are not bothered by the traces of corn it may contain) to fit the bottom of the pan. Place the paper in the pan, add the cake batter, and bake the cake. Cool it in the pan for 10 to 15 minutes after removing it from the oven. Run a sharp knife around the sides of the pan. Then place a wire rack on top of the cake, invert it, and lift off the pan. Remove the paper and hold a serving plate or another wire rack against the bottom of the cake and invert it again.

Pineapple Upside-Down Cake

There is no need to frost this easy-to-make cake because of the fruit topping.

> 1 c. pineapple canned in its own juice or fresh
>   pineapple with enough juice to cover it
> 1 c. pineapple juice concentrate, thawed
> 1/4 c. oil
> 3 c. barley flour
> 1 1/2 tsp. baking soda
> 1/2 tsp. unbuffered Vitamin C crystals
> 6 slices of fresh pineapple or pineapple canned
>   in its own juice, drained (about 2/3 of a
>   20-oz. can)
> A few red grapes or cherries (optional)

Puree the 1 c. pineapple together with its juice in a blender or food processor. Add the pineapple juice concentrate and oil and blend them again briefly. Oil a 9" by 9" cake pan. Arrange the slices of pineapple on the bottom of it, placing a seeded grape or pitted cherry in the center of each slice, if you wish to. Combine the flour, baking soda, and Vitamin C crystals in a large bowl. Add the pureed pineapple mixture and stir just until the liquid ingredients are mixed into the dry ingredients. Pour the batter into the prepared pan and bake the cake at 375° for 30 to 40 minutes, or until it is golden brown. Cool the cake in the pan for 10 minutes; then run a knife around the edges of the pan and invert it onto a serving dish. Makes one 9" square cake, about 9 servings.

This recipe is free of wheat, milk, eggs, corn, soy, yeast, and refined sugar.

Zucchini Cake

The zucchini adds moistness to this cake.

3 c. spelt flour
2 tsp. baking soda
1/4 tsp. salt (optional)
1 tsp. cinnamon
1/4 tsp. nutmeg
1/4 tsp. ground cloves
1/2 c. grated unsweetened coconut
2 c. grated zucchini
1 c. very small pieces of fresh pineapple or
    pineapple tidbits canned in their own
    juice, drained
1 1/4 c. pineapple juice concentrate, thawed
1/2 c. oil

In a large bowl, combine the flour, baking soda, salt, spices, and coconut. In a small bowl, combine the zucchini, pineapple, pineapple juice, and oil. Stir the liquid ingredients into the dry ingredients until they are just mixed in. Pour the batter into an oiled and floured 9" by 13" cake pan. Bake at 325° for 50 to 55 minutes, or until the cake is lightly browned and a toothpick inserted in its center comes out dry. Makes one 9" by 13" cake.

This recipe is free of wheat, milk, eggs, corn, soy, yeast, and refined sugar.

Date-Nut Bundt Cake

Your nonallergic guests will ask for second helpings when this rich cake is served.

1 1/2 c. quick rolled oats (uncooked)
1 1/2 c. boiling water
3/4 c. oil
3/4 c. cool water
1 1/2 c. oat flour
1 c. date sugar
1 1/4 tsp. baking soda
1/2 tsp. unbuffered Vitamin C crystals
1 tsp. salt (optional)
2 tsp. cinnamon
1/2 tsp. ground cloves
1 c. chopped pitted dates
1/2 c. finely chopped nuts

Combine the oats and boiling water in a large bowl. Allow them to cool for 5 to 10 minutes. Stir in the oil and cool water and beat the mixture until all the lumps are gone. In another bowl, stir together the flour, date sugar, baking soda, Vitamin C crystals, salt, spices, dates and nuts. Add them to the oatmeal mixture and stir it until they are just mixed in. Pour the batter into an oiled and floured 12 c. bundt pan or 8" by 8" cake pan. Bake it at 375° for 55 to 60 minutes. Cool the bundt cake in the pan for 30 minutes, then invert it onto a serving dish. The square cake may be served from the pan. If you want to frost this cake, drizzle the tube cake with "Date Glaze," page 180, or frost the square cake with 2/3 of a batch of "Date Frosting," page 180. Makes one bundt or 8" by 8" cake, 9 to 12 servings.

This recipe is free of wheat, milk, eggs, corn, soy, yeast, and refined sugar.

Apple Cake

Cakes made with spelt flour tend to become dry quickly. In this recipe, the apple and applesauce add moisture as well as flavor.

1 1/3 c. apple juice concentrate
3 c. spelt flour
2 tsp. baking soda
1 tsp. cinnamon

1/4 tsp. nutmeg
1/4 tsp. cloves
1/4 tsp. salt (optional)
1 c. grated or shredded peeled apple (about 1 medium)
2/3 c. unsweetened applesauce
1/2 c. oil
1 c. raisins (optional)

Boil the apple juice down to 2/3 c. in volume and allow it to cool. In a large bowl, combine the flour, baking soda, salt, and spices. In a small bowl, combine the grated apple, applesauce, juice, oil, and raisins. Stir the liquid ingredients into the dry ingredients until they are just mixed in. Pour the batter into an oiled and floured 9" by 13" cake pan. Bake the cake at 325° for 40 to 50 minutes, or until it is lightly browned and a toothpick inserted into its center comes out dry. Makes one 9" by 13" cake.

This recipe is free of wheat, milk, eggs, corn, soy, yeast, and refined sugar.

Spelt Carrot Cake

Although it is not quite as moist as "Rye Carrot Cake," below, this cake is still delicious.

Prepare the batter for "Apple Cake," above, except substitute 1 c. grated carrots for the grated apple. Bake it as directed above. Makes one 9" by 13" cake.

This recipe is free of wheat, milk, eggs, corn, soy, yeast, and refined sugar.

Rye Carrot Cake

This flavorful, moist cake is a favorite at our house.

2 1/2 c. rye flour
2 tsp. baking soda
1/2 tsp. Vitamin C crystals (Omit them if you are using
    the pineapple juice.)

1 1/2 tsp. cinnamon
1/4 tsp. cloves
1 c. raisins (optional)
1 1/2 c. shredded carrots
2 c. white grape juice OR 1 c. thawed pineapple juice
    concentrate plus 1 c. water
1/4 c. oil

In a large bowl, combine the flour, baking soda, Vitamin C crystals (if you are using them), spices, and raisins. In a small bowl, combine the carrots, juice, water (if you are using it), and oil. Stir the liquid ingredients into the dry ingredients until they are just mixed in. Pour the batter into an oiled and floured 9" by 9" cake pan. Bake the cake at 350° for 45 to 55 minutes, or until it is lightly browned and a toothpick inserted into its center comes out dry. Makes one 9" by 9" cake, or about 9 servings.

This recipe is free of wheat, milk, eggs, corn, soy, and refined sugar. If the raisins are omitted, it is also free of yeast.

Quinoa Carrot Cake

This carrot cake is both delicious and grain-free.

1 c. grated carrots
1 c. raisins (optional)
1 tsp. cinnamon
1/4 tsp. nutmeg
1/4 tsp. cloves
1 1/2 c. apple juice concentrate
3/8 c. (1/4 c. plus 2 tbsp.) oil
1 1/2 c. quinoa flour
1/2 c. tapioca flour
1 1/2 tsp. baking soda

Combine the carrots, raisins, spices, juice and oil in a saucepan. Bring them to a boil and simmer them, covered, for 5 minutes. Allow the mixture to cool to lukewarm or room temperature. In a large bowl, combine the quinoa flour, tapioca flour, and baking soda. Stir the liquid ingredients into the dry ingredients until they are just mixed in. Pour the batter into two oiled and floured 8" by 4" loaf pans. Bake the cakes at 325° for 40 to 50 minutes, or until they are lightly browned and a toothpick inserted into their centers comes out dry. This cake may appear to rise and then fall slightly during baking, but the texture will still be good. Makes two 8" by 4" cakes which freeze well.

This recipe is free of all grains (including wheat and corn), gluten, milk, eggs, soy, and refined sugar. If the raisins are omitted, it is also free of yeast.

Spice Cake

This sugar-free cake is moist and tasty. It is good plain or frosted with "Date Frosting," page 180.

> 4 c. oat, milo, or barley flour
> 1 c. date sugar, pressed through a strainer to remove lumps
> 2 tsp. baking soda
> 1/2 tsp. unbuffered Vitamin C crystals
> 2 tsp. cinnamon
> 3/4 tsp. cloves
> 1/2 tsp. allspice
> Pureed or thoroughly mashed bananas - 3 c. with oat or milo flour OR 4 c. with barley flour
> 3/4 c. oil
> 1 tsp. corn-free natural vanilla (optional)

In a large bowl, combine the flour, date sugar, baking soda, Vitamin C crystals, and spices. In a small bowl, combine the bananas, oil, and optional vanilla. Stir the liquid ingredients into the dry ingredients until they are just mixed. Pour the batter into an oiled and floured 9" by 13" cake pan, two oiled and floured 8" or 9" round cake pans, or 24 to 28 oiled and floured muffin cups. Bake the cake or cupcakes at 375° for 25 to 30 minutes, or until it is lightly browned and a toothpick inserted into its center comes out dry. If you are making a layer cake, cool the layers in the pans for 15 minutes and then remove them carefully because they are very fragile. (See the notes on layer cakes, page 167–168.) Makes one 9" by 13" cake, two 8" or 9" layers, or 24 to 28 cupcakes.

This recipe is free of wheat, milk, eggs, corn, soy, yeast, and refined sugar.

Stevia-Sweetened Spice Cake

This grain-free cake is a real treat for those who must avoid both sugar and fruit sweeteners. If you are just getting used to stevia, use the smaller amount.

> 2 1/4 c. amaranth flour
> 3/4 c. arrowroot
> 2 tsp. baking soda
> 1/2 tsp. unbuffered Vitamin C crystals
> 1 tsp. cinnamon
> 1/4 tsp. cloves
> 1/8 tsp. allspice
> 1/4 to 1/2 tsp. white stevia powder
> 1 c. water
> 1/4 c. oil

Combine the amaranth flour, arrowroot, baking soda, Vitamin C crystals, spices, and stevia in a large bowl. Mix together the water and oil, and stir them into the dry ingredients until they are just mixed in. (The batter will be stiff.) Put the batter into an oiled and floured 8" by 4" loaf pan and bake it at 350° for 30 to 40 minutes. Cool the cake in the pan for 10 minutes, and then remove it if you wish to. Makes one 8" by 4" cake, or about 6 servings.

This recipe is free of all grains (including wheat and corn), gluten, milk, eggs, soy, yeast, and refined sugar.

Shoo-Fly-Pie Cake

This cake, based on the traditional Pennsylvania Dutch pie, is sweet, spicy, and made with non-grain flours.

2 c. amaranth flour
2/3 c. arrowroot
1 tsp. baking soda
1/2 tsp. unbuffered Vitamin C crystals
1 1/2 tsp. cinnamon
1/2 tsp. nutmeg
1/2 tsp. cloves
3/4 c. molasses
1/2 c. water
1/4 c. oil

Combine the amaranth flour, arrowroot, baking soda, Vitamin C crystals, and spices in a large bowl. Mix together the molasses, water, and oil thoroughly and stir them into the dry ingredients until they are just mixed in. Put the batter into an oiled and floured 9" by 9" baking pan. Bake the cake at 350° for 25 to 30 minutes, or until a toothpick inserted in its center comes out dry. Makes one 9" by 9" cake, or about 9 servings.

This recipe is free of wheat, gluten, milk, eggs, corn, soy, and yeast. Although it is made with non-grain flours, it is not strictly grain-free because molasses is a member of the grain family.

Gingerbread

If you can tolerate it, vanilla goat's milk ice-cream, page 188, is delicious with this cake. This gingerbread can be made either with a grain or non-grain flour and sweetened with either molasses or apple juice.

2 c. spelt flour OR 1 1/2 c. amaranth flour plus 1/2 c. arrowroot OR 1 1/4 c. quinoa flour plus1/2 c. tapioca flour
1 tsp. baking soda
1/2 tsp. unbuffered Vitamin C crystals if you are using the molasses and water OR 1/4 tsp. if you are using the apple juice
3/4 tsp. ginger
1 tsp. cinnamon

1/2 c. water plus 1/2 c. molasses OR 1 c. apple juice
    concentrate, thawed
1/4 c. oil

Combine the flour(s), baking soda, Vitamin C crystals, and spices in a large bowl. Mix the molasses and water or the juice with the oil thoroughly and stir them into the dry ingredients until they are just mixed in. Put the batter into an oiled and floured 9" by 9" baking pan. Bake the cake at 350° for 30 to 35 minutes, or until a toothpick inserted in its center comes out dry. Makes one 9" by 9" cake, or about 9 servings.

This recipe is free of wheat, milk, eggs, corn, soy, and yeast. If it is made with the amaranth flour or quinoa flour, it is free of gluten. If it is made with the amaranth or quinoa flour and sweetened with the apple juice, it is free of all grains. If it is sweetened with the apple juice, it is free of refined sugar.

Devil's Food Cake

One of the challenges that the mother of an allergic child faces is making a birthday cake that nonallergic party guests will eat. This sugar-free cake with "Party Carob Frosting," page 182, will be enjoyed by all.

2 1/4 c. rye flour
1/3 c. carob powder, sifted to remove lumps
1 1/2 tsp. baking soda
1 c. grape juice concentrate, thawed
1/2 c. oil

Stir together the flour, carob powder, and baking soda in a large bowl. Mix the grape juice and oil and stir them into the dry ingredients until they are just mixed in. Put the batter into an oiled and floured 8" by 8" or 9" by 9" baking pan or an 8" or 9" round baking pan and bake the cake 350° for 25 to 30 minutes, or until a toothpick inserted into its center comes out dry. Cool it in the pan for 10 minutes and then remove the cake, if you wish to. This cake is not as fragile as some, and the recipe may be doubled to make a 2-layer cake. If you wish to frost this cake, use

a half batch of "Very Carob Frosting," page 181, or a full batch of
"German Chocolate Frosting," page 181, "Coconut Frosting,"
page 183, or "Party Carob Frosting," page 182. Makes one 8" or
9" cake, about 9 servings.

*This recipe is free of wheat, milk, eggs, corn, soy, yeast, and
refined sugar.*

Very Carob Cake

This layer cake is great for special occasions.

   2 1/4 c. quinoa flour
   3/4 c. tapioca flour
   1 1/2 c. carob powder, strained to remove lumps
   1 tbsp. baking soda
   2 c. apple juice concentrate, thawed
   1 c. oil

Stir together the quinoa flour, tapioca flour, carob powder, and
baking soda in a large bowl. Mix the apple juice and oil and stir
them into the dry ingredients until they are just mixed in. Put
the batter into two oiled and floured 8" or 9" round baking pans
and bake the cake at 350° for 30 to 35 minutes, or until a toothpick
inserted into its center comes out dry. Cool the cake in the pans
for 10 minutes and then remove it from the pans. This cake may
be frosted with "Very Carob Frosting," page 181, or a double batch
of "Coconut Frosting," page 183. Makes one 2-layer cake, or about
12 servings.

*This recipe is free of all grains (including wheat and corn),
gluten, milk, eggs, soy, yeast, and refined sugar.*

Banana Carob Cake

The bananas make this cake delightfully moist.

   3 c. barley flour
   1 1/4 c. carob powder, strained to remove lumps
   2/3 c. sugar

2 tsp. baking soda
1/2 tsp. unbuffered Vitamin C crystals
3 c. thoroughly mashed or pureed bananas
3/4 c. oil
1 tsp. corn-free natural vanilla (optional)

Combine the flour, carob powder, sugar, baking soda, and Vitamin C crystals in a large bowl. Mix together the bananas, oil, and vanilla, and stir them into the dry ingredients until they are just mixed in. Put the batter into two oiled and floured 8" or 9" round baking pans and bake the cake at 375° for 25 to 30 minutes, or until a toothpick inserted into its center comes out dry. Cool the cake in the pans for 10 minutes and then remove it from the pans. This cake may be frosted with "Very Carob Frosting," page 181, or a double batch of "German Chocolate Frosting," page 181, "Coconut Frosting," page 183, or "Party Carob Frosting," page 182. Makes one 2-layer cake, or about 12 servings.

This recipe is free of wheat, milk, eggs, corn, soy, and yeast.

Stevia-Sweetened Carob Cake

No one will even detect the stevia in this carob treat which contains no sugars of any kind, including fruit sugars.

1 1/2 c. quinoa flour
1/2 c. tapioca flour
1/2 c. carob powder which has been pressed through a
      strainer to remove any lumps
2 tsp. baking soda
1/2 tsp. unbuffered Vitamin C crystals
1/4 to 1/2 tsp. white stevia powder, or to taste
1 1/4 c. water
1/4 c. oil

Combine the quinoa flour, tapioca flour, carob powder, baking soda, Vitamin C crystals, and stevia in a large bowl. Mix together the water and oil and stir them into the dry ingredients until they are just mixed in. Pour the batter into an oiled and floured 8" by 4" loaf pan and bake the cake at 350° for 25 to 30 minutes. Cool it in the pan for 10 minutes, and then remove it if you wish to. Makes one 8" by 4" cake, or 6 to 8 servings.

This recipe is free of all grains (including wheat and corn), gluten, milk, eggs, soy, yeast, and refined sugar.

"German Chocolate" Cake

This cake is lighter than the previous carob cakes in both flavor and color, and can be made with either a grain or non-grain flour.

> 1 1/2 c. quinoa flour plus 3/4 c. tapioca flour OR 2 1/4 c.
>   rye flour
> 1/3 c. carob powder
> 1 1/2 tsp. baking soda
> 1 c. apple juice concentrate, thawed
> 1/2 c. oil

Combine the flour(s), carob powder, and baking soda in a large bowl. Mix the juice and oil and stir them into the dry ingredients until they are just mixed in. Put the batter into an oiled and floured 8" or 9" round or square baking pan and bake the cake at 350° for 25 to 30 minutes, or until a toothpick inserted in its center comes out dry. Cool it in the pan for 10 minutes and then remove it from the pan if you wish to. This cake is not as fragile as some, and the recipe may be doubled to make a 2-layer cake.

If you wish to frost this cake use a half batch of "Very Carob Frosting," page 181, or a full batch of "German Chocolate Frosting," page 181, "Coconut Frosting," page 183, or "Party Carob Frosting," page 182. Makes one 8" or 9" cake, about 9 servings.

This recipe is free of wheat, milk, eggs, corn, soy, yeast, and refined sugar. If it is made with the quinoa flour rather than the rye flour, it is free of gluten and all grains.

Date Frosting

This is especially good on "Spice Cake," page 173, or a square "Date-Nut Cake," page 169.

> 1 1/3 c. water
> 3 tbsp. oat or barley flour
> 2 c. date sugar

Remove any lumps in the date sugar by pressing it through a wire mesh strainer with the back of a spoon. Mix the water and flour in a small saucepan. Cook them over medium heat until they are thick, smooth, and bubbly, stirring them frequently. Remove the pan from the heat, add the date sugar, and beat the frosting until it is smooth. Frost the cake immediately. Makes enough frosting for one 9" by 13" cake or two 8" or 9" layers.

This recipe is free of wheat, milk, eggs, corn, soy, yeast, and refined sugar.

Date Glaze

Drizzle this on "Date-Nut Bundt Cake," page 169.

> 2/3 c. water
> 2 tbsp. oat flour
> 2/3 c. date sugar

Remove any lumps in the date sugar by pressingit through a wire mesh strainer with the back of a spoon. Mix the flour and water in a small saucepan. Cook the mixture over medium heat until it is thick, smooth, and bubbly, stirring it frequently. Remove it from the heat and add the date sugar. Beat it until it is smooth and drizzle it on the cake.

This recipe is free of wheat, milk, eggs, corn, soy, yeast, and refined sugar.

Very Carob Frosting

This not-too-sweet frosting was developed for "Very Carob Cake," page 177, but is good with other carob cakes too.

2 c. thoroughly mashed bananas
1/4 c. tapioca flour or arrowroot
1 3/4 c. carob powder

Beat all of the ingredients together with an electric mixer for about 2 minutes on high speed, or until the frosting is smooth. Frost the cake immediately. This recipe makes enough frosting for the tops and sides of two cake layers.

This recipe is free of all grains (including wheat and corn), gluten, milk, eggs, soy, yeast, and refined sugar.

"German Chocolate" Frosting

This is great on "German Chocolate' Cake," page 179, but is also good on almost any carob, fruit, carrot, zucchini, or spice cake.

1 c. apple juice concentrate OR 3/4 c. maple syrup
    OR 3/8 c. honey
1 c. finely shredded unsweetened coconut
1 c. finely chopped nuts

Boil the apple juice concentrate or maple syrup down to 3/8 c. volume (it will reach 3/8 c. about the time it starts to foam) or warm the honey. Add the coconut and nuts while it is still hot, mix it well, and spread it on the cake immediately. This frosting tastes tangy and is excellent on fruit cakes if it is made with the apple juice, and tastes more like traditional German chocolate cake frosting if it is made with the maple syrup or honey. This recipe makes enough frosting for one 8" or 9" cake.

This recipe is free of all grains (including wheat and corn), gluten, milk, eggs, soy, and yeast. If the apple juice concentrate is used, it is free of refined sugar.

Party Carob Frosting

This frosting makes a birthday cake special.

> 1 tbsp. rye or barley flour (Use the same kind of flour
>   as is used in the cake.)
> 1/3 c. water
> 1/3 c. butter or milk-free margarine (See the note
>   on which to use in the recipe.)
> 1/3 c. sugar
> 2/3 c. carob powder that has been pressed through a wire
>   mesh strainer to remove all lumps

Mix together the flour and water in a small saucepan and cook them over medium heat, stirring them frequently, until the mixture thickens and boils. Cool it to room temperature, stirring it frequently as it cools. With an electric mixer, cream the butter or margarine and sugar. (Note: Since this recipe will be used rarely, such as for a once-a-year birthday party treat, perhaps butter or margarine can be used. You will have to decide which is the "lesser of the two evils" in your situation, hydrogenated fat, such as margarine, or a dairy product, such as butter.) Beat in about 2 tbsp. of the cooled flour and water mixture, then beat in about 1/3 of the carob powder. Continue adding the flour and water mixture and carob powder alternately until they are used up. Beat the frosting until it is smooth and fluffy. This recipe makes enough frosting for the tops and sides of a 8" or 9" cake layer or to thinly frost a 13" by 9" cake or pan of "Rye Brownies," page 144. For a 2-layer birthday cake that your allergic children's friends will enjoy as much as your children do, double both this recipe and the "Devil's Food Cake" recipe, page 176.

This recipe is free of wheat, eggs, corn, soy, and yeast. It is free of milk if the butter is not used, but may contain soy or corn if the margarine used was made with those oils.

Coconut Frosting

This frosting can be used on any kind of cake, but it is especially good on carob cakes. Match the sweetener in the frosting to the sweetener in the cake you are using it on.

>   1 c. apple or pineapple juice concentrate OR 3/4 c. water
>   plus 1/2 c. beet or cane sugar OR 1/2 c. water
>   plus 1/2 c. molasses, honey, or maple syrup
>   3 tbsp. arrowroot OR 2 1/2 tbsp. tapioca flour
>   2 c. very finely shredded unsweetened coconut OR 3 c.
>   regular unsweetened shredded coconut

Mix the juice or the water and sugar, molasses, honey, or maple syrup with the arrowroot or tapioca flour in a saucepan. Cook the mixture, stirring it frequently, over medium heat until it thickens and boils. Stir in the coconut before it can cool off at all and immediately spread it on the top of the cake. (This frosting is best made with very finely shredded coconut, but if necessary, you can use regular shredded coconut. To obtain very finely shredded coconut, see "Sources of Special Foods," ch.16.) This recipe makes enough frosting for one 8" or 9" cake.

This recipe is free of all grains (including wheat and corn), gluten, milk, eggs, soy, and yeast. If it is made with the juice, it is free of refined sugar.

11

Ice Creams, Sorbets, Cones, and Sauces

Gone are the days when you needed rock salt, crushed ice, and a lot of hand cranking to make ice cream at home. Now you can make delicious ice creams and sorbets that will fit almost any diet with a minimum of effort. Modern ice cream makers feature a canister that you put into your freezer overnight before using it, eliminating the need for salt and ice. You do not have to crank the hand-cranked models continuously for the entire freezing period, and the electric models do all of the work for you. If you do not have an ice cream maker, directions are given in this chapter which allow you to make ice creams and sorbets using your food processor or blender. (If you are using a blender, the ice cream or sorbet may have to be processed in small batches.)

This chapter contains recipes for fruit-sweetened ice creams, sorbets, ice cream cones, and sauces for sundaes. There are a few recipes that are sweetened with honey for those who can tolerate it, and four ice cream and sorbet recipes that can be sweetened with stevia for those who must avoid even fruit sweeteners. Some of the recipes contain guar gum, which is a derivitave of a bean, as an optional ingredient. The purpose of the guar gum is to make the ice cream creamier and to slow down the formation of ice crystals in leftover ice cream stored in the freezer.

Making Ice Cream or Sorbet With a Food Processor or Blender

When you make ice cream or sorbet using your food processor or blender, you must freeze either most of or all of the ice cream or sorbet mixture in ice cube trays. How much you freeze depends on the characteristics of the mixture, and is specified in each recipe.

METHOD I:

This method is for sorbets made with stevia and for goat milk ice creams. Prepare the ice cream or sorbet mixture as directed in the recipe. Chill about 1/4 of the mixture to be frozen in the refrigerator and freeze the rest in ice cube trays until it is solid. Remove the cubes from the freezer and let them stand for 5 to 10 minutes at room temperature.

While they are standing at room temperature, chill the blender or food processor by blending about 1/3 of a container of cold water and a few regular ice cubes for one minute. Pour out the water and ice.

Place the chilled mixture from the refrigerator into the blender or processor. Add two of the frozen mixture cubes and blend them until they are smooth. Continue adding cubes two at a time and processing them until they are smooth after each addition until all of the cubes are used up. Place any ice cream or sorbet you do not eat immediately into the freezer.

METHOD II:

This method is for coconut milk ice creams and sorbets made with fruit juice concentrates, which do not freeze to rock-like firmness. Prepare the ice cream or sorbet mixture as directed in the recipe. Freeze all of the mixture in ice cube trays until it is solid. Chill the food processor or blender as in the second paragraph of "Method I." Remove the cubes from the freezer and immediately process them two at a time as in the third paragraph of "Method I."

Pina Colada "Ice Cream"

This rich and tasty treat is very easy to make because it contains only two ingredients.

> 1 1/2 c. coconut milk (1 14-oz. can)
> 1/2 c. pineapple juice concentrate, thawed

Combine the coconut milk and pineapple juice concentrate. Chill them thoroughly or overnight in the refrigerator and freeze the mixture according to the directions for your ice cream maker. If you do not have an ice cream maker, process it by "Method II," page 185. Makes about 1 1/2 pints of ice cream.

This recipe is free of all grains (including wheat and corn), gluten, milk, eggs, soy, yeast, and refined sugar.

Carob Ice Cream

This ice cream is delicious when made with the stevia; the carob completely masks the stevia taste.

> 2 c. goat milk plus 1/4 c. honey OR 2 1/4 c. goat milk
>   plus 1/4 tsp. white stevia powder
> 2 tbsp. carob powder
> 1 tsp. guar gum (optional)

Combine the milk, honey or stevia, carob powder, and guar gum, mixing them until the stevia is completely dissolved, if you are using it. Chill the mixture thoroughly or overnight in the refrigerator and freeze it as directed in the instructions for your ice cream maker. If you do not have an ice cream maker, process it by "Method I," page 185. Makes about 1 1/2 pints of ice cream.

This recipe is free of all grains (including wheat and corn), gluten, cow's milk, eggs, soy, and yeast. If the stevia is used, it is free of refined sugar.

Strawberry Ice Cream

This traditional favorite is delicious made with goat milk or coconut milk. You will not detect the flavor of the juice if you use the strawberry flavor.

        1 c. goat or coconut milk
        3/4 c. apple, pineapple, or unsweetened apple-white
             grape juice concentrate, thawed
        3/4 c. fresh or unsweetened frozen strawberries
        1 tsp. guar gum (optional)
        1/2 tsp. corn-free natural strawberry flavor (optional)

Puree the strawberries. (You should have about 1/2 c. of puree.) Stir in the milk, juice, guar gum, and optional flavor. Chill the mixture thoroughly or overnight in the refrigerator and freeze it according to the directions for your ice cream maker. If you do not have an ice cream maker, process it by "Method I," page 185. Makes about 1 1/2 pints of ice cream.

This recipe is free of all grains (including wheat and corn), gluten, cow's milk, eggs, soy, yeast, and refined sugar.

Peach Ice Cream

This is best when you make it from fresh peaches in the summertime, but you can also use frozen or canned peaches.

        1 c. goat or coconut milk
        3/4 c. apple, pineapple, or unsweetened apple-white
             grape juice concentrate, thawed
        3/4 c. fresh, unsweetened frozen, or drained water-packed
             canned peaches
        1 tsp. guar gum (optional)

Puree the peaches. (You should have about 1/2 c. of puree.) Stir in the milk, juice, and guar gum. Chill the mixture thoroughly or overnight in the refrigerator and freeze it according to the directions for your ice cream maker. If you do not have an ice cream maker, process it by "Method I," page 185. Makes about 1 1/2 pints of ice cream.

This recipe is free of all grains (including wheat and corn), gluten, cow's milk, eggs, soy, yeast, and refined sugar.

Orange Ice Cream

This tart and tangy ice cream will remind you of "Creamsicles."

    1 1/2 c. goat milk
    3/4 c. orange juice concentrate, thawed
    1/2 tsp. guar gum (optional)

Stir together the milk, orange juice concentrate, and guar gum until the guar gum is completely mixed in. Chill the mixture thoroughly or overnight in the refrigerator and freeze it according to the directions for your ice cream maker. If you do not have an ice cream maker, process it by "Method II," page 185. Makes about 1 1/2 pints of ice cream.

This recipe is free of all grains (including wheat and corn), gluten, cow's milk, eggs, soy, yeast, and refined sugar.

Vanilla Ice Cream

You can sweeten this family favorite with honey, fruit juice, or stevia. The fruit-juice-sweetened version has a delicious tangy twist.

    2 c. goat milk plus 1/4 c. honey OR 1 1/2 c.goat milk
       plus 3/4 c. unsweetened apple-white grape juice
       concentrate, thawed, OR 2 1/4 c. goat milk plus 1/4 tsp.
       white stevia powder
    3/4 tsp. corn-free natural vanilla
    Pinch of salt (optional)
    1 tsp. guar gum (optional)

Combine the honey, fruit juice, or stevia with the milk, vanilla, salt, and guar gum, mixing them until the stevia is completely dissolved, if you are using it. Chill the mixture thoroughly or overnight in the refrigerator and freeze it according to the directions for your ice cream maker. If you do not have an ice cream maker, process it by "Method I," page 185. Makes about 1 1/2 pints of ice cream.

This recipe is free of all grains (including wheat and corn), gluten, cow's milk, eggs, soy, and yeast. If the juice or stevia is used, it is also free of refined sugar.

Choose-Your-Flavor Ice Cream

"The Spicery Shoppe" makes a large variety of flavors to use in this ice cream.

Make "Vanilla Ice Cream," above, but substitute 3/4 tsp. almond, banana, cinnamon, coffee, maple, or any other flavor of corn-free natural flavoring for the vanilla. Makes about 1 1/2 pints of ice cream.

This recipe is free of all grains (including wheat and corn), gluten, cow's milk, eggs, soy, and yeast. If the juice or stevia is used, it is also free of refined sugar.

Carob Chip Ice Cream

The carob chips make plain vanilla ice cream special.

Make "Vanilla Ice Cream," above. Stir 1/4 c. milk-free unsweetened carob chips into it immediately after freezing it in your ice cream maker or processing it in your blender or food processor. Makes about 1 1/2 pints of ice cream.

This recipe is free of all grains (including wheat and corn), gluten, cow's milk, eggs, soy, and yeast. If the juice or stevia is used, it is also free of refined sugar.

Pineapple Sorbet

This is so easy to make with canned pineapple that you may want to always have a can of pineapple in your freezer so you can make it any time.

> 1 20-oz. can of pineapple packed in its own juice,
> OR 2 1/2 c. fresh pineapple with juice to cover

Freeze the pineapple in its juice overnight. If you are using the canned pineapple, you can freeze it in the can and in the morning run warm water on the can, remove both can ends, and slide the pineapple out. Break the frozen pineapple and juice into chunks and process it in a food processor or in small batches in a blender until it is smooth. Serve it immediately. Makes about 3 c. of sorbet, or 4 to 6 servings.

This recipe is free of all grains (including wheat and corn), gluten, milk, eggs, soy, yeast, and refined sugar.

Banaberry Sorbet

This is easy to make from frozen berries without any advance preparation.

> 2 ripe bananas
> 2 tbsp. honey (optional)
> 4 to 6 c. frozen strawberries, blueberries, or raspberries

Puree the bananas and optional honey in a food processor or blender until they are smooth. Gradually add the berries, processing after each addition, until the sorbet reaches the desired consistency. Serve it immediately. Makes about 4 c. of sorbet, or 6 to 8 servings.

This recipe is free of all grains (including wheat and corn), gluten, milk, eggs, soy, and yeast. If the honey is not used, it is free of refined sugar.

Apple Sorbet

This tastes like a frozen version of apple pie.

1 1/4 c. unsweetened applesauce
1 6-oz. can of frozen apple juice concentrate
1/2 tsp. cinnamon
1/4 tsp. nutmeg

Freeze the applesauce overnight in an ice cube tray. Remove the apple juice concentrate from the freezer and allow it to stand at room temperature for 10 to 15 minutes. Put the apple juice concentrate and spices in a food processor or blender and turn the machine on. Add the frozen applesauce cubes 2 at a time and process them until the sorbet is smooth after each addition. Serve it immediately. Makes about 2 c. of sorbet, or 4 servings.

This recipe is free of all grains (including wheat and corn), gluten, milk, eggs, soy, yeast, and refined sugar.

Cranberry Sorbet

Tart and tangy, this is a perfect light ending to a big holiday meal.

12 oz. fresh cranberries (about 4 c.)
1 1/2 c. apple or pineapple juice concentrate, thawed,
    OR 1 1/2 c. water plus 1/4 tsp. white stevia powder

Combine the cranberries with juice or water in a saucepan. Bring the mixture to a boil, reduce the heat, and simmer it, stirring it occasionally, for about 20 minutes, or until the cranberries have popped and lost their shape. If you are using the stevia, stir it in thoroughly. If you wish to remove the cranberry skins, which may be bitter, put the mixture through a food mill or press it through a strainer at this point. Chill the mixture thoroughly and freeze it according to the instructions for your ice cream maker. Or, to make the sorbet with a food processor or blender, if you are using the stevia, use "Method I" on page 185.

If you are using the apple juice, use "Method II" on page 185. Makes about 3 1/2 c. of sorbet, or 6 servings.

This recipe is free of all grains (including wheat and corn), gluten, milk, eggs, soy, yeast, and refined sugar.

Cantalope Sorbet

This is delicious in August when the cantalopes are at their peak.

2 medium-size sweet, ripe cantalopes

Peel the cantalopes, cut them into chunks, and puree them in a food processor or blender. Chill the puree thoroughly and freeze it according to the directions for your ice cream machine. Or, to make the sorbet with a food processor or blender, measure out 1 c. of the puree and chill it in the refrigerator. Freeze the rest of the puree in ice cube trays overnight or for several hours until the cubes are thoroughly frozen. Put the chilled puree into the food processor and blender and turn the machine on. Add the frozen cubes 2 at a time and process the sorbet until it is smooth after each addition. Serve it immediately. Makes about 4 c. of sorbet, or 6 to 8 servings.

This recipe is free of all grains (including wheat and corn), gluten, milk, eggs, soy, yeast, and refined sugar.

Kiwi Sorbet

This tangy and delicious sorbet can be sweetened with either fruit juice or stevia.

4 to 5 kiwi fruits
1/2 c. apple or pineapple juice concentrate, thawed,
    OR 1/2 c. water plus 1/16 tsp. white stevia powder,
    OR 1/2 c. water plus 1/2 tsp. stevia working solution,
    page 226

Peel the kiwis and cut them into chunks. Puree them in a food processor or blender, and measure out 1 1/2 c. of the puree. To the 1 1/2 c. of puree, add the juice or the water and stevia and blend the mixture again briefly. Chill the mixture thoroughly or overnight and freeze it according to the instructions for your ice cream maker. Or, to make the sorbet with a food processor or blender, if you are using the stevia, use "Method I" on page 185. If you are using the apple juice, use "Method II" on page 185. Makes about 2 1/4 c. of sorbet, or 4 servings.

This recipe is free of all grains (including wheat and corn), gluten, milk, eggs, soy, yeast, and refined sugar.

Ice Cream Cones

You can make ice cream cones with a krumkake, pizzelle, or ice cream cone iron. This is one of the rare recipes in which what kind of oil you use makes a difference. The cones are less likely to stick to the iron if you use coconut oil, although you can use other oils, if necessary, for any of the cones except the oat cones, which are quite fragile. If you can tolerate butter occasionally, substitute melted butter for the oil, and the cones will be easy to remove from the iron.

"Sugar" Cones:

2 c. rye flour OR 3 c. spelt flour
1/2 c. melted coconut or other oil
1 1/4 c. apple juice concentrate, thawed OR 1/2 c.
    water plus 3/4 c. apple juice concentrate, thawed,
    depending on the degree of sweetness desired

Amaranth Cones:

1 c. amaranth flour
1 c. arrowroot
1 tsp. baking soda
1/8 tsp. unbuffered Vitamin C crystals
1/4 c. melted coconut or other oil

1/4 c. honey
5/8 c. (1/2 c. plus 2 tbsp.) water

Carob-Rye Cones:

1 1/2 c. rye flour
1/2 c. carob powder
1/2 c. melted coconut or other oil
3/4 c. grape juice concentrate, thawed
1/2 c. water

Oat Cones:

1 c. oat flour
1 c. arrowroot
1/2 c. melted coconut oil
3/4 c. pineapple juice concentrate, thawed

Quinoa Cones:

1 1/2 c. quinoa flour
1/2 c. tapioca flour
1/2 tsp. baking soda
1/2 c. melted coconut or other oil
1 c. apple juice concentrate, thawed

Carob-Quinoa Cones:

1 c. quinoa flour
1/2 c. carob powder
1/2 c. tapioca flour
1/2 tsp. baking soda
1/2 c. melted coconut or other oil
1 c. apple juice concentrate, thawed

Choose one set of ingredients, above. Begin heating the iron. Combine the flour(s), carob powder (if it is used in the set of ingredients you have chosen), baking soda (if it is used), and Vitamin C crystals (if they are used) in a large electric mixer bowl. In a small bowl, stir together the oil, juice or honey, and water (if it is used), and pour them into the dry ingredients. Beat the dough on low speed until the flour is all moistened, then beat it on medium speed for one minute. Place the dough in the iron using heaping tablespoonfuls as a starting point as you determine how much dough you should put in to fill the iron when you close it. Cook each cone for 20 to 30 seconds, or until it is golden brown, and remove it from the iron using two forks. You may also have to experiment to determine what cooking time makes the cones easiest to remove. If you are using an oil other than coconut oil, spray or brush both the top and the bottom of the iron with oil after cooking each cone. If the cones stick after using coconut oil in the batter, brush the iron with melted coconut oil. Immediately after removing each cone from the iron, roll it into a cone shape. If you wish to have perfectly shaped cones, roll them around metal cone-shaped forms and allow them to cool before removing the forms. Makes 1 to 1 1/2 dozen cones.

This recipe is free of wheat, milk, eggs, corn, soy, and yeast. If the amaranth or either of the quinoa versions are made, it is free of gluten and all grains. If any version other than the amaranth version is made, it is free of refined sugar.

Strawberry Sauce

This is delicious served on pancakes and waffles as well as on almost any kind of ice cream or sorbet.

> 1 lb. unsweetened frozen strawberries, thawed
> (about 3 1/2 c.)
> 1/2 c. apple juice concentrate, thawed
> 2 tsp. arrowroot or tapioca flour

Stir the arrowroot or tapioca flour into the juice in a saucepan. Add the strawberries and cook the mixture over medium heat, stirring it often and cutting up the strawberries with the spoon as you stir, if you wish. When the sauce thickens and boils, remove it from the heat. Serve it warm or cold. Makes about 2 1/2 c. of sauce.

This recipe is free of all grains (including wheat and corn), gluten, milk, eggs, soy, yeast, and refined sugar.

Pineapple Sauce

This all-fruit sauce is excellent on "Pina Colada Ice Cream," page 186, cake, pancakes, or waffles.

> 1 8-oz. can crushed pineapple packed in its own juice
>   OR 3/4 c. finely chopped fresh pineapple
> Up to 1 c. pineapple juice
> 2 tsp. arrowroot or tapioca starch

If you are using canned pineapple, drain it and reserve the juice, adding enough additonal pineapple juice to bring its volume up to 1 c. (If you are using fresh pineapple, just use 1 c. of pineapple juice.) Stir the arrowroot or tapioca flour into the juice in a saucepan. Cook the mixture over medium heat, stirring it often, until it thickens and boils. Remove it from the heat and stir in the drained pineapple. Serve it warm or cold. Makes about 1 3/4 c. of sauce.

This recipe is free of all grains (including wheat and corn), gluten, milk, eggs, soy, yeast, and refined sugar.

Cherry Sauce

This is delicious over ice cream and breakfast foods, as well as on roast duck.

Make the cherry sauce according to the directions given in "Roast Duck with Cherry Sauce," page 88. Serve it warm or cold. Makes about 2 c. of sauce.

This recipe is free of all grains (including wheat and corn), gluten, milk, eggs, soy, yeast, and refined sugar.

Carob Syrup

Try this on strawberry, peach, or carob ice cream, as well as on vanilla ice cream. My children even like it on oatmeal.

        1/2 c. honey
        1/4 c. carob powder

Press the carob powder through a wire mesh strainer with the back of a spoon to remove any lumps. Mix the honey and carob powder together thoroughly and serve the sauce. Makes about 2/3 c. of sauce.

This recipe is free of all grains (including wheat and corn), gluten, milk, eggs, soy, and yeast.

12

Pastry, Other Fruit Desserts, and Puddings

Pie is one of almost everyone's favorite desserts and is a delicious way to capture the flavor and goodness of fresh summer fruit. But pies do not have to contain wheat flour, lard, hydrogenated shortening, or sugar to be delicious. This chapter provides recipes for wheat-free and grain-free pie crusts made with oil, fruit-sweetened pie fillings, fruit-sweetened cobblers, other fruit desserts, shortcakes, and puddings.

Pie crusts made with alternative flours and oil tend to break easily when you roll them. You can avoid this problem by pressing the dough into the pie plate and, if you wish to use a top crust, sprinkling crumbs of the dough over the top of the filling. If you wish to make a rolled crust, the spelt, rye, and barley pie crusts can be rolled out, with the spelt and rye doughs being the easiest to work with. Roll them on a well-floured pastry cloth using a cloth-covered, floured rolling pin. Then set the pie dish on the edge of the pastry cloth next to the rolled crust, pick up the edge of the cloth farthest away from the dish, and flip the crust and cloth over the pie dish. Peel off the pastry cloth from the crust and patch and trim the crust as needed. If you wish to make a two-crust pie, fill the bottom crust with the filling, repeat the rolling process with the top crust, and flip the crust over the filling. Patch and trim the top crust, prick it gently with a fork, and crimp the edges of the top and bottom crusts together. Then you will have a pie fit for a king.

Pie Crust

The barley crust is the most like a traditional wheat crust in taste and texture, but all of these crusts are delicious.

Quinoa:

    2 c. quinoa flour
    1 tsp. baking soda
    1/4 tsp. unbuffered Vitamin C crystals
    1/2 tsp. salt (optional)
    1/2 tsp. cinnamon (optional)
    1/2 c. oil
    1/4 to 3/8 c. (1/4 c. plus 2 tbsp.) water

Barley:

    3 c. barley flour
    1/2 tsp. salt (optional)
    1/2 c. oil
    3/8 c. (1/4 c. plus 2 tbsp.) water

Oat:

    3 c. oat flour
    1/2 tsp. salt (optional)
    1/2 c. oil
    1/4 c. water

Rye:

    2 1/2 c. rye flour
    1/2 tsp. salt (optional)
    2/3 c. oil
    1/4 c. water

Spelt:

3 c. spelt flour
1/2 tsp. salt (optional)
1/2 c. oil
1/3 c. water

Amaranth:

1 1/2 c. amaranth flour
3/4 c. arrowroot
1/2 tsp. salt (optional)
1/2 c. oil
1/4 c. water

Choose one set of ingredients above. In a large bowl, combine the flour(s) with the salt, or, for the quinoa crust, with the salt, baking soda, Vitamin C crystals, and cinnamon. Add the oil and blend it in thoroughly with a pastry cutter. Add the water and mix the dough until it begins to stick together, adding an extra 1 to 2 teaspoons of water if necessary. (For the quinoa crust, stir the flour mixture while you are adding the water until you have added enough to make the dough stick together.) Divide the dough in half. For one-crust pies, press each half of the dough into a glass pie dish, gently prick it with a fork, and bake it until the bottom of the crust begins to brown. The baking temperatures and times for each kind of crust are as follows:

Quinoa . . . . 20 to 25 minutes at 350°
Barley . . . . 15 to 18 minutes at 400°
Oat. . . . . 15 to 20 minutes at 400°
Rye. . . . . 15 to 20 minutes at 400°
Spelt. . . . . 18 to 22 minutes at 400°
Amaranth . . . . . . 15 to 18 minutes at 400°

For a two-crust pie, press half of the dough into the bottom of a glass pie dish, or roll out half of it as described on pages 198 and 199. Fill the crust with the filling of your choice. To top the pie, either crumble the second half of the dough and sprinkle it over the filling, or roll the second half of the dough out and place it on top of the pie as described on page 198-199. This recipe makes two single pie crusts or a more-than-adequate amount of pastry for a two-crust pie.

This recipe is free of wheat, milk, eggs, corn, soy, yeast, and refined sugar. If the quinoa or amaranth versions are used, it is also free of gluten and all grains.

Coconut Pie Crust

This grain-free pie crust makes a delicious pumpkin or cherry pie. It is best made with very finely shredded coconut.

> 2 c. very finely shredded (See "Sources of Special Foods,"
>   ch. 16.) or shredded unsweetened coconut
> Melted coconut oil - 3/8 c. (1/4 c. plus 2 tbsp.) with
>   very finely shredded coconut OR 1/4 c. with
>   shredded coconut

Thoroughly mix the coconut with the melted coconut oil and press it onto the bottom and sides of a glass pie dish. Bake the crust at 300° for 12 to 15 minutes, or until it begins to brown. Cool the crust completely and fill it with "Pumpkin Pie" filling, page 205, "Carob Pudding," page 214, or "Coconut Pudding," page 214. You may also fill this crust with any of the fruit pie fillings, pages 201-205, if you cook them until they are thickened and the fruit is tender and allow them to cool slightly before putting them into the crust. Makes one single pie crust.

This recipe is free of all grains (including wheat and corn), gluten, milk, eggs, soy, yeast, and refined sugar.

Apple Pie

You will never miss the sugar in this all-American favorite.

7/8 c. (3/4 c. plus 2 tbsp.) apple juice concentrate, divided
6 to 7 apples, peeled, cored, and sliced (about 5 c. of
    slices)
1 tsp. cinnamon
2 tbsp. tapioca flour OR 3 tbsp. quick-cooking tapioca
1 baked single pie crust OR 1 batch of pastry for a
    two-crust pie, page 199

If you are using the tapioca, allow it to soak in the apple juice
in a saucepan for 5 minutes, then add the apples and cinnamon,
bring them to a boil, and simmer them until they are tender. If
you are using the tapioca flour, simmer the apples and cinnamon
with 5/8 c. of the juice until the apples are tender. Mix the
remaining 1/4 c. juice with the tapioca flour, stir it into the apples,
and cook the mixture over medium heat until it has thickened.
For a one-crust pie, cool the apples for 10 minutes, then pour the
filling into the cooled, baked pie crust and refrigerate the pie.
For a two-crust pie, you do not need to simmer the apples until
they are tender. If you are using the tapioca, just bring the apple
mixture to a boil and put it into the crust. If you are using the
tapioca flour, just bring the apple mixture to a boil, stir in the
tapioca flour mixture, and simmer until it is thickened before
putting the filling into the crust. Bake a 2-crust pie for 10 minutes
in an oven that has been preheated to 400°, then turn down the
oven temperature to 350° and bake it for 40 to 50 minutes more,
or until the bottom crust of the pie begins to brown. Makes 1 pie,
or about 6 servings.

*This recipe is free of wheat, milk, eggs, corn, soy, yeast, and
refined sugar. If a quinoa, amaranth, or coconut pie crust is used,
it is also free of gluten and all grains.*

Peach Pie

*This is delicious made with fresh peaches in the summer, but
you can make it year-round by using canned or frozen peaches.*

7/8 c. (3/4 c. plus 2 tbsp.) apple juice concentrate, divided
5 c. of peeled, pitted, and sliced fresh peaches OR 5 c. of
    drained, canned, water-packed peaches OR 1 1/2

16-oz.bags of unsweetened frozen peaches
1/4 tsp. cinnamon (optional)
3 tbsp. tapioca flour or arrowroot
1 baked single pie crust OR 1 batch of pastry for a
     two-crust pie, page 199

If you are using fresh or frozen peaches, simmer the peaches and cinnamon with 5/8 c. of the juice until the peaches are just tender. If you are using canned peaches just combine the peaches and 5/8. c. of juice. Mix the remaining 1/4 c. juice with the tapioca flour or arrowroot, stir it into the peaches, and cook the mixture over medium heat until it has thickened. For a one-crust pie, cool the peaches for 10 minutes, then pour the filling into the cooled, baked pie crust and refrigerate the pie. For a two-crust pie, you do not need to simmer the peaches until they are tender. Just bring the peaches to a boil, stir in the tapioca flour or arrowroot mixture, and simmer the mixture until it is thickened before putting the filling into the crust. Bake a 2-crust pie for 10 minutes in an oven that has been preheated to 400°, then turn down the oven temperature to 350° and bake it for 40 to 50 minutes more, or until the bottom crust of the pie begins to brown. Makes 1 pie, or about 6 servings.

This recipe is free of wheat, milk, eggs, corn, soy, yeast, and refined sugar. If a quinoa, amaranth, or coconut pie crust is used, it is also free of gluten and all grains.

Blueberry Pie

This pie is easy to make and very delicious.

3/4 c. pineapple juice concentrate, thawed
2 tbsp. arrowroot
1 16-oz package frozen unsweetened blueberries
1 baked single pie crust OR 1 batch of pastry for a
     two-crust pie, page 199

Stir together the pineapple juice concentrate and arrowroot in a saucepan. Add the blueberries and cook the mixture over medium heat until it thickens and boils, stirring it frequently.

For a one-crust pie, cool the filling for 10 minutes, put it into a cooled, baked pie crust, and refrigerate the pie. For a two-crust pie, put the filling into the crusts and bake the pie for 10 minutes in an oven that has been preheated to 400°, then turn down the oven temperature to 350° and bake it for about 30 minutes more, or until the bottom crust of the pie begins to brown. Makes 1 pie, or about 6 servings.

This recipe is free of wheat, milk, eggs, corn, soy, yeast, and refined sugar. If a quinoa, amaranth, or coconut pie crust is used, it is also free of gluten and all grains.

Cherry Pie

The flavor of the cherries really shines in this sugar-free pie.

> 2 16-oz. cans unsweetened tart red pie cherries, drained
> 1 1/2 c. apple juice concentrate
> 1/4 c. tapioca
> 1 baked single pie crust OR 1 batch of pastry for a
>   two-crust pie, page 199

Boil the apple juice concentrate down to 3/4 c. in volume. Add the drained cherries and tapioca and let the mixture stand for 5 minutes. Then return it to a boil and simmer it for 5 minutes. For a one-crust pie, cool the filling for 10 minutes and put it into a cooled, baked pie crust. If you wish to, sprinkle the top of the filling with crumbs of leftover pie dough that have been baked on a cookie sheet or with coconut if a coconut crust is used. Refrigerate the pie. For a two-crust pie, put the filling into the crusts and bake the pie for 10 minutes in an oven that has been preheated to 400°, then turn down the oven temperature to 350° and bake it for about 30 minutes more, or until the bottom crust of the pie begins to brown. Makes 1 pie, or about 6 servings.

This recipe is free of wheat, milk, eggs, corn, soy, yeast, and refined sugar. If a quinoa, amaranth, or coconut pie crust is used, it is also free of gluten and all grains.

Grape Pie

You will be surprised at how flavorful this unusual fruit-sweet-ened pie is.

    4 c. seedless grapes
    1/2 c. unsweetened purple grape juice concentrate,
        thawed
    3 tbsp. quick-cooking tapioca
    1 batch of pastry for a two-crust pie, page 199

Roll out half of the pastry and put it into a glass pie dish (see pages 198-199), or pat half of it into the dish. Combine the grapes, juice, and tapioca and put them into the bottom crust. Roll out the top crust (see page 198-199) and cover the filling with it, or sprinkle the filling with crumbs of the other half of the dough. Bake the pie at 350° for 50 to 60 minutes, or until the bottom crust begins to brown. Makes 1 pie, or about 6 servings.

This recipe is free of wheat, milk, eggs, corn, soy, yeast, and refined sugar. If a quinoa or amaranth pie crust is used, it is also free of gluten and all grains.

Pumpkin Pie

This pie is too delicious to serve just on holidays.

    1 envelope unflavored gelatin OR 1 tbsp. coarse
        agar flakes OR 2 tsp. fine agar powder
    1 c. water
    1 16-oz. can pumpkin
    1 c. date sugar OR 1/4 tsp. white stevia powder
    1 tsp. cinnamon
    1 tsp. nutmeg
    1/4 tsp. ground cloves
    1/4 tsp. allspice
    1/4 tsp. ginger
    1 baked pie crust, page 199 or 201

Put the water in a saucepan and sprinkle the gelatin or agar on it. Bring it to a boil and heat it over medium heat until the gelatin or agar is dissolved. Add the pumpkin, date sugar or stevia, and spices and cook the mixture over medium heat, stirring it almost constantly, until it is warmed through. Pour the filling into the cooled baked pie crust and refrigerate the pie. Makes 1 pie, or about 6 servings.

This recipe is free of wheat, milk, eggs, corn, soy, yeast, and refined sugar. If the pie crust used is an amaranth, quinoa, or coconut crust, it is also free gluten and of all grains.

Easy Fruit Crumble

This recipe is as easy as it is delicious. To obtain millet flakes, see "Sources of Special Foods," ch. 16.

> 4 c. fresh blueberries or peeled and sliced apples or
>   peaches OR 4 c. drained water-packed canned peaches
>   OR 1 lb. frozen blueberries
> 1 c. date sugar, divided
> 1/4 c. arrowroot or tapioca flour
> 2 to 6 tbsp. water, divided
> 1 c. oatmeal or millet flakes, uncooked
> 1 tsp. cinnamon
> 1/4 c. oil

Combine 1/2 c. date sugar and the arrowroot or tapioca flour and stir them into the fruit in an 8" by 8" baking dish. If you are using fresh fruit, sprinkle 4 tbsp. water over the blueberries or apples or 2 tbsp. water over the peaches. In a small bowl, combine the cereal, date sugar, and cinnamon. Stir in the oil until the mixture is crumbly. Stir in 2 tbsp. of water. Sprinkle the mixture on top of the fruit. Bake it at 325° for 30 to 40 minutes, or until the topping browns and the fruit is tender when pierced with a fork. Makes 6 to 8 servings.

This recipe is free of wheat, milk, eggs, corn, soy, yeast, and refined sugar. If made with the millet flakes, it is also free of gluten.

Cherry Cobbler

This easy dessert is one of my favorites.

> 2 1-lb. cans water-packed tart pie cherries, drained, OR
>   4 c. fresh pitted pie cherries
> 1 1/2 c. apple juice concentrate
> 4 tsp. arrowroot or tapioca flour OR 2 tbsp. tapioca
> 1 batch of any "Cobbler Topping," page 210

Boil down the apple juice concentrate to 3/4 c. volume and allow it to cool slightly. Stir in the arrowroot, tapioca flour, or tapioca. If you are using the tapioca, allow the mixture to stand for 5 minutes. Stir in the cherries and bring the mixture to a boil. If you are using the arrowroot or tapioca flour, simmer it until it is thickened and clear. (You do not have to simmer it if you use the tapioca.) Put the cherry mixture into a 2 1/2-quart casserole. Make the cobbler topping and put it on top of the fruit. Bake it at 350° for 25 to 35 minutes, or until the topping begins to brown. Makes 6 to 8 servings.

This recipe is free of wheat, milk, eggs, corn, soy, yeast, and refined sugar. If it is made with amaranth or quinoa topping, it is also free of gluten and all grains.

Blueberry Cobbler

This delicious cobbler can be made all year' round using fresh or frozen blueberries.

> 4 c. fresh blueberries OR 1 1-lb bag unsweetened frozen
>   blueberries
> 1/2 c. apple or pineapple juice concentrate, thawed
> 4 tsp. arrowroot or tapioca flour
> 1 batch of any "Cobbler Topping," page 210

Stir the arrowroot or tapioca flour into the juice in a saucepan. Add the fruit, bring the mixture to a boil, and simmer it until it is thickened and clear. Put it into a 2 1/2-quart casserole. Make the cobbler topping and put it on top of the fruit. Bake it at 350°

for 25 to 35 minutes or until the topping begins to brown. Makes 6 to 8 servings.

This recipe is free of wheat, milk, eggs, corn, soy, yeast, and refined sugar. If it is made with amaranth or quinoa topping, it is also free of gluten and all grains.

Peach Cobbler

This is any easy way to enjoy fresh peaches in the summertime, but can also be made with frozen peaches at any time of the year.

> 4 c. sliced fresh peaches OR 1 1-lb. bag unsweetened
>   frozen peaches
> 1/2 c. apple or pineapple juice concentrate, thawed
> 4 tsp. arrowroot or tapioca flour OR 2 tbsp. tapioca
> 1 batch of any "Cobbler Topping," page 210

Stir the arrowroot, tapioca flour, or tapioca into the juice in a saucepan. If you are using the tapioca, let it stand for 5 minutes. Add the peaches and bring the mixture to a boil. If you are using the arrowroot or tapioca flour, simmer it until it is thickened and clear. (You do not have to simmer it if you use the tapioca.) Put the peach mixture into a 2 1/2-quart casserole. Make the cobbler topping and put it on top of the fruit. Bake it at 350° for 25 to 35 minutes or until the topping begins to brown. Makes 6 to 8 servings.

This recipe is free of wheat, milk, eggs, corn, soy, yeast, and refined sugar. If it is made with amaranth or quinoa topping, it is also free of gluten and all grains.

Apple Cobbler

This is as delicious and homey as apple pie but not as much work to make.

> 4 to 5 apples, peeled, cored, and sliced to make 3 1/2
>   to 4 c. of slices
> 1/2 c. apple juice concentrate, thawed

4 tsp. arrowroot or tapioca flour OR 2 tbsp. tapioca
1 batch of any "Cobbler Topping," page 210

Stir the arrowroot, tapioca flour, or tapioca into the juice in a saucepan. If you are using the tapioca, let it stand for 5 minutes. Add the apples and bring the mixture to a boil. If you are using the arrowroot or tapioca flour, simmer it until it is thickened and clear. (You do not have to simmer it if you use the tapioca.) Put the apple mixture into a 2 1/2-quart casserole. Make the cobbler topping and put it on top of the fruit. Bake it at 350° for 25 to 35 minutes or until the topping begins to brown. Makes 6 to 8 servings.

This recipe is free of wheat, milk, eggs, corn, soy, yeast, and refined sugar. If it is made with amaranth or quinoa topping, it is also free of gluten and all grains.

Rhubarb Cobbler

This a great way to prepare rhubarb without using sugar.

3 c. sliced rhubarb
1 c. pineapple juice concentrate
4 tsp. arrowroot or tapioca flour
1 batch of any "Cobbler Topping," page 210

Boil down the pineapple juice concentrate to 1/2 c. volume and allow it to cool slightly. Stir in the arrowroot or tapioca flour. Add the rhubarb and bring the mixture to a boil, simmering it until it is thickened and clear. Put it into a 2 1/2-quart casserole. Make the cobbler topping and put it on top of the fruit. Bake it at 350° for 25 to 35 minutes, or until the topping begins to brown. Makes 6 to 8 servings.

This recipe is free of wheat, milk, eggs, corn, soy, yeast, and refined sugar. If it is made with amaranth or quinoa topping, it is also free of gluten and all grains.

Bing Cherry Cobbler

The dark, sweet fruit makes a pleasing contrast to the topping in this cobbler.

> 4 c. pitted fresh bing (dark) cherries OR 1 1-lb. bag
>   frozen unsweetened bing cherries
> 1/2 c. apple or pineapple juice concentrate, thawed
> 4 tsp. arrowroot or tapioca flour
> 1 batch of any "Cobbler Topping," page 210

Stir the arrowroot or tapioca flour into the juice in a saucepan. Add the fruit, bring it to a boil, and simmer it until it is thickened and clear. Put it into a 2 1/2-quart casserole. Make the cobbler topping and put it on top of the fruit. Bake it at 350° for 25 to 35 minutes or until the topping begins to brown. Makes 6 to 8 servings.

This recipe is free of wheat, milk, eggs, corn, soy, yeast, and refined sugar. If it is made with amaranth or quinoa topping, it is also free of gluten and all grains.

Cobbler Topping

Here are a variety of cobbler toppings to mix and match with whatever fruit you choose.

Barley:

> 7/8 c. (3/4 c. plus 2 tbsp.) barley flour
> 3/4 tsp. baking soda
> 1/8 tsp. unbuffered Vitamin C crystals
> 3/8 c. (1/4 c. plus 2 tbsp.) apple or pineapple juice
>   concentrate, thawed
> 2 tbsp. oil

Rye:

> 3/4 c. rye flour
> 3/4 tsp. baking soda

1/8 tsp. unbuffered Vitamin C crystals
3/8 c. (1/4 c. plus 2 tbsp.) apple or pineapple juice
    concentrate, thawed
2 tbsp. oil

Spelt:

7/8 c. (3/4 c. plus 2 tbsp.) spelt flour
3/4 tsp. baking soda
1/8 tsp. unbuffered Vitamin C crystals
3/8 c. (1/4 c. plus 2 tbsp.) apple juice concentrate, thawed
2 tbsp. oil

Amaranth:

3/4 c. amaranth flour
1/4 c. arrowroot
3/4 tsp. baking soda
1/8 tsp. unbuffered Vitamin C crystals
3/8 c. (1/4 c. plus 2 tbsp.) apple or pineapple juice
    concentrate, thawed
2 tbsp. oil

Quinoa:

5/8 c. (1/2 c. plus 2 tbsp.) quinoa flour
2 tbsp. tapioca flour
3/4 tsp. baking soda
1/8 tsp. unbuffered Vitamin C crystals
3/8 c. (1/4 c. plus 2 tbsp.) apple or pineapple juice
    concentrate, thawed
2 tbsp. oil

Choose one set of ingredients, above. Combine the flour(s), baking soda, and Vitamin C crystals in a large bowl. Mix together the juice and oil and stir them into the dry ingredients until they are just mixed in. Put the topping over the fruit mixture in the casserole dish and bake it at 350° for 25 to 35 minutes, or until the topping is slightly browned. Makes 6 to 8 servings.

This recipe is free of wheat, milk, eggs, corn, soy, yeast, and refined sugar. If the amaranth or quinoa versions are made, it is also free of gluten and all grains.

Shortcake

This is great with any kind of fruit.

A double batch of any "Cobbler Topping," above
Additional oil and flour

Make the cobbler topping as directed in the recipe. Spread it in an oiled and floured 8" round or square pan. Bake it at 350° for 25 to 30 minutes or until it is lightly browned. Cool it in the pan for 10 minutes, then remove it and allow it to cool completely on a wire rack. Cut it into wedges or squares. If you wish to, you may split each piece in half horizontally by carefully slicing it with a serrated knife. Serve it with fresh, thawed frozen, or canned fruit. Makes 6 to 9 servings.

This recipe is free of wheat, milk, eggs, corn, soy, yeast, and refined sugar. If the amaranth or quinoa versions are made, it is also free of gluten and all grains.

Apple Tapioca

This sugar-free dessert is delicious when made with fresh Jonathan apples in the fall.

7 c. peeled, cored, and thinly sliced apples
   (about 10 apples)
1 c. thawed apple juice concentrate, divided
3 tbsp. tapioca
1 1/2 tsp. cinnamon

Combine the apples, 1/2 c. of the juice, and the cinnamon in a saucepan, bring the mixture to a boil, and simmer it until the apples are tender, about 15 to 30 minutes, depending on the apples.

While the apples are cooking, combine the remaining 1/2 c. juice and the tapioca and allow them to stand for at least 5 minutes. When the apples are tender, stir the tapioca mixture into them, return them to a boil, and simmer them for an additional 3 to 5 minutes. Allow the pudding to stand for at least 20 minutes before serving it. Makes about 8 servings.

This recipe is free of all grains (including wheat and corn), gluten, milk, eggs, soy, yeast, and refined sugar.

Quinoa Pudding

This is a delicious grain-, milk-, and sugar-free takeoff on rice pudding.

    1 c. quinoa, thoroughly washed
    2 c. water
    1 c. apple juice concentrate, thawed, OR 1/4 tsp. white
        stevia powder plus an additional l c. water
    1 tsp. cinnamon
    1/2 c. raisins or finely chopped dried pears (optional)

Combine the quinoa and 2 c. water in a saucepan, bring it to a boil, and simmer it for 20 minutes, or until the quinoa is translucent. (If you wish to, you may use 3 c. cooked quinoa instead.) Add the apple juice concentrate or the stevia and additional water, the cinnamon, and the dried fruit and simmer the mixture for 10 to 15 minutes more, or until the liquid is absorbed. Or, if you would rather bake the pudding, combine the cooked quinoa, juice or stevia plus water, cinnamon, and fruit in a 1 1/2-quart covered casserole and bake it at 350° for 20 to 30 minutes, or until the liquid is absorbed. Sprinkle the top of the pudding with cinnamon and serve it warm. Makes 4 to 6 servings.

This recipe is free of all grains (including wheat and corn), gluten, milk, eggs, soy, yeast, and refined sugar.

Carob Pudding

This pudding is delicious sweetened with either honey or stevia.

> 2 c. goat or coconut milk plus 1/3 c. honey OR 2 1/4 c.
>   goat or coconut milk plus 1/8 tsp. white stevia powder
> 5 tbsp. arrowroot
> 1/4 c. carob powder
> 2 tsp. corn-free natural vanilla (optional)

Stir together the carob powder, arrowroot, and stevia (if you are using it) in a saucepan. Add 1/2 c. of the milk and stir the mixture until it is smooth. Add the rest of the milk and the honey (if you are using it), and cook it over medium heat until it thickens and begins to boil. Stir in the vanilla and serve the pudding warm or cold. Makes 4 servings.

This recipe is free of all grains (including wheat and corn), gluten, cow's milk, eggs, soy, yeast. If the stevia is used, it is also free of refined sugar.

Coconut Pudding or Finger Pudding

This is delicious in a "Coconut Pie Crust," page 201, with coconut sprinkled on top.

> 1 14-oz. can coconut milk (1 2/3 c.)
> 1/4 c. honey OR 1/8 tsp. white stevia powder
> 1/4 c. tapioca flour or arrowroot for a soft pudding
>   OR 3/8 c.(1/4 c. plus 2 tbsp.) water chestnut
>   starch for a finger pudding
> Unsweetened grated coconut (optional)

Combine the coconut milk, honey or stevia, and starch in a saucepan and bring the mixture to a boil. Cook it over medium heat, stirring it occasionally at first and then constantly as it begins to thicken, until it is very thick. For the soft pudding, pour it into a bowl or individual dessert glasses, sprinkle it with coconut if you wish, and serve it warm or cold with a spoon. For the finger pudding, pour it into an oiled 8" by 8" pan and sprinkle it with grated coconut, if you wish. Refrigerate it until it is very cold, cut it into squares, and serve it on plates. Makes 4 to 6 servings of soft pudding, or 6 to 9 servings of finger pudding.

This recipe is free of all grains (including wheat and corn), gluten, milk, eggs, soy, and yeast. If the stevia is used, it is also free of refined sugar.

Tapioca Pudding

This pudding is good if you make it with either the honey or the stevia. For a change from "plain vanilla," try it with "The Spicery Shoppe" alcohol-free, corn-free natural flavorings. It is especially delicious with their almond, banana, lemon, orange, or maple flavorings. (See "Sources of Special Foods," ch. 16.)

 2 3/4 c. goat milk
 1/4 c. honey OR 1/8 tsp. white stevia powder
 1/4 c. quick-cooking tapioca
 1/4 c. tapioca flour
 1 tsp. corn-free natural vanilla or other flavoring
   (optional)

Combine the milk, honey or stevia, and tapioca in a saucepan and allow them to stand for at least 5 minutes. Stir in the tapioca flour and cook the mixture over medium heat, stirring it almost constantly, until it comes to a full boil. Stir in the flavoring. Chill it thoroughly before serving it. Makes about 6 servings.

This recipe is free of all grains (including wheat and corn), gluten, cow's milk, eggs, soy, and yeast. If the stevia is used, it is also free of refined sugar.

13

Beverages, Condiments, and Miscellaneous Recipes and Notes

This chapter contains recipes for some of the little things that go along with a meal that make it special. There are recipes for beverages, condiments that will liven up burgers of any kind, cranberry sauce or jelly for the holidays, stevia-sweetened "Mock Maple Syrup" for breakfast, and several types of snacks. This chapter also contains tips about substitutions, altitude, etc.

Hot Carob

This comforting beverage is delicious when you make it with either the honey or the stevia.

>   1 tbsp. carob powder
>   2 tbsp. hot water
>   1 c. goat milk
>   2 tbsp. honey OR 1/16 tsp. white stevia powder
>   OR 1/2 tsp. stevia working solution, page 226.

Combine the carob powder and water in a saucepan and stir them to remove the lumps in the carob. Add the goat milk and sweetener and heat the mixture until it just begins to steam. Makes 1 serving which is just the right size to fill a 10-oz mug.

This recipe is free of all grains (including wheat and corn), gluten, cow's milk, eggs, soy, and yeast. If the stevia is used it is free of refined sugar.

Dacopa Au Lait

Dacopa, a beverage made from roasted dahlia roots, is delicious with a little coconut or goat milk in it. See "Sources of Special Foods," ch. 16, for where to obtain it.

> 2 tsp. dacopa crystals
> 1 c. boiling water
> 3 tbsp. goat or coconut milk (optional)
> 1 tsp. honey (optional)

Put the dacopa crystals in a 10-oz. mug. Stir in the boiling water until the crystals dissolve. Then stir in the milk and honey. Makes one serving.

This recipe is free of all grains (including wheat and corn), gluten, cow's milk, eggs, soy, and yeast. If the honey is omitted it is free of refined sugar.

Fruit Shake

Let your imagination soar as you devise combinations of milks, juices, and fruits to use in this recipe. Some good ones are coconut milk with banana and honey, pineapple juice with banana, and apple juice with kiwi.

> 3/4 c. chilled coconut or goat milk or fruit juice
> 3/4 c. frozen berries or other frozen fruit that has
>   been cut into small pieces OR 1 small or 1/2 large
>   frozen banana, cut into chunks
> 1 tbsp. honey OR 2 tbsp. frozen fruit juice concentrate
>   (optional)

Puree all the ingredients together in a blender. Makes one large or two small servings.

This recipe is free of all grains (including wheat and corn), gluten, cow's milk, eggs, soy, and yeast. If the honey is omitted it is free of refined sugar.

Carob Soda

This is delicious with "Carob Ice Cream," page 186, "Strawberry Ice Cream," page 187, or "Vanilla Ice Cream," page 188.

    3 tbsp. "Carob Syrup," page 197
    3/4 c. chilled carbonated water
    1 to 2 ice cubes OR one scoop of ice cream

In a glass, mix the carob syrup thoroughly with 1/4 c. of the water. Add the rest of the water and the ice, if you are using it. Top it with the ice cream, if you are using it. Makes one serving.

This recipe is free of all grains (including wheat and corn), gluten, cow's milk, eggs, soy, and yeast.

Donna Gates' Lemonade or Cranberry Cooler

Donna Gates, president of a Washington, D.C. area Candida support group, reports that these beverages help group members satisfy their desire for something sweet without aggravating their yeast problems. These beverage recipes will soon be published in her book, The Body Ecology Diet.

    1/2 c. lemon juice OR 3/4 c. pure unsweetened
        cranberry juice, such as Knudsen's "Just Cranberry,"
        OR 1/3 c. cranberry juice concentrate, such as Hain
        Cranberry Juice Concentrate
    1/8 tsp. white stevia powder
    4 c. cold water or chilled carbonated water

Mix the juice and stevia together until the stevia is completely dissolved. Add the water and serve the drink. Makes about 4 servings.

This recipe is free of all grains (including wheat and corn), gluten, milk, eggs, soy, yeast, and refined sugar.

Grandma's Cranberry Sauce or Jelly

This recipe is adapted from one my mother has been making for holidays for as long as I can remember.

> 12 oz. fresh cranberries (about 4 c.)
> 1 1/2 to 2 1/2 c. (the amount depending on the degree
>   of sweetness desired) apple or pineapple juice
>   concentrate, thawed OR 3/4 c.water plus 1/4 tsp.
>   white stevia powder

If you are using the fruit juice, boil it down to half of its original volume (to 3/4 to 1 1/4 c.). Combine the water or juice with the cranberries in a saucepan, bring them to a boil, and simmer them, stirring them often, for 15 to 20 minutes, or until the cranberries have popped. If you are using the stevia, thoroughly stir it into the sauce at this point. Refrigerate the sauce until serving time. Makes about 2 c. of cranberry sauce.

If you prefer cranberry jelly, after cooking the sauce and adding the stevia (if you are using it), put the sauce through a food mill or press it through a strainer. Refrigerate the jelly until serving time. (Children tend to prefer the jelly because the cranberry skins, which may be bitter, have been removed.) Makes about 1 2/3 c. cranberry jelly.

This recipe is free of all grains (including wheat and corn), gluten, milk, eggs, soy, yeast, and refined sugar.

Mock Maple Syrup

Here is something to put on pancakes or waffles for people who must avoid fruit sugars as well as refined sweeteners.

1 tsp. arrowroot OR 1 1/2 tsp. tapioca flour
1 c. water
1/8 tsp. white stevia powder
1/2 tsp. corn-free natural maple flavoring
1/2 tsp. corn-free natural vanilla (optional)

Stir the arrowroot or tapioca flour into the water in a saucepan. Bring it to a boil. The mixture will thicken slightly and become clear. Stir in the stevia and flavorings until the stevia is completely dissolved and serve the syrup. Any leftover syrup may be refrigerated and, if necessary, reheated to redissolve the starch. Makes about 1 c. of syrup.

This recipe is free of all grains (including wheat and corn), gluten, milk, eggs, soy, yeast, and refined sugar.

Easy Catsup

If you can tolerate canned tomato products, this is a quick and easy way to make something yummy to put on your burgers.

1 6-oz. can tomato paste
1/2 c. water plus 1/4 c. thawed apple or pineapple juice
    concentrate OR 3/4 c. water plus 1/8 tsp. white
    stevia powder
2 tsp. finely chopped onion OR 1/2 tsp. dry onion
    flakes (optional)
1 whole clove
1/2 tsp. salt
2 tsp. tart tasting unbuffered Vitamin C crystals,
    such as Vital Life brand

Combine the tomato sauce, juice or water plus stevia, onion, clove, and salt in a saucepan and bring them to a boil. Simmer them, covered, for 30 to 45 minutes, stirring them at least every 5 to 10 minutes. Remove the clove and stir in the Vitamin C crystals. Makes about 3/4 to 1 c. catsup.

This recipe is free of all grains (including wheat and corn), gluten, milk, eggs, soy, yeast, and refined sugar.

Fresh Tomato Catsup

This recipe is adapted from the one my mother uses to put up tomatoes from her garden.

    2 lbs. Italian plum or Roma tomatoes
    1 tsp. finely minced onion (optional)
    1/2 tsp. dry mustard
    1 tsp. salt (optional)
    Dash of pepper (optional)
    4 slices of pineapple plus 3/4 c. pineapple juice
        OR 1/16 to 1/8 tsp. white stevia powder OR 1/2 to
        1 tsp. stevia working solution, page 226
    1 tsp. tart tasting unbuffered Vitamin C crystals, such as
        Vital Life brand

Puree the tomatoes in a food processor or blender to yield about 4 c. of puree. If you are using the pineapple, puree it in the pineapple juice. In a saucepan, combine the tomatoes, onion, mustard, salt, pepper, and pineapple or stevia. Bring the mixture to a boil, reduce the heat, and simmer it, stirring it often, for about one hour, or until it is thick. Stir in the Vitamin C. Makes 2 c. of catsup.

This recipe is free of all grains (including wheat and corn), gluten, milk, eggs, soy, yeast, and refined sugar. If you make it with the stevia, it is suitable for use on a strict low-yeast diet.

Mild Mustard

This tastes like ordinary mustard but does not contain vinegar.

    2 tsp. dry mustard
    1 c. water
    3 tsp. arrowroot
    1/4 tsp. tumeric
    1/2 tsp. salt (optional)
    1 tsp. tart tasting unbuffered Vitamin C crystals,
        such as Vital Life brand

Combine the dry mustard and water in a saucepan and allow them to stand for 10 minutes. Stir in the arrowroot, tumeric, and salt and heat the mixture over medium heat, stirring it often, until it thickens and boils. Stir in the Vitamin C crystals and refrigerate the mustard. Makes about 1 c. of mustard.

This recipe is free of all grains (including wheat and corn), gluten, milk, eggs, soy, yeast, and refined sugar.

Hot Mustard

This mustard is for those who like it hot.

> 1/4 c. dry mild dijon style mustard (See "Sources
> of Special Foods," ch. 16.)
> 3 tbsp. water

Mix the mustard and water together. Refrigerate the mustard. Makes about 1/3 c. of mustard.

This recipe is free of all grains (including wheat and corn), gluten, milk, eggs, soy, yeast, and refined sugar.

Cucumber Relish

This recipe developed by Marge Jones is from The Yeast Connection Cookbook. It is delicious with burgers of all kinds in place of pickles.

> 2 tbsp. water
> 1/4 tsp. tart tasting unbuffered Vitamin C crystals,
> such as Vital Life brand
> 3 cucumbers
> Salt
> Freshly ground black pepper to taste (optional)
> 2 tbsp. fresh dill, finely chopped OR 2 tsp. dried dill

In a small cup, mix the water and Vitamin C crystals; set them aside. Peel the cucumbers and cut them in half lengthwise. Remove the seeds with a spoon or melon-baller, and discard them.

Shred the cucumbers in a food processor or by hand. Salt them lightly and place them in a strainer for 10 to 15 minutes to drain. Press them lightly with your hand, then turn them into a bowl. When the Vitamin C crystals dissolve in the water, add the mixture to the cucumbers. Add the dill and mix well. Cover and refrigerate at least 2 hours. Before serving taste and add salt if needed. Makes about 3 c. of relish.

This recipe is free of all grains (including wheat and corn), gluten, milk, eggs, soy, yeast, and refined sugar.

Gorp

This is a great snack to take along on outings.

   2 c. cashew pieces
   1 1/2 c. raisins
   1 c. milk-free unsweetened carob chips

Mix together the cashew pieces, raisins, and carob chips and enjoy. Try your own combinations of dried fruits and nuts. A rule of thumb is to use smaller amounts of smaller-size ingredients. Makes about 3 1/2 c. of gorp.

This recipe is free of all grains (including wheat and corn), gluten, milk, eggs, soy, yeast, and refined sugar.

Fruit Roll-Ups

Kids love having these for a sugar-free and nutritious snack.

Strawberry, Raspberry, or Cherry:
   1 lb. of fresh strawberries or raspberries
      OR a 1-lb. bag of frozen, unsweetened
      strawberries or bing cherries
   4 c. unsweetened applesauce

Banana:
   About 12 large bananas

Peach:
> 4 lbs. fresh peaches OR 3 1-lb. bags of frozen
>   unsweetened peaches OR about 5 1/2 1-lb. cans of
>   water-packed canned peaches, drained

Grape:
> About 4 1-lb. cans water-packed canned pears, drained,
>   yielding 4 2/3 c pear puree
> 1 1/3 c. grape juice concentrate, thawed

Apple:
> 6 c. unsweetened applesauce
> 1 1/2 tsp. cinnamon

Choose one set of ingredients, above. If you are using fresh fruit, peel or clean it and cut it into chunks. Combine all of the ingredients in a food processor or blender and puree them to yield about 6 c. of pureed fruit. Cover the trays of a food dehydrator or cover cookie sheets, platters, and trays with cellophane or heavy plastic wrap. Put 1/3 c. to 3/8 c. portions of the pureed fruit onto the cellophane or plastic wrap and spread them out into 7" circles, so that the puree is about 1/4" thick. Dry them in a dehydrator for about 10 to 12 hours at 135° or out in the sun, covered with netting, on a hot (90°), dry day for 10 to 12 hours. You can tell that the fruit leather has dried long enough when it does not have any sticky spots, but also is not so dry that it is brittle. Cut the cellophane or plastic wrap so that the individual circles are separated and roll them up. Makes 14 to 16 fruit roll-ups.

This recipe is free of all grains (including wheat and corn), gluten, milk, eggs, soy, yeast, and refined sugar.

Carob Fudge

This occasional treat doesn't last long around our house.

> 5/8 c. (1/2 c. plus 2 tbsp.) honey
> 2 tbsp. oil
> 1/2 c. carob powder

3/4 c. powdered goat milk
2 tbsp. finely chopped nuts (optional)

Thoroughly mix together the honey and oil. Add the carob powder and powdered milk and beat the fudge until it is smooth. Knead in the nuts, if you wish to use them. Spread the fudge in a lightly oiled pie dish, refrigerate it, and cut it into 3/4" squares just before serving it. Store the fudge refrigerated in the pie dish, because it tends to spread. Makes about 50 squares.

This recipe is free of all grains (including wheat and corn), gluten, milk, eggs, soy, and yeast.

Candy Canes

This is a Christmas treat to keep the corn-allergic child from feeling left out.

3/4 c. water
3 c. cane or beet sugar
1/4 tsp. cream of tartar
Coconut oil or butter
1/4 tsp. natural spearmint oil

Bring the water to a boil in a saucepan. Add the sugar and cream of tartar and stir the mixture until the sugar dissolves. When the mixture returns to a boil, use a brush and hot water to thoroughly wash down any sugar crystals on the sides of the pan into the sugar solution. Put a candy thermometer into the pan so it is in the solution but not touching the bottom of the pan. Cook the solution without stirring it until the temperature on the thermometer reaches 312° at sea level, or 100° above the temperature of boiling water in your area. (See "The Effect of Altitude on Candy Making," page 227.) While the sugar solution is boiling, warm the coconut oil until it just begins to melt and use it or butter to thoroughly grease a marble slab or a very large heavy stoneware platter. Watch the candy thermometer continuously as the solution nears its final temperature. When it reaches the right temperature immediately pour it onto the marble slab or platter. As the edges of the candy cool, lift them toward the center with a candy scraper or metal knife-type of spatula. When the candy is partially cooled, sprinkle the spearmint oil over its surface and continue to work it with the scraper or spatula. When it is barely cool enough to handle, form it into a ball and pull it until it takes on a sheen, about 20 pulls. Form it into a rope, cut it into pieces, and form them into cane shapes. Allow the candy canes to harden on the marble slab or platter. Makes 8 to 10 10" candy canes.

This recipe is free of all grains (including wheat and corn), gluten, milk, eggs, soy, and yeast.

Stevia Working Solution

This solution allows you to add amounts of stevia too small to be measured as a powder to recipes.

> 1 tsp. white stevia powder
> 2 tbsp. plus 2 tsp. water

Put the stevia powder into the water and stir it until it is completely dissolved. Any solution that you do not use immediately may be refrigerated for future use. Making a solution makes it easier to measure small amounts of stevia accurately. For example:

> 2 tsp. solution = 1/4 tsp. white powder
> 1 tsp. solution = 1/8 tsp. white powder
> 1/2 tsp. solution = 1/16 tsp. white powder
> 1/4 tsp. solution = 1/32 tsp. white powder.

This recipe is free of all grains (including wheat and corn), gluten, milk, eggs, soy, yeast, and refined sugar.

Notes and Tips On...

...SUBSTITUTIONS: Many ingredients occur together repeatedly in these recipes (apple with quinoa, grape with rye, etc.) because I use them together on the same day of my family's rotation schedule. To fit your family's rotation schedule, substitute any fruit juice, fruit juice concentrate, or fruit puree (such as applesauce) for another fruit juice, etc. You can use arrowroot and tapioca flour interchangeably in baking. Substituting the various alternative flours for each other may require other modifications in the recipe, but do not be afraid to try substitutions. Also, if you use a very finely milled flour or a coarsely milled or blender-ground flour you may have to change the amount of liquid used in the recipe.

...FLOURING CAKE PANS, PASTRY CLOTHS, ETC: Always use the same kind of flour used in the recipe.

...MEASURING LESS THAN 1/4 TSP. OF STEVIA OR OTHER INGREDIENTS: Fill the 1/4 tsp. measuring spoon with stevia or the ingredient to be measured, level it off with a knife, and then, using a dinner knife with a rounded end, cut the powder in the spoon in half and scrape half of it out of the spoon and back into its container to measure 1/8 tsp. If 1/16 tsp. is required, cut the remaining 1/8 tsp. in half again and scrape half of it out. Use what remains in the spoon. Or, use "Stevia Working Solution," page 226, to measure very small amounts of stevia.

...THE EFFECT OF ALTITUDE ON BAKING: All of the recipes in this cookbook were developed at an altitude of about 5,000 feet. Many of them have been used at lower altitudes without difficulty. Since they are not for delicate baked products, such as angel food cakes, etc., there is little chance of difficulty at lower altitudes. However, if you do encounter difficulty, the following changes may be made in the recipe:

1. Increase the amount of baking soda and Vitamin C crystals by 1/4 of the amount called for in the recipe.
2. Decrease the amount of liquid by 2 to 3 tablespoons per cup of liquid called for.
3. Decrease the baking temperature by 25°.

...THE EFFECT OF ALTITUDE ON CANDY MAKING: When making candy at any altitude except sea level, you should check the boiling temperature of water in your area before starting.

Bring a pan of water to a boil with a candy thermometer in the water but not touching the bottom of the pan. Let it boil for a few minutes; then read the temperature on the thermometer. Subtract this temperature from 212°, then subtract this difference from the sea level final temperature to cook the candy to given in the recipe.

...THE "FREE OF" COMMENTS AT THE END OF THE RECIPES: Wheat and corn are listed separately because they are the most common allergens among the grains. Recipes containing honey, maple syrup, or molasses are not listed as being free of refined sugar. Molasses is partially refined, maple syrup has been greatly concentrated, and honey has been refined and concentrated by the bees. Recipes containing fruit juice concentrates or date sugar (which is ground dried dates) are listed as being free of refined sugar because they are not refined sweeteners and fruit sugars are often well tolerated in moderate amounts.

14

Nutritional Values
of
Alternative Flours

COMPARATIVE NUTRITIVE VALUES OF ALTERNATIVE FLOURS

Per 100 Gram Portions (Raw Dry Weight)

	AMARANTH	ARROWROOT	BARLEY	BUCKWHEAT	CASSAVA (TAPIOCA)	CHESTNUT	GARBANZO	MILLET	OATS	QUINOA	RICE	RYE	SPELT	TEFF	WHEAT (FOR COMPARISON)
Energy (Kcal)	358	362	349	360	352	362	368	368	357	351	390	362	382	332	361
Protein (g)	12.9	0	8.2	11.7	0.6	6.1	20.1	9.9	13.0	12.3	8.2	12.1	14.3	8.7	12.7
Fat (g)	7.2	0	1.0	2.4	0.2	3.7	6.6	4.1	6.5	6.1	2.6	2.2	2.9	1.9	3.3
Carbohydrates (g)	65.1	87.5	78.8	72.9	86.4	76.2	59.6	72.9	63.0	67.7	83.5	73.4	74.5	75.5	71.7
Calcium (mg)	247	0	16	114	10	50	100	20.0	59.7	112	39.3	38.0	6.9	146	37.0
Magnesium (mg)			37	252				167	169		91.7	133			160
Iron (mg)	3.4	0	2.0	3.1	0.4	3.2	7.0	6.8	3.9	7.5	1.6	3.7	4.2	4.9	4.3
Zinc (mg)		0.07									1.96	3.25	3.4		2.7
Vitamin A (IU)	0	0	0	0	0		33.4	0	0	0	0	0	41.0	0	0
Vitamin E (IU)		tr.						0.05	1.40		0.49	1.65			1.40
Vitamin C (mg)	3.0	0	0	0	0		0	0	0	3.00	0	0	0		0
Thiamin (mg)	0.14	0	0.12	0.60	0	0.23	0.12	0.73	0.52	0.36	0.29	0.43	0.65	0.38	0.66
Riboflavin (mg)	0.32	0	0.05		0	0.37	0.33	0.38	0.13	0.42	0.07	0.22	0.23	0.14	0.12
Niacin (mg)	1.00	0	3.10	4.40	0	1.00	0.70	2.30	0.52	1.40	4.58	1.60	8.46	1.90	4.40

ESSENTIAL AMINO ACIDS IN MG.

Per 100 Grams of Food

	AMARANTH	ARROWROOT	BARLEY	BUCKWHEAT	CASSAVA (TAPIOCA)	CHESTNUT	GARBANZO	MILLET	OATS	QUINOA	RICE	RYE	SPELT	TEFF	WHEAT (FOR COMPARISON)
Arginine			555	178				409	876			541		337	602
Histadine			248	34				165	292	496		261		188	299
Isoleucine			421	46				562	526	513	390	414	560	378	426
Leucine			784	64				1059	1012	903	714	728	900	724	871
Lysine			406	67				262	517	843	324	401	275	273	374
Methionine			196	22				222	232	168	147	172	400	226	190
Phenylalanine			603	41				427	698	574	416	522	700	207	589
Threonine			389	43				204	462	524	324	395	560	334	382
Tryptophan			180	19				68	176		92	87	180	146	
Valine			592	54				566	711	629	580	561	580	491	577

AMINO ACID PROFILE OF HUMAN MILK*

Per 12 Grams of Protein

Arginine	460 mg.
Histadine	300 mg.
Isoleucine	480 mg.
Leucine	1040 mg.
Lysine	810 mg.
Methionine	190 mg.
Phenylalanine	410 mg.
Threonine	530 mg.
Tryptophan	200 mg.
Valine	540 mg.

*Human milk is the ideal protein for human beings, so its amino acid profile is given for comparison to the amino acid profiles of alternative flours.

The nutritional values for alternative flours and human milk were derived from the following sources:

Considine, Douglas M. and Glenn D. Considine. *Foods and Food Production Encyclopedia*. Van Nostrand Reinhold Company, 1982, pages 153, 352, 1289, 1355, 1356, 1696, 2124.

Ensminger, Audrey H., M. E. Ensminger, James E. Konlande, and John R. K. Robson, M.D. *Foods and Nutrition Encyclopedia*, Volumes 1 and 2. Pegus Press, Clovis, California, 1983, pages 830 to 833, 840, 841, 910, 911, and 1879.

Strehlow, Wighard. *The Wonder Food Spelt*. 1989, pages 10 & 11.

Wood, Rebecca. *Quinoa the Supergrain*. Japan Publications, Inc., Tokyo, 1989, page 36.

15

Food Family Tables

TABLE 1

ALPHABETICAL LISTING OF FOODS WITH THEIR LOCATIONS IN TABLES 2 AND 3

A

Abalone—p.254
Agar, <u>Gelidium species</u>—p.240
Agar, <u>Gracillaria species</u>—p.241
Aguamiel (sweetener from
    the maguey plant)—p.252
Albacore—p.258
Alfalfa—p.245
Algin, or alginic acid—p.241
Alligator—p.259
Allspice—p.247
Almond—p.245
Aloe vera—p.252
Amaranth—p.243
Anchovy—p.255
Anise—p.248
Antelope—p.261
Apple—p.245
Apricot—p.245

Arrowroot, Dasheen—p.252
Arrowroot, East Indian—p.253
Arrowroot, Fiji—p.253
Arrowroot, Florida—p.242
Arrowroot, Musa—p.253
Arrowroot, Queensland—p.253
Arrowroot, West Indian—p.253
Artichoke, Globe—p.250
Artichoke, Jerusalem—p.250
Asparagus—p.252
Avocado—p.244

B

Bamboo shoots—p.251
Banana—p.253
Barberry—p.243
Barley—p.251
Basil—p.249
Bass, Black—p.257
Bass, Freshwater—p.257
Bass, Sea—p.257
Baker's Yeast—p.240
Bayleaf—p.243
Bean, Aduki, Black, Garbanzo,
    Kidney, Lima, Lupine, Navy,
    Pinto, Soy, White, etc.—p.245

Bear—p.260
Beef—p.261
Beet—p.243
Beet Sugar—p.243
Belgian Endive—p.250
Berries—See listing under
    individual berry names
Bison—p.261
Blackberry—p.244
Blackfish—p.256
Blueberry—p.248
Bluefish—p.258
Boar, Wild—p.261
Bonito—p.258
Boysenberry—p.244
Brazil Nut—p.248
Breadfruit—p.242
Brewer's Yeast—p.240
Broccoli—p.244
Brussel Sprouts—p.244
Buckwheat—p.242
Buffalo—p.261
Butterfish—p.257
Butternut (White Walnut)—p.243

C

Cabbage, all varieties—p.244
Cabbage-palm—p.252
Camel—p.261
Camote—p.249
Cane Sugar—p.251
Canola (oil and seeds)—p.244
Cantalope—p.249
Caper—p.244
Carageen—p.241
Carambola—p.246
Caraway—p.248
Cardamon—p.253
Caribou—p.261
Carob Bean, Carob Bean
    Gum—p.245
Carob Flour or Powder
    (from carob bean pod)—p.245
Carp—p.256
Carrot—p.248
Cashew—p.246
Cassava—p.246
Castor Oil—p.246

Catfish, Freshwater—p.256
Catfish, Sea—p.256
Cauliflower—p.244
Celeriac—p.248
Celery—p.248
Celery Leaf or Seed—p.248
Ceriman—p.252
Chamomile—p.250
Chard—p.243
Cheese Molds—p.240
Cheese—In the same family
    as the animal that produced the
    milk from which they are made
Cherimoya—p.243
Cherry—p.245
Chervil—p.248
Chestnut—p.243
Chestnut, Water—p.251
Chicken—p.260
Chicken Eggs—p.259
Chickpea (Garbanzo Bean)—p.245
Chicle (Chewing Gum
    Base)—p.248
Chicory—p.250
Chives—p.252
Chlorella species—p.241
Chocolate—p.247
Chokecherry—p.245
Chub—p.256
Cider, Apple—p.245
Cinnamon—p.244
Citron—p.246
Clam, Soft-shelled—p.254
Clam, Thick-shelled—p.254
Cloves—p.247
Cockle—p.254
Cocoa—p.247
Coconut, Coconut Meal,
    Coconut Oil—p.252
Cod—p.256
Coffee—p.249
Cola Nut—p.247
Collards—p.244
Coriander—p.248
Corn—p.251
Cottonseed (Oil)—p.247
Crab, all varieties—p.255
Cranberry—p.248
Crappie—p.257

Crayfish—p.255
Cream of Tartar—p.246
Cress, all varieties—p.244
Croaker—p.257
Crocodile—p.259
Cucumber—p.250
Cumin—p.248
"Currant," commercial
    dried—p.247
Currant, True—p.244
Cusk—p.256
Custard Apple—p.243
Cuttlefish—p.254

D

Dab—p.259
Dacopa (beverage made from
    Dahlia root)—p.250
Dandelion—p.250
Date, all varieties—p.251
Date Sugar—p.252
Deer—p.261
Dewberry—p.244
Dill—p.248
Dolphin—p.260
Dolphinfish (Mahi Mahi)—p.257
Dory, all varieties except
    Oreo Dory—p.257
Dory, Oreo—p.257
Dove—p.260
Drum—p.257
Duck—p.259
Duck Eggs—p.259
Dulse—p.241

E

Eel—p.256
Eggplant—p.249
Eggs, Chicken—p.259
Eggs, other—In the same families
    as the animals that produce
    them
Elk—p.261
Endive, all varieties—p.250
Escarole—p.250
Eucalyptus—p.247
Evening Primrose (Oil)—p.247

F

Fennel—p.248
Fig—p.242
Filbert—p.243
Flaxseed (and oil)—p.246
Flounder—p.259
Frog—p.259

G

Garbanzo Bean and Flour—p.245
Garlic—p.252
Ginger—p.253
Ginseng—p.248
Goat—p.261
Goose—p.259
Goose Eggs—p.259
Gooseberry—p.244
Grape, all varieties—p.246
Grapefruit—p.246
Grenadine—p.248
Groundnut—p.251
Grouper—p.257
Grouse—p.260
Guava—p.247
Guinea-fowl—p.260
Gum Acacia—p.245
Gum Arabic—p.245
Gum Tragacanth—p.245

H

Haddock—p.256
Hake—p.256
Halibut, California
    (lefteyed)—p.258
Halibut (righteyed)—p.258
Harvestfish—p.257
Herring—p.255
Hibiscus—p.247
Hickory Nut—p.243
Hoki—p.256
Hops—p.242
Horse—p.261
Horseradish—p.244
Huckleberry—p.248

T

V

W

Y

Z

TABLE 2

FOOD FAMILIES OF THE PLANT KINGDOM[1,2]

I. Division Mycophyta (molds and yeasts)
  A. Subdivision Eumycotina
    1. Class Ascomycetes
      a. Subclass Hemiascomycetidae
        [1] Order Saccharomycetaceae
          [a] FAMILY SACCHAROMYCETACEAE
            BAKER'S YEAST
            BREWER'S YEAST
        [2] Order Eurotiales
          [a] FAMILY EUROTIACEAE
            CITRIC ACID PRODUCING MOLDS
              (Aspergillus species)
            CHEESE MOLDS
              Penicillium roqueforti
              P. camemberti
              P. species (other cheeses)
    2. Class Basidiomycetes
      a. Subclass Homobasidiomycetidae
        [1] Order Agaricales
          [a] MUSHROOM FAMILIES
            (BOLETACEAE, RUSSULACEAE,
            AGARICACEAE)
              MUSHROOMS
              PUFFBALLS
              TRUFFLES
II. Division Rhodophyta
  A. Class Rhodophyceae
    1. Subclass Florideophycidae
      a. Order Nemalionales
        [1] FAMILY GELIDIACEAE
          AGAR (Gelidium species)
      b. Order Gigartinales
        [1] FAMILY GRACILARIACEAE

AGAR (<u>Gracillaria sp.</u>)

EDIBLE SEAWEEDS of <u>Gracillaria</u>

<u>species</u>

   [2] FAMILY GIGARTINACEAE

CARAGEEN (<u>Chondrus sp.</u>)

IRISH MOSS (an edible seaweed,

<u>Chondrus crispus</u>)

  c. Order Palmariales

    [1] FAMILY PALMARIACEAE

DULSE (an edible seaweed)

 2. Subclass Bangiophycidae

  a. Order Bangiales

    [1] FAMILY BANGIACEAE

NORI (an edible seaweed)

III. Division Phaeophyta

  A. Class Phyophyceae

   1. Order Laminariales

    a. FAMILY LAMINARIACEAE

KOMBU

EDIBLE SEAWEEDS of <u>Laminaria</u>

<u>species</u>

    b. FAMILY ALARIACEAE

WAKAME

  B. MANY FAMILIES OF BROWN ALGAE

KELP (an edible seaweed)

ALGIN OR ALGINIC ACID

(food additive)

IV. Division Chlorophyta

  A. Class Cholorphyceae

   1. Order Chlorococcales

    a. FAMILY OOCYSTACEAE

<u>CHLORELLA SPECIES</u>

(a nutritional supplement)

V. Divison Cyanophyta

  A. Class Cyanophyceae

   1. Order Oscilliatoriales

    a. FAMILY NOSTOCINACEAE

SPIRULINA SPECIES
(a nutritional supplement)

VI. Division Pteropsida
   A. Class Gymnospermae
      1. Order Cycadales
         a. CYCAD FAMILY (CYCADACEAE)
               FLORIDA ARROWROOT
      2. Order Coniferales
         a. PINE FAMILY (PINACEAE)
               JUNIPER (used to make gin)
               PINE NUTS
   B. Subdivision Angiospermae
      1. Class Dicotyledones
         a. Subclass Apetale
           [1] Order Piperales
              [a] PEPPER FAMILY (PIPERACEAE)
                  BLACK PEPPER
                  WHITE PEPPER
           [2] Order Proteales
              [a] PROTEA FAMILY (PROTEACEAE)
                  MACADAMIA NUT
           [3] Order Urticales
              [a] MULBERRY FAMILY (MORACEAE)
                  MULBERRY
                  FIG
                  BREADFRUIT
              [b] HEMP FAMILY (CANNABINACEAE)
                  HOPS (used in making beer)
           [4] Order Polygonales
              [a] BUCKWHEAT FAMILY
                  (POLYGONACEAE)
                  BUCKWHEAT
                  RHUBARB
                  SORREL
           [5] Order Juglandales
              [a] WALNUT FAMILY (JUGLANDACEAE)
                  BLACK WALNUT

WHITE WALNUT (BUTTERNUT)
ENGLISH WALNUT
PECAN
HICKORY NUT

[6] Order Fagales
  [a] BEECH FAMILY (FAGACEAE)
    CHESTNUT
  [b] BIRCH FAMILY (BETULACEAE)
    FILBERT
    NATURAL WINTERGREEN FLAVOR

[7] Order Chenopodiales
  [a] GOOSEFOOT FAMILY
  (CHENOPODIACEAE)
    BEET
    SUGAR BEET
    CHARD
    SPINACH
    QUINOA
  [b] AMARANTH FAMILY
  (AMARANTHAECAE)
    AMARANTH

[8] Order Ranales
  [a] WATER LILY FAMILY
  (NYMPHAEACEAE)
    LOTUS (flour)
  [b] CUSTARD APPLE FAMILY
  (ANONACEAE)
    CUSTARD APPLE
    CHERIMOYA
    PAPAW
  [c] NUTMEG FAMILY (MYRISTICACEAE)
    NUTMEG
    MACE
  [d] BARBERRY FAMILY
  (BERBERIDACEAE)
    BARBERRY
    MANDRAKE (also called MAYAPPLE)

[e] LAUREL FAMILY (LAURACEAE)
    AVOCADO
    BAYLEAF
    CINNAMON
    SASSAFRAS
[9] Order Papaverales
  [a] POPPY FAMILY (PAPAVERACEAE)
    POPPYSEED
    CAPER[3]
  [b] MUSTARD FAMILY (CRUCIFERAE)
    BROCCOLI
    BRUSSEL SPROUTS
    CABBAGE (ALL VARIETIES)
    CANOLA (OIL AND SEEDS)
    CAULIFLOWER
    COLLARDS
    CRESS (CURLY, GARDEN,
      UPLAND, AND WATER)
    HORSERADISH
    KALE
    KOHLRABI
    MUSTARD (GREENS AND SEED)
    RADISH
    RUTABAGA
    TURNIP
b. Subclass Polypetale
  [l] Order Rosales
    [a] GOOSEBERRY FAMILY
      (GROSSULARIACEAE)[4]
      GOOSEBERRY
      TRUE CURRANT
    [b] ROSE FAMILY (ROSACEAE)
      BLACKBERRY
      BOYSENBERRY
      DEWBERRY
      LOGANBERRY
      LONGBERRY

RASPBERRY
STRAWBERRY
YOUNGBERRY
[c] APPLE FAMILY (POMACEAE)[5]
APPLE
APPLE CIDER
CIDER VINEGAR
LOQUAT
PEAR
QUINCE
ROSEHIP
[d] PLUM FAMILY (DRUPACEAE)
ALMOND
APRICOT
CHERRY
CHOKECHERRY
NECTARINE
PEACH
PLUM
[e] PEA FAMILY (LEGUMINOSAE)
(1) Subfamily Mimosaceae
GUM ACACIA
GUM ARABIC
GUM TRAGACANTH
SENNA
(2) Subfamily Caesalpinoideae
TAMARIND (a seasoning)
(3) Subfamily Papilionoideae
ALFALFA
BEAN (ADUKI, BLACK, KIDNEY,
    LIMA, NAVY, PINTO, SOY,
    WHITE, etc.)
BLACK-EYED PEA
CHICKPEA (GARBANZO BEAN)
GREEN PEA
KUDZU
LENTIL

LICORICE
LOCUST (CAROB) BEAN
LUPINE BEAN (and flour)
PEANUT

[2] Order Gerinales

   [a] FLAX FAMILY (LINACEAE)
      FLAXSEED (and oil)

   [b] OXALIS FAMILY (OXALIDACEAE)
      CARAMBOLA

   [c] SPURGE FAMILY (EUPHORBIACEAE)
      CASTOR OIL
      CASSAVA
      TAPIOCA

   [d] RUE (CITRUS) FAMILY (RUTACEAE)
      CITRON
      GRAPEFRUIT
      KUMQUAT
      LEMON
      LIME
      ORANGE
      TANGELO
      TANGERINE

[3] Order Salpindales

   [a] CASHEW FAMILIY (ANACARDIACEAE)
      CASHEW
      MANGO
      PISTACHIO

   [b] HOLLY FAMILY (AQUAFOLIACEAE)
      YERBA MATE (beverage)

   [c] MAPLE FAMILY (ACERACEAE)
      MAPLE SUGAR
      MAPLE SYRUP

[4] Order Rhamnales

   [a] GRAPE FAMILY (VITACEAE)
      CREAM OF TARTAR
      GRAPE
      WINE AND WINE VINEGAR

RAISIN
COMMERCIAL DRIED
"CURRANTS"
[5] Order Malvales
  [a] MALLOW FAMILY (MALVACEAE)
      COTTONSEED (oil)
      HIBISCUS
      OKRA
  [b] STERICULA FAMILY
    (STERICULIACEAE)
      CHOCOLATE
      COCOA
      COLA NUT
[6] Order Guttiferales
  [a] DILLENIA FAMILY (DILLENIACEAE)
      KIWI FRUIT
[7] Order Parietales
  [a] TEA FAMILY (THEACEAE)
      BLACK TEA
      GREEN TEA
  [b] PASSIONFLOWER FAMILY
    (PASSIFLORACEAE)
      PASSION FRUIT
  [c] PAPAYA FAMILY (PAPAYACEAE)
      PAPAYA
[8] Order Myrtales
  [a] MYRTLE FAMILY (MYRTACEAE)
      ALLSPICE
      CLOVES
      EUCALYPTUS
      GUAVA
  [b] EVENING PRIMROSE FAMILY
    (ONAGRACEAE)
      EVENING PRIMROSE OIL
  [c] POMEGRANITE FAMILY
    (PUNICACEAE)
      POMEGRANITE

GRENADINE
(derived from pomegranite)
[d] SAPUCAYA FAMILY
(LECYTHIDACEAE)
BRAZIL NUT
PARADISE NUT
[9] Order Umbellales
[a] GINSENG FAMILY (ARALIACEAE)
GINSENG, ALL VARIETIES
[b] PARSLEY FAMILY (UMBELLIFERAE)
ANISE
CARAWAY
CARROT
CELERIAC
CELERY, CELERY SEED AND LEAF
CHERVIL
CORIANDER
CUMIN
DILL
FENNEL
PARSLEY
PARSNIP
c. Subclass Sympetale
[l] Order Ericales
[a] BLUEBERRY FAMILY
(VACCINIACEAE)
BLUEBERRY
CRANBERRY
HUCKLEBERRY
[2] Order Ebenales
[a] EBONY FAMILY (EBENACEAE)
PERSIMMON
[b] SAPODILLA FAMILY (SAPOTACEAE)
CHICLE (CHEWING GUM BASE)
GUTTA PERCHA
(DENTAL MATERIAL)

[3] Order Gentianales
  [a] OLIVE FAMILY (OLEACEAE)
      BLACK OLIVE
      GREEN OLIVE
      OLIVE OIL
[4] Order Polemoniales
  [a] MORNING-GLORY FAMILY
    (CONVOLVULACEAE)
      JICAMA[6]
      SWEET POTATO
      WHITE SWEET POTATO (CAMOTE)
  [b] MINT FAMILY (LABIATAE)
      BASIL
      MARJORAM
      MENTHOL
      MINT
      OREGANO
      PEPPERMINT
      ROSEMARY
      SAGE
      SAVORY
      SPEARMINT
      THYME
  [c] POTATO FAMILY (SOLANACEAE)
      EGGPLANT
      PAPRIKA
      PEPPER - BELL, CAYENNE, CHILI
      TOBACCO
      TOMATO
      WHITE POTATO
[5] Order Rubiales
  [a] MADDER FAMILY (RUBIACEAE)
      COFFEE
[6] Order Curcurbitales
  [a] GOURD FAMILY (CURCURBITACEAE)
      CANTALOPE
      CASABA MELON

CRENSHAW MELON
CUCUMBER
HONEYDEW MELON
MUSKMELON
PERSIAN MELON
PUMPKIN (and PUMPKIN SEEDS)
SUMMER SQUASH (CROOKNECK,
　STRAIGHTNECK, YELLOW,
　ZUCCHINI)
WATERMELON
WINTER SQUASH
　(ACORN, BUTTERNUT, HUBBARD,
　PATTYPAN, SPAGHETTI)

[7] Order Campanulales
  [a] COMPOSITE FAMILY
    (1) Group Tubuliflorae
      (a) Tribe Heliantheae
        DAHLIA (DACOPA BEVERAGE)
        JERUSALEM ARTICHOKE
        SUNFLOWER (SEEDS AND OIL)
      (b) Tribe Anthemideae
        CHAMOMILE
        STEVIA (SWEETENER)
        TARRAGON
      (c) Tribe Cynareae
        GLOBE ARTICHOKE
        SAFFLOWER (OIL)
    (2) Group Liguliflorae
      (a) Tribe Cichorieae
        BELGIAN ENDIVE
        CHICORY
        DANDELION
        ENDIVE
        ESCAROLE
        LETTUCE
        ROMAINE
        SALSIFY

        [8] Order Tubiflorae
          [a] Suborder Solanineae
             (1) PEDALIUM FAMILY
                   (PEDALIACEAE)
                   SESAME (SEEDS, OIL, AND MEAL)

2. Class Monocotyledones
    a. Order Graminales
        [1] SEDGE FAMILY (CYPERACEAE)
              GROUNDNUT
              WATER CHESTNUT
        [2] GRAIN FAMILY (GRAMINEAE)
          [a] Subfamily Poateae
             (1) Tribe Bambuseae
                  BAMBOO SHOOTS
             (2) Tribe Hordeae
                  BARLEY
                  KAMUT
                  RYE
                  SPELT
                  TRITICALE
                  WHEAT
             (3) Tribe Aveneae
                  OATS
             (4) Tribe Festuceae
                  TEFF
             (5) Tribe Orizeae
                  RICE
                  WILD RICE
          [b] Subfamily Panicateae
             (1) Tribe Paniceae
                  MILLET
             (2) Tribe Andropogoneae
                  MILO
                  MOLASSES
                  SORGHUM
                  SUGAR CANE AND CANE SUGAR

        (3) Tribe Tripsaceae
           CORN
  b. Order Palmales
    [l] PALM FAMILY (PALMACEAE)
        CABBAGE-PALM
        COCONUT (MEAL AND OIL)
        DATE AND DATE SUGAR
        SAGO (STARCH AND SOURCE
          OF VITAMIN C)
  c. Order Arales
    [l] ARUM FAMILY (ARACEAE)
        CERIMAN (TROPICAL FRUIT)
        DASHEEN ARROWROOT
        MALANGA
        POI
        TARO
  d. Order Xyridales
    [l] PINEAPPLE FAMILY (BROMELIACEAE)
        PINEAPPLE
  e. Order Liliales
    [l] LILY FAMILY (LILIACEAE)
        ALOE VERA
        ASPARAGUS
        CHIVES
        GARLIC
        LEEKS
        ONION
        SARSAPARILLA
        SHALLOT
    [2] YAM FAMILY (DIOSCOREACEAE)
        NAME
        TRUE YAM
    [3] AMARYLLIS FAMILY
      (AMARYLLIDACEAE)
        AGAVE (source of tequilla)
        AGUAMIEL (sweetener derived
          from the maguey plant)

       [4] IRIS FAMILY (IRIDACEAE)
          SAFFRON
       [5] TACCA FAMILY (TACCACEAE)
          FIJI ARROWROOT

f. Order Scitaminales
       [1] CANNA FAMILY (CANNACEAE)
          QUEENSLAND ARROWROOT
       [2] BANANA FAMILY (MUSACEAE)
          BANANA
          MUSA ARROWROOT
          PLANTAIN
       [3] GINGER FAMILY (ZINGIBERACEAE)
          CARDAMON
          EAST INDIAN ARROWROOT
          GINGER
          TUMERIC
       [4] ARROWROOT FAMILY (MARANTACEAE)
          WEST INDIAN ARROWROOT

g. Order Orchidales
       [1] ORCHID FAMILY (ORCHIDACEAE)
          VANILLA

TABLE 3

FOOD FAMILIES OF THE ANIMAL KINGDOM[7]

I. Phylum Mollusca
   A. Class Gastropoda
      1. Order Prosobranchia
         a. ABALONE FAMILY (HALIOTIDAE)
            ABALONE
      2. Order Pulmonata
         a. SNAIL FAMILY (HELICIDAE)
            EDIBLE SNAILS
   B. Class Pelecypoda (Bivalvia)
      1. Order Filibranchia
         a. MUSSEL FAMILY (MYTILIDAE)
            MUSSEL
         b. SCALLOP FAMILY (PECTINIDAE)
            SCALLOP
         c. OYSTER FAMILY (OSTREIDAE)
            OYSTER
      2. Order Eulamellibranchia
         a. THICK-SHELLED CLAM FAMILY (VENERIDAE)
            THICK-SHELLED CLAM
         b. SOFT-SHELLED CLAM FAMILY (MYACIDAE)
            SOFT-SHELLED CLAM
         c. COCKLE FAMILY (CARDIACIDAE)
            COCKLE
   C. Class Cephalopoda
      1. Order Dibranchia
         a. SQUID FAMILY (LOLIGINIDAE)
            SQUID
            CUTTLEFISH
      2. Order Octopoda
         a. OCTOPUS FAMILY (OCTOPODIDAE)
            OCTOPUS
II. Phylum Arthropoda
   A. Subphylum Mandibulata

1. Class Crustacea
   a. Subclass Malocostraca
      [1] Order Decapoda
         [a] PRAWN FAMILY (PENEIDAE)
            PRAWN
            SHRIMP
         [b] LOBSTER FAMILY (HOMARIDAE)
            CRAYFISH
            LOBSTER
         [c] CRAB FAMILY (PAGURIDAE)
            CRAB (ALL VARIETIES)

III. Phylum Chordata
   A. Subphylum Vertebrata
      1. Class Osteichthyes
         a. Superorder Chondrostei
            [1] Order Acipenseroidei
               [a] STURGEON FAMILY
                   (ACIPENSERIFORMES)
                   STURGEON (CAVIAR)
         b. Superorder Teleostei
            [1] Order Isopondyli
               [a] HERRING FAMILY (CLUPEIDAE)
                   HERRING
                   MENHADEN
                   SARDINE
                   SHAD
               [b] ANCHOVY FAMILY (ENGRAULIDAE)
                   ANCHOVY
               [c] Suborder Salmonoidea
                  (1) SALMON FAMILY (SALMONIDAE)
                      SALMON (ALL VARIETIES)
                      TROUT (ALL FRESHWATER
                        VARIETIES)
                  (2) SMELT FAMILY (OSMERIDAE)
                      SMELT
                  (3) WHITEFISH FAMILY
                      (COREGONIDAE)

                            WHITEFISH
[2] Order Haplomi
    [a] PIKE FAMILY (ESOCIDAE)
                            BLACKFISH
                            MUSKELLUNGE
                            PICKEREL
                            PIKE
[3] Order Ostariophysi
    [a] SUCKER FAMILY (CATASTOMIDAE)
                            SUCKER
    [b] MINNOW FAMILY (CYPRINIDAE)
                            CARP
                            CHUB
                            MINNOW
    [c] Suborder Siluroidea
        (1) CATFISH FAMILY (SILURIDAE)
                            FRESHWATER CATFISH
        (2) SEA CATFISH FAMILY (ARIIDAE)
                            SEA CATFISH
[4] Order Apodes
    [a] EEL FAMILY (ANGUILLIFORMES)
                            EEL
[5] Order Acanthini
    [a] CODFISH FAMILY
        (1) Subfamily Lotinae (Cusk)
                            CUSK
        (2) Subfamily Merluccinae (Hake)
                            HAKE
                            HOKI
        (3) Subfamily Gadinae (Cod)
                            COD (ALSO CALLED SCROD)
                            HADDOCK
                            POLLACK
                            WHITING
[6] Order Berycomorphi
    [a] ROUGHY FAMILY (TRACHICHTHYIDAE)
                            ORANGE ROUGHY

OTHER TYPES OF ROUGHY
[7] Order Zeomorphi
    [a] DORY FAMILY (ZEIDAE)
        JOHN DORY
        OTHER TYPES OF DORY
    [b] OREO FAMILY (OREOSOMATIDAE)
        OREO DORY
[8] Order Percomorphi
    [a] Suborder Callionymoidea
        (1) BUTTERFISH FAMILY (PHOLIDAE)
            BUTTERFISH
            HARVESTFISH
    [b] Suborder Percoidea
        (1) SEA BASS FAMILY (SERRANIDAE)
            GROUPER
            SEA BASS
        (2) DOLPHINFISH FAMILY
            (CORYPHAENIDAE)
            DOLPHINFISH (ALSO CALLED
                MAHI MAHI)
        (3) PERCH FAMILY (PERCIDAE)
            PERCH
            WALLEYE
        (4) SNAPPER FAMILY (LUTJANIDAE)
            MUTTON SNAPPER
            RED SNAPPER
            OTHER TYPES OF SNAPPER
        (5) SUNFISH FAMILY
            (CENTRARCHIDAE)
            BLACK BASS
            CRAPPIE
            FRESHWATER BASS
            SUNFISH
        (6) CROAKER FAMILY (SCIAENIDAE)
            CROAKER (ALL VARIETIES)
            DRUM
            SEA TROUT

    (7) JACK FAMILY (CARANGIDAE)
         JACK
         POMPANO
    (8) BLUEFISH FAMILY (POMATOMIDAE)
         BLUEFISH
    (9) PORGY FAMILY (SPARIDAE)
         PORGY

[c] Suborder Scombroidea
    (1) MACKEREL FAMILY (SCOMBRIDAE)
         MACKEREL
    (2) BONITO FAMILY (CYBIDAE)
         BONITO
    (3) TUNA FAMILY (THUNNIDAE)
         ALBACORE
         TUNA
    (4) SWORDFISH FAMILY (XIPHIDAE)
         SWORDFISH
    (5) SAILFISH FAMILY (ISTIOPHORIDAE)
         MARLIN
         SAILFISH

[d] Suborder Mugiloidea
    (1) MULLET FAMILY (MUGILIDAE)
         MULLET
    (2) SILVERSIDE FAMILY (ATHERINIDAE)
         SILVERSIDE

[e] Suborder Scorpaenoidea
    (1) SCORPIONFISH FAMILY
         (SCORPAENIDAE)
         SCORPIONFISH

[9] Order Heterosomata
  [a] Suborder Pleuronectoidea[8]
    (1) TURBOT FAMILY (BOTHIDAE)
         TURBOT
         CALIFORNIA HALIBUT (LEFTEYED)
    (2) HALIBUT FAMILY
         (PLEURONECTIDAE)
         HALIBUT (RIGHTEYED)

         (3) FLOUNDER FAMILY
            (HIPPOGLOSSIDAE)
            DAB
            FLOUNDER
            PLAICE
         (4) SOLE FAMILY (SOLEDAE)
            SOLE
      [10] Order Lophiformes
        [a] Suborder Lophoidei
         (1) ANGLERFISH FAMILY (LOPHIDAE)
            MONKFISH

2. Class Amphibia
    a. Order Salientia
      [1] FROG FAMILY (RANIDAE)
         FROG

3. Class Reptilia
    a. Order Testudines (or Chelonia)
      [1] TURTLE FAMILY (CHELONIDAE)
         TERAPIN
         TURTLE
    b. Order Crocodylia
      [1] ALLIGATOR FAMILY (ALLIGATORIDAE)
         ALLIGATOR
      [2] CROCODILE FAMILY (CROCODYLIDAE)
         CROCODILE
    c. Order Squamata
      [1] Superorder Serpentes
        [a] MANY SNAKE FAMILIES
         SNAKES

4. Class Aves
    a. Superorder Neognathae
      [1] Order Anseriformes
        [a] DUCK FAMILY (ANATIDAE)
         DUCK (AND DUCK EGGS)
         GOOSE (AND GOOSE EGGS)
      [2] Order Galliformes
        [a] GROUSE FAMILY (TETRAONIDAE)

GROUSE (ALSO CALLED PARTRIDGE)
[b] PHEASANT FAMILY (PHASIANIDAE)
CHICKEN (AND CHICKEN EGGS)
PHEASANT
QUAIL
[c] TURKEY FAMILY (MELEAGRIDIDAE)
TURKEY (AND TURKEY EGGS)
[d] GUINEA-FOWL FAMILY (NUMIDIDAE)
GUINEA-FOWL
(AND GUINEA-FOWL EGGS)
[3] Order Columbiformes
[a] DOVE FAMILY (COLUMBIDAE)
DOVE
PIGEON (ALSO CALLED SQUAB)
5. Class Mammmalia
a. Order Marsupialia
[1] OPOSSUM FAMILY (DIDELPHIDAE)
OPOSSUM
b. Order Lagomorpha
[1] HARE FAMILY (LEPORIDAE)
RABBIT
c. Order Rodentia
[1] Suborder Sciuromorpha
[a] SQUIRREL FAMILY (SCIURIDAE)
SQUIRREL
d. Order Cetacea
[1] WHALE FAMILIES (BALAENOPTERIDAE,
BALAENIDAE, RHACHIANOPTERIDAE,
AND PHYSETERIDAE)
WHALE (ALL VARIETIES)
[2] DOLPHIN FAMILY (DELPHINIDAE)
DOLPHIN
e. Order Carnivora
[1] Suborder Fissipeda
[a] BEAR FAMILY (URSIDAE)
BEAR

f. Order Perissodactyla
   [1] HORSE FAMILY (EQUIDAE)
         HORSE
g. Order Artiodactyla
   [1] Suborder Suiformes
      [a] SWINE FAMILY (SUIDAE)
            DOMESTIC PIG (PORK)
            WILD BOAR
   [2] Suborder Tylopoda
      [a] CAMEL FAMILY (CAMELIDAE)
            CAMEL AND CAMEL MILK
            LLAMA AND LLAMA MILK
   [3] Suborder Ruminantia
      [a] DEER FAMILY (CERVIDAE)
            CARIBOU
            DEER (VENISON)
            ELK
            MOOSE
            REINDEER
      [b] PRONGHORN FAMILY
         (ANTILOCUPRIDAE)
            PRONGHORN
      [c] ANTELOPE FAMILY (ANTILOPINAE)
            ANTELOPE
      [d] CATTLE FAMILY (BOVIDAE)
         (1) Subfamily Bovinae
            BEEF
            BISON (AMERICAN BUFFALO)
            BUFFALO (CAPE, WATER, ETC.)
            OX
            MILK AND BYPRODUCTS FROM
               THESE ANIMALS
         (2) Subfamily Caprinae
            GOAT
            SHEEP (LAMB)
            MILK AND BYPRODUCTS FROM
               THESE ANIMALS

1. According to the most recent classification schemes, fungi and algae are no longer included in the plant kingdom, but have been assigned to kingdoms of their own. However, for purposes of this book, we will consider all foods as either plants or animals.

2. The classification of plants in Table 2 was derived from the following sources:

   Alexopoulos, Constantine John, *Introductory Mycology*, Second Edition, John Wiley and Sons, Inc., New York, 1962.

   Alexopoulos, C. J. and H. C. Bold, *Algae and Fungi*, The Macmillan Company, New York, 1967.

   Lobban, Christopher S. and Michael J. Wynne, *The Biology of Seaweeds*, Blackwell Scientific Publications, Oxford, England, 1981.

   Phaff, H. J., M. W. Miller, and E. M. Mrak, *The Life of Yeasts*, Harvard University Press, 1966.

   Rendle, Alfred Barton, *The Classification of Flowering Plants*, Volumes 1 and 2, Second Edition, Cambridge University Press, London, 1967.

   Round, F. E., *The Biology of Algae*, Second Edition, Edward Arnold Publishers Limited, Bath, England, 1973.

3. Capers are sometimes classified in a separate family from poppyseeds, the Capparidaceae family.

4. The Grossulariaceae (gooseberry) family members are sometimes classified in the Saxifragaceae family.

5. The members of the apple familly (Pomaceae) are sometimes classified as a tribe of the family Rosaceae.

6. Jicama is sometimes classified in the legume family rather than the morning glory family by botanists. However, allergy doctors agree with the botanists that classify it in the morning glory family, so it is included in the morning glory family in Table 2.

7. The classification of animals in Table 3 was dervied from the following sources:

   The Larousse Encyclopedia of Animal Life, McGraw-Hill Book Company, New York, 1967.

   The New Larousse Encyclopedia of Animal Life, Bonanza Books, New York, 1981.

   Rothschild, Lord, *A Classification of Living Animals*, John Wiley and Sons, Inc., New York, New York, 1961.

8. The foods in the suborder Pleuronectoidea are sometimes classified together as one food family.

16

Sources of Special Foods and Products

This is a listing of the manufacturers of many of the special foods and products used in the recipes in this book, as well as some mail-order distributors of these products. Your health food store can order foods from these sources, or your can order directly from many of them yourself. Sources are not listed for all of the special foods used in this book because many of them are available at almost any health food store.

ACETIC ACID, DEHYDRATED:

Ener-G Foods, Inc.
5960 First Avenue South
P. O. Box 84487
Seattle, Washington 98124
(800) 331-5222; in Washington (800) 325-9788

AMARANTH, WHOLE, FLOUR, AND PUFFED:

Nu-World Amaranth, Inc.
P. O. Box 2202
Naperville, Illinois 60540
(708) 369-6819

Allergy Resources, Inc.
745 Powderhorn
Monument, Colorado 80132
(719) 488-3630 or (800) USE-FLAX

BUFFALO AND GAME MEATS:

Game Sales International, Inc.
P.O. Box 5314
444 Washington Street
Loveland, Colorado 80537
(303) 667-4090 or (800) 729-2090

Czimer Food, Inc.
13136 W. 159th Street
Lockport, Illinois 60441
(708) 301-7152

CANOLA SEEDS

West Star Farms Canola Seeds
Westar Foods
P.O. Box AA
Del Norte, Colorado 81132
(719) 657-0322

CAROB CHIPS, MILK-FREE UNSWEETENED:

Simple Foods, Inc.
1200 Hertel Avenue
Buffalo, New York 14216
(800) 234-8850

Allergy Resources, Inc. (see above)

CASSAVA MEAL (See Tuber Flours for Cassava Flour):

G. B. Ratto & Co. International Grocers
821 Washington Street
Oakland, California 94607
(800) 325-3483; in California (800) 228-3515

CHESTNUT FLOUR

G. B. Ratto & Co. International Grocers (see above)

COCONUT, FINELY SHREDDED UNSWEETENED:

Jerry's Nut House, Inc.
2101 Humboldt Street
Denver, Colorado 80205
(303) 861-2262

COCONUT MILK, 100%

Allergy Resources, Inc. (see p. 264)

DACOPA (BEVERAGE FROM DAHLIA TUBERS):

California Natural Products
P. O. Box 1219
Lathrop, California 95330
(209) 858-2525

An Ounce of Prevention
8200 E. Phillips Place
Englewood, Colorado 80112
(303) 770-8808

Allergy Resources, Inc. (see p. 264)

FLAVORINGS, CORN-FREE, ALCOHOL-FREE, NATURAL:

Saint John's Herb Garden
7711 Hill Mead Road
Bowie, Maryland 20715
(301) 262-5302

The Spicery Shoppe
Flavorchem
1525 Brook Drive
Downers Grove, Illinois 60515
(708) 932-8100 or (800) 323-1301

An Ounce of Prevention (see above)

GOAT CHEESE:

North Farm Cooperative
204 Regas Road
Madison, Wisconsin 53714
(608) 241-2667

GOAT MILK, ULTRAPASTEURIZED FRESH, CANNED, AND DRIED:

Jackson-Mitchell Pharmaceuticals, Inc.
P.O. Box 934
Turlock, California 95381
(800) 343-1185

GUAR GUM:

Fruitful Yield
5005 W. Oakton
Skokie, Illinois 60077
(708) 679-8882

Allergy Resources, Inc. (see p. 264)

MILLET FLAKES:

Allergy Resources, Inc. (see p. 264)

MILO FLOUR:

Allergy Resources, Inc. (see p. 264)

Special Foods
9207 Shotgun Court
Springfield, Virginia 22153
(703) 644-0991

MUSTARD, DRY MILD DIJON:

G. B. Ratto & Co. International Grocers (see p. 264)

PARCHMENT PAPER:

California Nutritional Products
5242 Bolsa Avenue, Suite 3
Huntington Beach, California 92647
(714) 893-0017

PASTA:

AMARANTH:

Special Foods (see above)

BARLEY:

Special Foods (see p. 266)

BEAN THREAD NOODLES:

Eden Foods, Inc.
701 Tecumseh Road
Clinton, Michigan 49236
(800) 248-0301 or (517) 456-7424

BUCKWHEAT (100% SOBA):

Eden Foods, Inc. (see above)

CORN:

DeBoles Nutritional Foods, Inc.
2120 Jericho Turnpike
Garden City Park, New York 11040
(516) 742-1825

KUDZU-KIRI
(KUDZU AND SWEET POTATO STARCHES):

Eden Foods, Inc. (see above)

Allergy Resources, Inc. (see p. 264)

LENTIL:

Special Foods (see p. 266)

MILLET:

Special Foods (see p. 266)

MILO:

Special Foods (see p. 266)

OAT:

Special Foods (see p. 266)

QUINOA:
100% Quinoa:

Special Foods (see p. 266)

Containing Corn:

> The Quinoa Corporation
> P.O. Box 1039
> 24248 Crenshaw Boulevard, Suite 220
> Torrance, California 90505
> (213) 530-8666

RICE:

> Eden Foods, Inc. (see p. 267)

RYE:

> Special Foods (see p. 266)

SPELT:

> Purity Foods, Inc.
> 2871 W. Jolly Road
> Okemos, Michigan 48864
> (517) 351-9231

> An Ounce of Prevention (see p. 265)

> Allergy Resources, Inc. (see p. 264)

SPECIAL TUBERS (WHITE SWEET POTATO, CASSAVA, MALANGA, YAM):

> Special Foods (see p. 266)

QUINOA, WHOLE AND FLOUR:

> The Quinoa Corporation (see above)

> Allergy Resources, Inc. (see p. 264)

ROTATION DIETS (CUSTOMIZED) WITH COMPATIBLE RECIPES:

> A.D.A.P.T. Allergy Cooking and Diet Consultations
> 1877 Polk Avenue
> Louisville, Colorado 80027
> (303) 666-8253

SPELT, WHOLE AND FLOUR:

Purity Foods, Inc. (see p. 268)

An Ounce of Prevention (see p. 265)

STEVIA:

Allergy Resources, Inc. (see p. 264)

2nd Opinion
P. O. Box 69046
Portland, Oregon 97201
(800) 999-6922 or (503) 228-0711

Fran's Herbal Rainbow
P. O. Box 212
Bellwood, Illinois 60104
(708) 547-1213

TAPIOCA FLOUR:

Ener-G Foods, Inc. (see p. 263)

TEFF, WHOLE AND FLOUR;

Maskal Teff
1318 Willow
Caldwell, Idaho 83605
(208) 454-3330

Allergy Resources, Inc. (see p. 264)

TUBER FLOURS (WHITE SWEET POTATO, CASSAVA, MALANGA, YAM, ETC., including recipes):

Special Foods (see p. 266)

VITAMIN C, UNBUFFERED:

Aller–C Powder Carrot Source Vitamin C
L. C. and Associates
5581 Woodsong Drive
Atlanta, Georgia 30338
(404) 396-8675

An Ounce of Prevention (see p. 265)

Klaire Laboratories, Inc. (Vital Life Brand—corn source, but so highly purified as to be considered synthetic)
P. O. Box 618
Carlsbad, California 92008
(714) 438-1083

Bronson Pharmaceuticals (excellent in baking—corn source, but so highly purified as to be considered synthetic)
4526 Rinetti Lane
La Canada, California 91011
(213) 790-2646

WATER CHESTNUT FLOUR:

Special Foods (see p. 266)

YEAST, QUICK-RISE, CORN- AND PRESERVATIVE-FREE:

Red Star Quick-Rise Yeast
Universal Foods Corporation
Consumer Service Center
433 E. Michigan Street
Milwaukee, Wisconsin 53202
(414) 271-6755

MISCELLANEOUS SOURCES OF MANY FOODS AND PRODUCTS BY PHONE OR MAIL ORDER:

An Ounce of Prevention (see p. 265)

(Spelt flour and pasta, Vital Life Vitamin C, many other vitamins, dacopa, flavorings, cosmetics, cleaning products, air and water filters, cellophane bags, books, etc.)

Allergy Resources, Inc. (see p. 264)
(Flours, including arrowroot and tapioca flour, cereals, pasta, many other foods, vitamins, cleaning supplies, filters, bedding, etc.)

G. B. Ratto & Co. International Grocers (see p. 264)
(International and unusual foods of all kinds)

References

These books complement the information contained in this cookbook. If This Is Tuesday, It Must Be Chicken gives much detailed information about rotation diets, as well as some recipes. The Allergy Self-Help Cookbook is a treasure house of recipes; the reason my book does not contain more amaranth recipes is because Mrs. Jones has done such a thorough job with amaranth in her book. And The Yeast Connection Cookbook is a must for those with yeast problems. This is by no means an exhaustive list of references. There are many other very informative books available at your library, bookstore, and doctor's office.

Crook, William G., M.D. and Marjorie Hurt Jones, R.N. *The Yeast Connection Cookbook*. Professional Books, Jackson, Tennessee 38301, 1989.

Golos, Natalie, and Frances Golos Golbitz. *If This Is Tuesday, It Must Be Chicken*. Keats Publishing, Inc., New Canaan, Connecticut, 1983.

Jones, Marjorie Hurt, R.N. *The Allergy Self-Help Cookbook*. Rodale Press, Emmaus, Pennsylvania, 1984.

Jones, Marjorie Hurt, R.N. *Superfoods*. Mast Enterprises, Inc., 2615 N. Fourth Street, #616, Coeur d'Alene, Idaho 83814, 1990.

Allergen Avoidance Index

The purpose of this index is to help you find foods that avoid specific allergens. The foods are listed by chapter categories.

Guide to Symbols:

X   = Free of the ingredient, or the statement at the top
       of the column is true

X*   = Free of the ingredient or the statement at the top
       of the column is true if optional ingredients in the recipe
       are omitted

A   = An alternative (goat or sheep) milk product is used in
       the recipe, but it is free of cow's milk

A*   = The recipe is free of cow's milk if optional ingredients
       are used, and is also free of alternative (goat or sheep)
       milk if optional ingredients are omitted

M   = Free of meat

T   = Free of tomatoes

F   = The recipe contains feta cheese, and is suitable for
       use on a low yeast diet if goat or sheep feta cheese
       is tolerated.

MUFFINS, CRACKERS, BREAKFAST FOODS, AND BREADS MADE WITHOUT YEAST

	PAGE	FREE OF ALL GRAINS	FREE OF GLUTEN	FREE OF WHEAT	FREE OF CORN	FREE OF MILK	FREE OF EGGS	FREE OF SOY	FREE OF YEAST	FREE OF REFINED SUGAR	FREE OF FRUIT	FREE OF OTHER	SUITABLE FOR STRICT LOW-YEAST DIET
APPLE & SPICE MUFFINS	28	X	X	X	X	X	X	X	X	X			
APPLESAUCE BREAD	45	X	X	X	X	X	X	X	X	X			
BANANA BREAD	46	X*	X*	X	X	X	X	X	X	X			
BANANA MUFFINS	33	X	X	X	X	X	X	X	X	X			
BARLEY BISCUITS	50			X	X	X	X	X	X	X	X		X
BARLEY MUFFINS	30			X	X	X	X	X	X	X	X		X
BARLEY PANCAKES	42			X	X	X	X	X	X	X*	X		X*
BARLEY SANDWICH BREAD	48			X	X	X	X	X	X	X	X		X
BARLEY WAFFLES	44			X	X	X	X	X	X	X	X		X
BLUEBERRY MUFFINS	33	X*	X*	X	X	X	X	X	X	X*			
CANOLA SEED CRACKERS	38	X*	X*	X	X	X	X	X	X	X	X		X
CASSAVA CRACKERS	40	X	X	X	X	X	X	X	X	X	X		X
CHESTNUT WAFERS	39	X	X	X	X	X	X	X	X	X	X		X
COCONUT MILK WAFERS	37	X	X	X	X	X	X	X	X	X	X		X
"GRAHAM" CRACKERS	35	X	X	X	X	X	X	X	X	X			
MILLET SURPRISE MUFFINS	31		X	X	X	X	X	X	X	X			
MILO CRACKERS	37			X	X	X	X	X	X	X	X		X
NO-YEAST BREAD	46	X*	X*	X	X	X	X	X	X	X	X		X
NO-YEAST SANDWICH BUNS	48	X*	X*	X	X	X	X	X	X	X	X		X
OAT BISCUITS	50			X	X	X	X	X	X	X	X		X
OAT CRACKERS	36			X	X	X	X	X	X	X	X		X
OAT MUFFINS	29			X	X	X	X	X	X	X	X		X
PEAR MUFFINS	29	X	X	X	X	X	X	X	X	X			

MUFFINS, CRACKERS, BREAKFAST FOODS, AND BREADS
MADE WITHOUT YEAST (CONT'D)

	PAGE	FREE OF ALL GRAINS	FREE OF GLUTEN	FREE OF WHEAT	FREE OF CORN	FREE OF MILK	FREE OF EGGS	FREE OF SOY	FREE OF YEAST	FREE OF REFINED SUGAR	FREE OF FRUIT	FREE OF OTHER	SUITABLE FOR STRICT LOW-YEAST DIET
PINEAPPLE MUFFINS	28		X*	X	X	X	X	X	X	X			
QUINOA CRACKERS	35	X	X	X	X	X	X	X	X	X	X		X
QUINOA GRANOLA	40	X	X	X	X	X	X	X	X	X			
QUINOA PANCAKES	43	X	X	X	X	X	X	X	X	X	X*		X*
RYE PANCAKES	41			X	X	X	X	X	X	X	X*		X*
RYE SURPRISE MUFFINS	32			X	X	X	X	X	X	X*	X*		
SALTINES	36			X	X	X	X	X	X	X	X		X
SPELT BISCUITS	51			X	X	X	X	X	X	X	X		X
SPELT BISCUIT SANDWICH BUNS	52			X	X	X	X	X	X	X	X		X
SPELT PANCAKES	43			X	X	X	X	X	X	X	X*		X*
SPELT SANDWICH BREAD	49			X	X	X	X	X	X	X	X		X
SPELT SURPRISE MUFFINS	31			X	X	X	X	X	X	X			
STEVIA-SWEETENED SPICE MUFFINS	34	X	X	X	X	X	X	X	X	X	X		X
TEETHING BISCUITS	52	X*	X*	X	X	X	X	X	X	X			

YEAST RAISED BREADS AND BAKED GOODS

	PAGE	FREE OF ALL GRAINS	FREE OF GLUTEN	FREE OF WHEAT	FREE OF CORN	FREE OF MILK	FREE OF EGGS	FREE OF SOY	FREE OF YEAST	FREE OF REFINED SUGAR	FREE OF FRUIT	FREE OF OTHER	SUITABLE FOR STRICT LOW-YEAST DIET
BARLEY SANDWICH BUNS	60			X	X	X	X	X		X*	X*		
CINNAMON ROLLS	66			X	X	X	X	X		X*	X*		
CINNAMON SWIRL BREAD	64			X	X	X	X	X		X*			
ENGLISH MUFFINS	63			X	X	X	X	X		X			
NO-FRY DOUGHNUTS	67	X*	X*	X	X	X	X	X		X*			
OAT YEAST BREAD	56			X	X	X	X	X		X			
PITA (POCKET) BREAD	62			X	X	X	X	X		X			
PRETZELS	62			X	X	X	X	X		X			
QUICK BARLEY YEAST BREAD	59			X	X	X	X	X		X*	X*		
QUINOA YEAST BREAD	57	X	X	X	X	X	X	X		X			
RAISIN BREAD	57	X	X	X	X	X	X	X		X			
RYE SANDWICH BUNS	59			X	X	X	X	X		X			
RYE YEAST BREAD	58			X	X	X	X	X		X			
SPELT SANDWICH OR DINNER BUNS	61			X	X	X	X	X		X			
SPELT SWEET ROLL DOUGH	64			X	X	X	X	X		X*	X*		
SPELT YEAST BREAD	60			X	X	X	X	X		X			
TEA RING	65			X	X	X	X	X		X*			

MAIN DISHES

	PAGE	FREE OF ALL GRAINS	FREE OF GLUTEN	FREE OF WHEAT	FREE OF CORN	FREE OF MILK	FREE OF EGGS	FREE OF SOY	FREE OF YEAST	FREE OF REFINED SUGAR	FREE OF FRUIT	FREE OF OTHER	SUITABLE FOR STRICT LOW-YEAST DIET
BISCUIT TOPPING FOR CASSEROLES	77	X*	X*	X	X	X	X	X	X	X	X	M	X
BEAN-N-BISCUIT	80	X*	X*	X	X	X	X	X	X	X	X	M	
BRAISED BUFFALO BURGERS	93	X	X	X	X	X	X	X	X	X	X		X
BRAISED GOAT	91	X	X	X	X	X	X	X	X	X	X		X
BUFFALO LOAF	92	X	X	X	X	X	X	X	X*	X	X*		X*
BUFF-N-BISCUIT	78	X*	X*	X	X	X	X	X	X	X	X		X
CRISPY BROILED FISH	87	X	X	X	X	X	X	X	X	X	X		X
CRISPY OVEN-FRIED CHICKEN	89	X*	X*	X	X	X	X	X	X	X	X		X
CROCKPOT GAME ROAST	83	X	X	X	X	X	X	X	X	X	X		X
DUCK-N-BISCUIT	79	X*	X*	X	X	X	X	X	X	X	X		X
GAME CHILI	86	X	X	X	X	X	X	X	X	X	X		
GAME ROAST DINNER	83	X	X	X	X	X	X	X	X	X	X		X
GAME STEW	84	X	X	X	X	X	X	X	X	X	X		X
GAME STROGANOFF	82	X*	X*	X	X	X	X	X	X*	X	X*		X*
GOAT RIBS	91	X	X	X	X	X	X	X	X*	X	X*		X*
GOLDEN GAME STEW	86	X	X	X	X	X	X	X	X	X	X		X
ITALIAN RICE MEAL IN A BOWL	74		X	X	X	A	X	X		X	X	M	
ITALIAN-STYLE BAKED RABBIT	89	X	X	X	X	X	X	X	X*	X	X*		X*
LENTIL BURGERS	94	X	X	X	X	X	X	X	X	X	X	M	
MACARONI AND CHEESE	81	X*	X*	X	X	A	X	X	X*	X	X	M	F*
NO MEAT OR TOMATO CHILI	73	X	X	X	X	X	X	X	X	X	X	M,T	
PASTIES	76			X	X	X	X	X		X	X		

MAIN DISHES (CONT'D)

	PAGE	FREE OF ALL GRAINS	FREE OF GLUTEN	FREE OF WHEAT	FREE OF CORN	FREE OF MILK	FREE OF EGGS	FREE OF SOY	FREE OF YEAST	FREE OF REFINED SUGAR	FREE OF FRUIT	FREE OF OTHER	SUITABLE FOR STRICT LOW-YEAST DIET
QUINOA STUFFED PEPPERS	72	X	X	X	X	X	X	X	X	X	X	M,T	X
ROAST DUCK WITH CHERRY SAUCE	88	X	X	X	X	X	X	X	X	X			
SALMON LOAF OR PATTIES	87	X*	X*	X	X	X	X	X	X	X	X		X
SLOPPY GOAT SANDWICHES	92	X*	X*	X	X	X	X	X	X*	X	X*		X*
STUFFED ACORN SQUASH	71	X	X	X	X	A	X	X	X	X		M	F*
STUFFED ZUCCHINI	70	X*	X*	X	X	A	X	X		X	X	M	
TENDER GOAT CHOPS OR STEAK	90	X	X	X	X	X	X	X	X	X	X		X
TURKEY POT PIE	75	X*	X*	X	X	X	X	X	X	X	X		X
TWO-FOOD-FAMILY VEGETARIAN CHILI	73	X	X	X	X	X	X	X*	X	X	X	M	
ZUCCHINI STEW	85	X	X	X	X	X	X	X	X	X	X		X*

PASTA AND ETHNIC DISHES

	PAGE	FREE OF ALL GRAINS	FREE OF GLUTEN	FREE OF WHEAT	FREE OF CORN	FREE OF MILK	FREE OF EGGS	FREE OF SOY	FREE OF YEAST	FREE OF REFINED SUGAR	FREE OF FRUIT	FREE OF OTHER	SUITABLE FOR STRICT LOW-YEAST DIET
AVOCADO SAUCE	115	X	X	X	X	X	X	X	X	X	X		X
EASY MEAT SAUCE FOR LASAGNE	104	X	X	X	X	X	X	X		X	X		
EASY PIZZA SAUCE	104	X	X	X	X	X	X	X		X	X	M	
EASY SPAGHETTI SAUCE WITH MEATBALLS	103	X	X	X	X	X	X	X		X	X		
EASY VEGETARIAN SPAGHETTI SAUCE	101	X	X	X	X	X	X	X		X	X	M	
ENCHILADA CASSEROLE	116	X*	X*	X	X	A*	X	X	X*	X	X	M	
FRESH TOMATO SAUCE	102	X	X	X	X	X	X	X	X	X	X	M	X
GARLIC, PEPPER, AND OIL SAUCE	101	X*	X*	X	X	X	X	X	X	X	X	M,T	X
LASAGNE	106	X*	X*	X	X	A	X	X	X*	X	X	M*	F*
MANICOTTI	105	X*	X*	X	X	A	X	X	X*	X	X	M	F*
MEXICAN SAUCE	114	X	X	X	X	X	X	X	X*	X	X	M	X*
ORIENTAL GAME OR CHICKEN	117	X*	X*	X	X	X	X	X	X	X	X		X
PASTA E FAGIOLI	111	X*	X*	X	X	X	X	X	X	X	X	M*	
PASTA FOR ROLLING BY HAND	96	X*	X*	X	X	X	X	X	X	X	X		X
PASTA MADE WITH AN EXTRUSION MACHINE	99	X*	X*	X	X	X	X	X	X	X	X		X
PESTO	100	X	X	X	X	X	X	X	X	X	X	M,T	X
PESTO PIZZA	110	X*	X*	X	X	A*	X	X	X*	X	X	M,T	X*
PIZZA	108	X*	X*	X	X	A*	X	X	X*	X	X	M*	X*
POLENTA	106	X*	X	X	X*	A*	X	X	X*	X	X	M	X*
QUICK REFRIED BEANS	113	X	X	X	X	X	X	X	X	X	X	M	
TORTILLAS	112	X*	X*	X	X	X	X	X	X	X	X		X
TOSTADAS	115	X*	X*	X	X	A*	X	X	X*	X	X	M	X*

VEGETABLES, SIDE DISHES, AND SOUPS

	PAGE	FREE OF ALL GRAINS	FREE OF GLUTEN	FREE OF WHEAT	FREE OF CORN	FREE OF MILK	FREE OF EGGS	FREE OF SOY	FREE OF YEAST	FREE OF REFINED SUGAR	FREE OF FRUIT	FREE OF OTHER	SUITABLE FOR STRICT LOW-YEAST DIET
"CREAM" OF VEGETABLE SOUP	125	X	X	X	X	X	X	X	X	X	X	M	X
DRIED BEANS	120	X	X	X	X	X	X	X	X	X	X		
DUCK SOUP	126	X	X	X	X	X	X	X	X	X	X		X
HARVARD BEETS	118	X	X	X	X	X	X	X	X	X	X*		X*
QUINOA POULTRY STUFFING OR SIDE DISH	122	X	X	X	X	X	X	X	X	X	X	M	X
SPLIT PEA SOUP	123	X	X	X	X	X	X	X	X	X	X	M	
SUGAR AND TOMATO-FREE BAKED BEANS	121	X	X	X	X	X	X	X	X	X	X*	M,T	
TWO-FOOD-FAMILY BLACK BEAN SOUP	124	X	X	X	X	X	X	X	X	X	X	M	
TWO-FOOD-FAMILY CHICKEN SOUP	127	X*	X*	X	X	X	X	X	X	X	X		X
TWO-FOOD-FAMILY LENTIL SOUP	122	X	X	X	X	X	X	X	X	X	X	M	
VEGETABLES WITH CHEESE SAUCE	119	X*	X*	X	X	A	X	X	X*	X	X		F*

SALADS AND DRESSINGS

	PAGE	FREE OF ALL GRAINS	FREE OF GLUTEN	FREE OF WHEAT	FREE OF CORN	FREE OF MILK	FREE OF EGGS	FREE OF SOY	FREE OF YEAST	FREE OF REFINED SUGAR	FREE OF FRUIT	FREE OF OTHER	SUITABLE FOR STRICT LOW-YEAST DIET
AVOCADO AND ALMOND SALAD	138	X	X	X	X	X	X	X	X	X			
AVOCADO-CANOLA SEED DRESSING	130	X	X	X	X	X	X	X	X	X	X		X
BEET SALAD	134	X	X	X	X	X	X	X	X	X	X		X
BELGIAN ENDIVE SALAD	136	X*	X*	X	X	A*	X	X	X*	X	X		X*
CARROT AND OLIVE SALAD	133	X	X	X	X	X	X	X	X	X	X		X
CHRISTMAS SALAD	137	X	X	X	X	X	X	X	X	X			
COLESLAW	132	X	X	X	X	X	X	X	X	X	X		X
CUCUMBER-AVOCADO SALAD	132	X	X	X	X	X	X	X	X	X	X		X
CUCUMBER SALAD	133	X	X	X	X	X	X	X	X	X	X		X
FRUITY SALAD DRESSING	129	X	X	X	X	X	X	X	X	X			
GARBANZO BEAN SALAD	135	X	X	X	X	X	X	X	X	X	X		
ITALIAN DRESSING	129	X	X	X	X	X	X	X	X	X	X		X
ONE-FOOD-FAMILY CRUNCH SALAD	134	X	X	X	X	X	X	X	X	X	X		X
PASTA SALAD	139	X*	X*	X	X	X	X	X	X	X	X		X*
PINE NUT DRESSING	131	X	X	X	X	X	X	X	X	X	X		X
PITA OR TORTILLA SALAD	141	X*	X*	X	X	A*	X	X	X*	X	X		X*
RABBIT SALAD	142	X	X	X	X	X	X	X	X	X	X		X
SPINACH SALAD	135	X*	X*	X	X	A*	X	X	X	X	X		F*
THREE BEAN SALAD	140	X	X	X	X	X	X	X	X	X	X*		
WALDORF SALAD	131	X	X	X	X	X	X	X	X	X			

COOKIES

	PAGE	FREE OF ALL GRAINS	FREE OF GLUTEN	FREE OF WHEAT	FREE OF CORN	FREE OF MILK	FREE OF EGGS	FREE OF SOY	FREE OF YEAST	FREE OF REFINED SUGAR	FREE OF FRUIT	FREE OF OTHER	SUITABLE FOR STRICT LOW-YEAST DIET
CAROB SANDWICH COOKIES	151		X	X	X	X	X	X	X				
CAROB WAFERS	161	X	X	X	X	X	X	X	X	X	X		X
CARROT COOKIES	146	X*	X*	X	X	X	X	X	X	X	X*		X*
CASHEW BUTTER COOKIES	161		X	X	X	X	X	X	X		X		
COOKIE PRESS COOKIES	153	X*	X*	X	X	X	X	X	X	X*	X*		
FIG NEWTONS	152	X*	X*	X	X	X*	X	X	X	X			
FRAZELLE	164	X*	X*	X	X	X	X	X	X		X		
GINGERBREAD CUTOUT COOKIES	160	X*	X	X	X	X	X	X	X*		X*		
GINGERBREAD MEN	156		X	X	X	X	X	X	X*		X*		
GINGERSNAPS	158		X	X	X	X	X	X	X		X		
MAPLE BARS	165		X	X	X	X	X	X	X		X*		
MAPLE COOKIES	159		X	X	X	X	X	X	X*		X*		
MILLET OR TEFF APPLE COOKIES	147		X	X	X	X	X	X	X	X			
MIX AND MATCH COOKIES	163		X	X	X	X	X	X	X*		X*		
OATMEAL RAISIN COOKIES	146		X	X	X	X	X	X	X	X			
NO-GRAIN CAROB SANDWICH COOKIES	161	X*	X	X	X	X	X	X	X	X*	X*		X*
PINEAPPLE-COCONUT COOKIES	145		X	X	X	X	X	X	X				
PIZZELLES	153	X*	X*	X	X	X	X	X	X	X*	X*		
QUINOA ALMOND COOKIES	164	X	X	X	X	X	X	X	X	X*	X*		
QUINOA BROWNIES	144	X	X	X	X	X	X	X	X	X	X*		X*
QUINOA CAROB CHIP COOKIES	148	X	X	X	X	X	X	X	X	X	X*		X*

COOKIES (CONT'D)

	PAGE	FREE OF ALL GRAINS	FREE OF GLUTEN	FREE OF WHEAT	FREE OF CORN	FREE OF MILK	FREE OF EGGS	FREE OF SOY	FREE OF YEAST	FREE OF REFINED SUGAR	FREE OF FRUIT	FREE OF OTHER	SUITABLE FOR STRICT LOW-YEAST DIET
RYE BROWNIES	144			X	X	X	X	X	X	X			
SANDWICH COOKIES	157			X	X	X	X	X	X	X*	X		X*
SHORTBREAD	149	X*	X*	X	X	X	X	X	X	X*	X*		
SPELT CAROB CHIP COOKIES	149			X	X	X	X	X	X	X			
SUGAR AND SPICE COOKIES	158	X*	X	X	X	X	X	X	X		X		
SUGAR COOKIES	156			X	X	X	X	X	X	X*	X		X*

CAKES AND FROSTINGS

	PAGE	FREE OF ALL GRAINS	FREE OF GLUTEN	FREE OF WHEAT	FREE OF CORN	FREE OF MILK	FREE OF EGGS	FREE OF SOY	FREE OF YEAST	FREE OF REFINED SUGAR	FREE OF FRUIT	FREE OF OTHER	SUITABLE FOR STRICT LOW-YEAST DIET
APPLE CAKE	170			X	X	X	X	X	X	X			
BANANA CAROB CAKE	177			X	X	X	X	X	X				
COCONUT FROSTING	183	X	X	X	X	X	X	X	X	X*	X*		
DATE FROSTING	180			X	X	X	X	X	X	X			
DATE GLAZE	180			X	X	X	X	X	X	X			
DATE NUT BUNDT CAKE	169			X	X	X	X	X	X	X			
DEVIL'S FOOD CAKE	176			X	X	X	X	X	X	X			
"GERMAN CHOCOLATE" CAKE	179	X*	X*	X	X	X	X	X	X	X			
"GERMAN CHOCOLATE" FROSTING	181	X	X	X	X	X	X	X	X	X*	X*		
GINGERBREAD	175	X*	X*	X	X	X	X	X	X	X*	X*		
PARTY CAROB FROSTING	182			X	X	X*	X	X	X		X		
PINEAPPLE UPSIDE-DOWN CAKE	168			X	X	X	X	X	X	X			
QUINOA CARROT CAKE	172	X	X	X	X	X	X	X	X*	X			
RYE CARROT CAKE	171			X	X	X	X	X	X*	X			
SHOO-FLY-PIE CAKE	174		X	X	X	X	X	X	X		X		
SPELT CARROT CAKE	171			X	X	X	X	X	X	X			
SPICE CAKE	173			X	X	X	X	X	X	X			
STEVIA-SWEETENED CAROB CAKE	178	X	X	X	X	X	X	X	X	X	X		X
STEVIA-SWEETENED SPICE CAKE	174	X	X	X	X	X	X	X	X	X	X		X
VERY CAROB CAKE	177	X	X	X	X	X	X	X	X	X			
VERY CAROB FROSTING	181	X	X	X	X	X	X	X	X	X			
ZUCCHINI CAKE	169			X	X	X	X	X	X	X			

ICE CREAMS, SORBETS, CONES, AND SAUCES

	PAGE	FREE OF ALL GRAINS	FREE OF GLUTEN	FREE OF WHEAT	FREE OF CORN	FREE OF MILK	FREE OF EGGS	FREE OF SOY	FREE OF YEAST	FREE OF REFINED SUGAR	FREE OF FRUIT	FREE OF OTHER	SUITABLE FOR STRICT LOW-YEAST DIET
APPLE SORBET	191	X	X	X	X	X	X	X	X	X			
BANABERRY SORBET	190	X	X	X	X	X	X	X	X	X*			
CANTALOPE SORBET	192	X	X	X	X	X	X	X	X	X			
CAROB CHIP ICE CREAM	189	X	X	X	X	A	X	X	X	X*	X*		X*
CAROB ICE CREAM	186	X	X	X	X	A	X	X	X	X*	X		X*
CAROB SYRUP	197	X	X	X	X	X	X	X	X		X		
CHERRY SAUCE	196	X	X	X	X	X	X	X	X	X			
CHOOSE-YOUR-FLAVOR ICE CREAM	189	X	X	X	X	A	X	X	X	X*	X*		X*
CRANBERRY SORBET	191	X	X	X	X	X	X	X	X	X			
ICE CREAM CONES	193	X*	X*	X	X	X	X	X	X	X*	X*		
KIWI SORBET	192	X	X	X	X	X	X	X	X	X			
ORANGE ICE CREAM	188	X	X	X	X	A	X	X	X	X			
PEACH ICE CREAM	187	X	X	X	X	A*	X	X	X	X			
PINA COLADA "ICE CREAM'	186	X	X	X	X	X	X	X	X	X			
PINEAPPLE SAUCE	196	X	X	X	X	X	X	X	X	X			
PINEAPPLE SORBET	190	X	X	X	X	X	X	X	X	X			
STRAWBERRY ICE CREAM	187	X	X	X	X	A*	X	X	X	X			
STRAWBERRY SAUCE	195	X	X	X	X	X	X	X	X	X			
VANILLA ICE CREAM	188	X	X	X	X	A	X	X	X	X*	X*		X*

PASTRY, OTHER FRUIT DESSERTS, AND PUDDINGS

	PAGE	FREE OF ALL GRAINS	FREE OF GLUTEN	FREE OF WHEAT	FREE OF CORN	FREE OF MILK	FREE OF EGGS	FREE OF SOY	FREE OF YEAST	FREE OF REFINED SUGAR	FREE OF FRUIT	FREE OF OTHER	SUITABLE FOR STRICT LOW-YEAST DIET
APPLE COBBLER	208	X*	X*	X	X	X	X	X	X	X			
APPLE PIE	201	X*	X*	X	X	X	X	X	X	X			
APPLE TAPIOCA	212	X	X	X	X	X	X	X	X	X			
BING CHERRY COBBLER	210	X*	X*	X	X	X	X	X	X	X			
BLUEBERRY COBBLER	207	X*	X*	X	X	X	X	X	X	X			
BLUEBERRY PIE	203	X*	X*	X	X	X	X	X	X	X			
CAROB PUDDING	214	X	X	X	X	A*	X	X	X	X*	X		X*
CHERRY COBBLER	207	X*	X*	X	X	X	X	X	X	X			
CHERRY PIE	204	X*	X*	X	X	X	X	X	X	X			
COBBLER TOPPING	210	X*	X*	X	X	X	X	X	X	X			
COCONUT PIE CRUST	201	X	X	X	X	X	X	X	X	X	X		X
COCONUT PUDDING OR FINGER PUDDING	214	X	X	X	X	X	X	X	X	X*	X		X*
EASY FRUIT CRUMBLE	206		X*	X	X	X	X	X	X	X			
GRAPE PIE	205	X*	X*	X	X	X	X	X	X	X			
PEACH COBBLER	208	X*	X*	X	X	X	X	X	X	X			
PEACH PIE	202	X*	X*	X	X	X	X	X	X	X			
PIE CRUST	199	X*	X*	X	X	X	X	X	X	X	X		X
PUMPKIN PIE	205	X*	X*	X	X	X	X	X	X	X	X*		X*
QUINOA PUDDING	213	X	X	X	X	X	X	X	X	X	X*		X*
RHUBARB COBBLER	209	X*	X*	X	X	X	X	X	X	X			
SHORTCAKE	212	X*	X*	X	X	X	X	X	X	X			
TAPIOCA PUDDING	215	X	X	X	X	A	X	X	X	X*	X		X*

BEVERAGES, CONDIMENTS, AND MISCELLANEOUS RECIPES

	PAGE	FREE OF ALL GRAINS	FREE OF GLUTEN	FREE OF WHEAT	FREE OF CORN	FREE OF MILK	FREE OF EGGS	FREE OF SOY	FREE OF YEAST	FREE OF REFINED SUGAR	FREE OF FRUIT	FREE OF OTHER	SUITABLE FOR STRICT LOW-YEAST DIET
CANDY CANES	225	X	X	X	X	X	X	X	X		X		
CAROB FUDGE	224	X	X	X	X	A	X	X	X		X		
CAROB SODA	218	X	X	X	X	A*	X	X	X		X*		
CUCUMBER RELISH	222	X	X	X	X	X	X	X	X	X	X		X
DACOPA AU LAIT	217	X	X	X	X	A*	X	X	X	X*	X		X*
D. GATES LEMONADE OR CRANBERRY COOLER	218	X	X	X	X	X	X	X	X	X			X
EASY CATSUP	220	X	X	X	X	X	X	X	X	X	X*		
FRESH TOMATO CATSUP	221	X	X	X	X	X	X	X	X	X	X*		X*
FRUIT ROLL-UPS	223	X	X	X	X	X	X	X	X	X			
FRUIT SHAKE	217	X	X	X	X	A*	X	X	X	X*			˙
GORP	223	X	X	X	X	X	X	X	X	X			
GRANDMAS CRANBERRY SAUCE OR JELLY	219	X	X	X	X	X	X	X	X	X			
HOT CAROB	216	X	X	X	X	A	X	X	X	X*	X		X*
HOT MUSTARD	222	X	X	X	X	X	X	X	X	X	X		X
MILD MUSTARD	221	X	X	X	X	X	X	X	X	X	X		X
MOCK MAPLE SYRUP	219	X	X	X	X	X	X	X	X	X	X		X
STEVIA WORKING SOLUTION	226	X	X	X	X	X	X	X	X	X	X		X

Index to the Recipes by Major Grains or Grain Alternatives

"It's barley day. What can I eat?" This index provides an easy way to find the answer to a question that occurs commonly on a rotation diet by listing the recipes in this book according to the major grain or grain alternative that they contain. The recipes that do not contain a grain or grain alternative, such as those for ice creams, most of the main dishes, etc., are not listed in this index.

AMARANTH

Amaranth is used in conjunction with arrowroot in most of these recipes.

Muffins, Crackers, Breakfast Foods and Breads Made Without Yeast:

Stevia-Sweetened Spice Muffins—p.34
Canola Seed Crackers—p.38
Banana Bread—p.45
No-Yeast Bread—p.46
No-Yeast Sandwich Buns—p.48
Teething Biscuits—p.52

Main Dishes:

Stuffed Zucchini—p.70
Turkey Pot Pie—p.75
Biscuit Topping for Casseroles—p.77
Buff-n-Biscuit—p.78
Duck-n-Biscuit—p.79

Bean-n-Biscuit—p.80
Salmon Loaf or Patties—p.87
Sloppy Goat Sandwiches made with amaranth
    "No-Yeast Bread,"—p.92

Pasta and Ethnic Dishes:

Pasta for Rolling by Hand—p.96
Manicotti—p.105
Lasagne—p.106
Pizza—p.108
Pesto Pizza—p.110
Tortillas—p.112
Tostadas—p.115
Enchilada Casserole—p.116
Oriental Game or Chicken served with puffed
    amaranth—p.117

Salads and Dressings:

Spinach Salad with amaranth "Canola Seed Crackers,"—p.135
Belgian Endive Salad with amaranth
    "Canola Seed Crackers,"— p.136
Pita or Tortilla Salad with amaranth tortillas—p.141

Cookies:

Shortbread—p.149
Fig Newtons—p.152
Pizzelles—p.153
Cookie Press Cookies—p.153
Frazelle—p.164

Cakes and Frostings:

Stevia-Sweetened Spice Cake—p.174
Shoo-Fly-Pie Cake—p.174
Gingerbread—p.175

Ice Creams, Sorbets, Cones, and Sauces:

Ice Cream Cones—p.193

Pastry and Other Desserts:

Pie Crust—p.199-201
Apple Pie—p.201
Peach Pie—p.202
Blueberrry Pie—p.203
Cherry Pie—p.204
Grape Pie—p.205
Pumpkin Pie—p.205
Cherry Cobbler—p.207
Blueberry Cobbler—p.207
Peach Cobbler—p.208
Apple Cobbler—p.208
Rhubarb Cobbler—p.209
Bing Cherry Cobbler—p.210
Cobbler Topping—p.210
Shortcake—p.212

ARROWROOT

In addition to the recipes in this list, arrowroot is used in most of the amaranth recipes, above.

Main Dishes:

No-Meat or Tomato Chili—p.73
Game Stroganoff—p.82
Roast Duck with Cherry Sauce—p.88
Buffalo Loaf—p.92
Braised Buffalo Burgers—p.93
Lentil Burgers—p.94

Pasta and Ethnic Dishes:

Oriental Game or Chicken—p.117

Vegetables, Side Dishes, and Soups:

Harvard Beets—p.118
Vegetables with Cheese Sauce—p.119

Cakes and Frostings:

Very Carob Frosting—p.181
Coconut Frosting—p.183

Ice Creams, Sorbets, Cones, and Sauces:

Strawberry Sauce—p.195
Pineapple Sauce—p.196
Cherry Sauce—p.196

Pastry and Other Desserts:

Carob Pudding—p.214
Coconut Pudding—p.214

Beverages, Condiments, and Miscellaneous Recipes:

Mock Maple Syrup—p.219
Mild Mustard—p.222

BARLEY

Muffins, Crackers, Breakfast Foods and Breads Made Without Yeast:

Barley Muffins—p.30
Blueberry Muffins—p.33
Canola Seed Crackers—p.38
Barley Pancakes—p.42
Barley Waffles—p.44
No-Yeast Bread—p.46
No-Yeast Sandwich Buns—p.48
Barley Sandwich Bread—p.48
Barley Biscuits—p.50

Yeast Raised Breads and Baked Goods:

Quick Barley Yeast Bread—p.59
Barley Sandwich Buns—p.60

Main Dishes:

Stuffed Zucchini—p.70
Turkey Pot Pie—p.75
Biscuit Topping for Casseroles—p.77
Buff-n-Biscuit—p.78
Duck-n-Biscuit—p.79
Bean-n-Biscuit—p.80
Macaroni and Cheese made using homemade or
    commercial barley pasta—p.81
Salmon Loaf or Patties—p.87
Crispy Oven-Fried Chicken—p.89
Sloppy Goat Sandwiches made with barley "No-Yeast Bread"
    or "Quick Barley Yeast Bread,"—p.92

Pasta and Ethnic Dishes:

Pasta for Rolling by Hand—p.96
Pasta Made with an Extrusion Machine—p.99
Pasta Sauces served with homemade or
    commercial barley pasta—p.100-104
Manicotti—p.105
Lasagne—p.106
Pizza—p.108
Pesto Pizza—p.110
Pasta e fagioli made with homemade or
    commercial barley pasta—p.111
Oriental Game or Chicken served with homemade or
    commercial barley pasta—p.117

Vegetables, Side Dishes, and Soups:

Vegetables with cheese sauce—p.119
Two-Food-Family Chicken Soup with barley or homemade or
    commercial barley pasta—p.127

Salads and Dressings:

Spinach Salad with barley "Canola Seed Crackers,"—p.135
Belgian Endive Salad with barley "Canola Seed
  Crackers,"—p.136
Pasta Salad made with homemade or commercial
  barley pasta—p.139

Cookies:

Shortbread—p.149
Cookie Press Cookies—p.153
Sugar Cookies—p.156
Sandwich Cookies—p.157
Gingersnaps—p.158
Mix and Match Cookies—p.163

Cakes and Frostings:

Pineapple Upside Down Cake—p.168
Spice Cake—p.173
Banana Carob Cake—p.178
Date Frosting—p.180
Party Carob Frosting—p.182

Pastry and Other Desserts:

Pie Crust—p.199-201
Apple Pie—p.201
Peach Pie—p.202
Blueberrry Pie—p.203
Cherry Pie—p.204
Grape Pie—p.205
Pumpkin Pie—p.205
Cherry Cobbler—p.207
Blueberry Cobbler—p.207
Peach Cobbler—p.208
Apple Cobbler—p.208
Rhubarb Cobbler—p.209
Bing Cherry Cobbler—p.210

Pasta and Ethnic Dishes:

Pasta for Rolling by Hand—p.96
Pasta Sauces served with homemade chestnut
    pasta—p.100-104
Manicotti—p.105
Lasagne—p.106
Pizza—p.108
Pesto Pizza—p.110
Pasta e fagioli made with homemade chestnut pasta—p.111
Oriental Game or Chicken served with
    homemade chestnut pasta—p.117

Vegetables, Side Dishes, and Soups:

Two-Food-Family Chicken Soup with homemade
    chestnut pasta—p.127

GARBANZO

Pasta and Ethnic Dishes:

Tortillas—p.112
Tostadas—p.115
Enchilada Casserole—p.116

Salads and Dressings:

Pita or Tortilla Salad with garbanzo tortillas—p.141

MILLET

Muffins, Crackers, Breakfast Foods and Breads Made Without Yeast:

Millet Surprise Muffins—p.31

Main Dishes:

Macaroni and Cheese made using commercial millet
   pasta—p.81

Pasta and Ethnic Dishes:

Pasta Sauces served with commercial millet pasta—p.100-104
Pasta e fagioli made with commercial millet pasta—p.111
Oriental Game or Chicken served with
   commercial millet pasta—p.117

Vegetables, Side Dishes, and Soups:

Two-Food-Family Chicken Soup with homemade or
   commercial millet pasta—p.127

Salads and Dressings:

Pasta Salad made with commercial millet pasta—p.139

Cookies:

Millet or Teff Apple Cookies—p.147

Pastry and Other Desserts:

Easy Fruit Crumble—p.206

MILO

Muffins, Crackers, Breakfast Foods and Breads Made Without Yeast:

Pineapple Muffins—p.28
Milo Crackers—p.37

Main Dishes:

Macaroni and Cheese made using commercial milo
   pasta—p.81

Pasta and Ethnic Dishes:

Pasta Sauces served with commercial milo pasta—p.100-104
Pasta e fagioli made with commercial milo pasta—p.111
Oriental Game or Chicken served with commercial
    milo pasta—p.117

Vegetables, Side Dishes, and Soups:

Two-Food-Family Chicken Soup with commercial
    milo pasta—p.127

Salads and Dressings:

Spinach Salad with "Milo Crackers,"—p.135
Belgian Endive Salad with "Milo Crackers,"—p.136
Pasta Salad made with commercial milo pasta—p.139

Cakes and Frostings:

Spice Cake—p.173

OAT

Muffins, Crackers, Breakfast Foods and Breads Made
Without Yeast:

Oat Muffins—p.29
Blueberry Muffins—p.33
Oat Crackers—p.36
Oat Biscuits—p.50

Yeast Raised Breads and Baked Goods:

Oat Yeast Bread—p.56

Main Dishes:

Turkey Pot Pie—p.75
Macaroni and Cheese made using commercial oat pasta—p.81
Crispy Oven-Fried Chicken—p.89

Pastry and Other Desserts:

Pie Crust—p.199-201
Apple Pie—p.201
Peach Pie—p.202
Blueberrry Pie—p.203
Cherry Pie—p.204
Grape Pie—p.205
Pumpkin Pie—p.205
Easy Fruit Crumble—p.206

QUINOA

Quinoa flour is used in conjunction with tapioca flour in most of these recipes.

Muffins, Crackers, Breakfast Foods and Breads Made Without Yeast:

Apple and Spice Muffins—p.28
Pear Muffins—p.29
Blueberry Muffins—p.33
Stevia-Sweetened Spice Muffins—p.34
Quinoa Crackers—p.35
"Graham" Crackers—p.35
Quinoa Granola—p.40
Quinoa Pancakes—p.43
Applesauce Bread—p.46
No-Yeast Bread—p.46
No-Yeast Sandwich Buns—p.49
Teething Biscuits—p.52

Yeast Raised Breads and Baked Goods:

Quinoa Yeast Bread—p.56
Raisin Bread—p.57
No-Fry Doughnuts—p.67

Salads and Dressings:

Cookies:

Cakes and Frostings:

Ice Creams, Sorbets, Cones, and Sauces:

Pastry and Other Desserts:

RICE

Main Dishes:

Pasta and Ethnic Dishes:

Vegetables, Side Dishes, and Soups:

Salads and Dressings:

RYE

Muffins, Crackers, Breakfast Foods and Breads Made Without Yeast:

Pastry and Other Desserts:

SPELT

Muffins, Crackers, Breakfast Foods and Breads Made Without Yeast:

Yeast Raised Breads and Baked Goods:

Main Dishes:

Pasta and Ethnic Dishes:

Oriental Game or Chicken served with homemade or commercial spelt pasta—p.117

Vegetables, Side Dishes, and Soups:

Two-Food-Family Chicken Soup with homemade or commercial spelt pasta—p.127

Salads and Dressings:

Spinach Salad with "Saltines,"—p.135
Belgian Endive Salad with "Saltines,"—p.136
Pasta Salad made with homemade or commercial spelt pasta—p.139
Pita or Tortilla Salad with "Pita Bread" or spelt tortillas—p.141

Cookies:

Carrot Cookies—p.146
Spelt Carob Chip Cookies—p.149
Shortbread—p.149
Pizzelles—p.153
Cookie Press Cookies—p.153
Gingerbread Men—p.156
Sugar Cookies—p.156
Sandwich Cookies—p.157
Frazelle—p.164

Cakes and Frostings:

Zucchini Cake—p.169
Apple Cake—p.170
Spelt Carrot Cake—p.171
Gingerbread—p.175

Ice Creams, Sorbets, Cones, and Sauces:

Ice Cream Cones—p.193

TAPIOCA

In addition to the recipes in this list, tapioca flour is used in most of the quinoa flour recipes, above.

TEFF

WATER CHESTNUT

General Index
(Recipes are in italics.)

Books by Starburst Publishers
(Partial listing—full list available on request)

Allergy Cooking With Ease   —Nicolette N. Dumke

A book designed to provide a wide variety of recipes to meet many different types of dietary and social needs, and, whenever possible, save you time in food preparation. Includes: Recipes for those special foods that most food allergy patients think they will never eat again; Timesaving tricks; and Allergen Avoidance Index.

(trade paper-opens flat)   ISBN 091498442X   **$12.95**

The World's Oldest Health Plan   —Kathleen O'Bannon Baldinger

Subtitled: *Health, Nutrition and Healing from the Bible.* Offers a complete health plan for body, mind and spirit, just as Jesus did. It includes programs for diet, exercise and mental health. Contains foods and recipes to lower cholesterol and blood pressure, improve the immune system and other bodily functions, reduce stress, reduce or cure constipation, eliminate insomnia, reduce forgetfulness, confusion and anger, increase circulation and thinking ability, eliminate "yeast" problems, improve digestion, and much more.

(trade paper-opens flat)   ISBN 0914984578   **$14.95**

The Low-Fat Supermarket   —Judith & Scott Smith

A comprehensive reference of over 4,500 brand name products that derive less than 30% of their calories from fat. Information provided includes total calories, fat, cholesterol and sodium content. Organized according to the sections of a supermarket. Your answer to a healthier you.

(trade paper)   ISBN 0914984438   **$10.95**

Dr. Kaplan's Highway To Health   —Eric Scott Kaplan

Subtitled: *A Guide to THINNING and WINNING.* A comprehensive guide to the formulas and principles of: FAT LOSS, EXERCISE, VITAMINS, SUCCESS and HAPPINESS. It emphasizes **Maximum Metabolism** through diet modification—fat and carbohydrate modification, coupled with exercise and the removal of sugar, stimulating the body to utilize stored and dietary fat for energy. Dr. Kaplan will teach you a natural approach to food combinations—what you can eat in quantity and what foods such as sugar, white flour and salt to modify or eliminate so *you can eat more and weigh less.*

(hard cover)   ISBN 091498456X   **$21.95**

Stay Well Without Going Broke   —Gulling, Renner, & Vargas

Subtitled: *Winning the War Over Medical Bills.* Provides a blueprint for how health care consumers can take more responsibility for monitoring their own health and the cost of its care—a crucial cornerstone of the health care reform movement today. Contains inside information from doctors, pharmacists and hospital personnel on how to get cost-effective care without sacrificing quality. Offers legal strategies to protect your rights when illness is terminal.

(hard cover)   ISBN 0914984527   **$22.95**

Books by Starburst Publishers—cont'd.

The New American Family
—Artlip, Artlip, & Saltzman

American men and women are remarrying at an astounding rate, and nearly 60% of the remarriages involve children under the age of eighteen. Unfortunately, over half of these remarriages also end in divorce, with half of the "redivorces" occuring within five years. The New American Family tells it like it is. It gives examples and personal experiences that help you to see that the second time around is no picnic. It provides practical, good sense suggestions and guidelines for making your new American family the one you always dreamed of.

(trade paper) ISBN 0914984446 **$10.95**

Dragon Slaying For Parents
—Tom Prinz

Subtitled: *Removing The Excess Baggage So You Can Be The Parent You Want To Be*. Shows how Dragons such as Codependency, Low Self-Esteem and other hidden factors interfere with effective parenting. This book by a marriage, family, and child counselor, is for all parents—to assist them with the difficult task of raising responsible and confident children in the 1990's. It is written especially for parents who believe they have "tried everything!"

(trade paper) ISBN 0914984357 **$9.95**

A Woman's Guide To Spiritual Power
—Nancy L. Dorner

Subtitled: *Through Scriptural Prayer*. Do your prayers seem to go "against a brick wall?" Does God sometimes seem far away or non-existent? If your answer is "Yes," *You* are not alone. Prayer must be the cornerstone of your relationship to God. "This book is a powerful tool for anyone who is serious about prayer and discipleship."— Florence Littauer

(trade paper) ISBN 0914984470 **$9.95**

Common Sense Management & Motivation
—Roy H. Holmes

Teaches the principles of motivating subordinate personnel via good human relations, It is written from practical "how-to" experience rather than classroom theory. Specific subjects covered include: Basic motivation psychology, Effective communication, Delegating, Goal-setting, Confronting, and Leadership qualities. A must book for all existing or aspiring supervisors, managers, business leaders, and anyone else interested in managing and motivating people.

(hard cover) ISBN 0914984497 **$16.95**

Alzheimer's—Does "The System" Care?
—Ted & Paula Valenti

Experts consider Alzheimer's disease to be the "disease of the century." More than half the one million elderly people residing in American nursing homes have "senile dementia." This book reveals a unique observation as to the cause of Alzheimer's and the care of its victims.

(hard cover) ISBN 0914984179 **$14.95**